My Father and I

My Father and I

The Marais and the
Queerness of Community

D AVID C ARON

Cornell University Press

ITHACA AND LONDON

First published 2009 by Cornell University Press

Printed in the United States of America

Library of Congress Cataloging-in-Publication Data

Caron, David (David Henri)
    My father and I : the Marais and the queerness of community / David Caron.
        p. cm.
    Includes bibliographical references and index.
    ISBN 978-0-8014-4773-0 (cloth : alk. paper)
    1. Marais (Paris, France)—History.   2. Gay community—France—Paris—History.
3. Jewish neighborhoods—France—Paris—History.   4. Homosexuality—France—Paris—
History.   5. Jews—France—Paris—History.   6. Gottlieb, Joseph, 1919–2004.
7. Caron, David (David Henri)—Family.   I. Title.
    DC752.M37C37   2009
    306.76'6092244361—dc22
2008043686

Cornell University Press strives to use environmentally responsible sup-
pliers and materials to the fullest extent possible in the publishing of
its books. Such materials include vegetable-based, low-VOC inks and
acid-free papers that are recycled, totally chlorine-free, or partly composed
of nonwood fibers. For further information, visit our website at
www.cornellpress.cornell.edu.

Cloth printing   10 9 8 7 6 5 4 3 2 1

In memory of Joseph Gottlieb, my father
And for all my other friends

Contents

IOU

Every book is a community. This one is no exception. I have written it neither for myself nor by myself. It bears the imprint of many friendships and
many sources of support, moral and otherwise. Throughout this long process, I have relied on the kindness of strangers and on the tough and tender
demands of those close to me.

My father's dream was to own a bookstore. He never did, but with this
book, which is his, he will now be in bookstores. I only wish he had been
around to see what he inspired. My writing has allowed me to grow closer
to him and to make up for so many years of misunderstanding. I miss him
every day.

I am particularly indebted to my friends Ross Chambers and Cyril Royer,
who have been precious interlocutors from day one. Thinking with them
was a challenge and a joy, and they made this book better. Along with Ross
and Cyril, Alejandro Herrero-Olaizola and Juli Highfill have given me far
more than I could possibly acknowledge here. Jarrod Hayes, Cristina
Moreiras-Menor, Martine Delvaux, and Liu Haiyong also deserve special
recognition for their friendship, advice, and encouragements. I also thank
Lawrence D. Kritzman and Michael Sibalis, who read the manuscript for
Cornell University Press and contributed much to its improvement. Peter J.
Potter was an ideal editor, wonderfully supportive, engaged, and generous.
Thank you all so much.

Dilettantism is a lovely ideal but it is also a luxury. A luxury I don't have.
Without the support of institutional structures, I could never do what I love
to do—read, write and, think about stuff—and do it for a living. For that I
am truly grateful. First of all, I want to acknowledge the various units at the
University of Michigan that have made this book possible thanks to their

generous support: the Department of Romance Languages and Literatures; the College of Literature, Science and the Arts; the Office of the Vice Provost for Research; and the Rackham School of Graduate Studies. I was also very fortunate to have received a fellowship from the National Endowment for the Humanities, which allowed me to conduct crucial research in Paris for a year. Another fellowship, at the University of Michigan's Institute for the Humanities, helped me greatly in advancing my thinking and writing. Many thanks to all involved in one way or another: Martine Antle, Marie Lathers, David Halperin, Peggy McCracken, Marie-Hélène Huet, David Carroll, Didier Eribon, and Daniel Herwitz.

And there are all the friends in France and elsewhere, the old ones, the new ones, and those whose names I never even knew. *I'll sing them all and we'll stay all night!* This is ultimately a book on friendship, and their love and hospitality have proved my point about community. When bad things happened—and they happened often during the writing of this book—they were there to help. In addition to those already mentioned, and in no particular order: Annabelle, Alain, Denis, Laurent, Thierry, Anna, Gowen, Nico, Guillaume, Krysztof, Gilles, Bruno, Babar, Michael, Johnny Boy, Tetsuya, Mindy, Patty, Ed, Fred, Jean-Louis, Ronan, Amar, Sylvie, Xavier, Lilian, René-Pierre, Bruno, Kali, Mika, Sophie, Kane, Iannis, Laetitia, Lijun, Marie, Caroline, Didier, and Hervé who didn't make it. And my family, of course. 还有我的那只小浣熊，那么勇敢，那么善良。

―――――――

AN earlier version of the prologue, "My Father and I," was published in *GLQ* in 2005 (vol. 11, 265–282). Many thanks to the publisher, Duke University Press, for permission to reprint it here. Small sections of chapters 3 and 5 have appeared in *Entre Hommes: French and Francophone Masculinities in Culture and Theory* in 2008, edited by Todd Reeser and Lewis Seifert (251–266) and in *Gay Shame,* also in 2008, edited by David Halperin and Valerie Traub. Many thanks to the editors and the University of Delaware Press and the University of Chicago Press respectively for permission to reprint parts of these essays here.

DAVID CARON

Ann Arbor, Michigan

My Father and I

"It isn't fun to be free alone."
ALFRED JARRY

Prologue:
My Father and I

My relationship with my father was a disaster. Or at least that's how it often felt to me. Let me give you an example. One day in the fall of 1998, my father and I took a little walk through the Marais, the old and emblematic Jewish neighborhood of Paris where he once lived and worked. My father, who by then lived in Caen, Normandy, was visiting my sister in Paris and took the opportunity to do a little shopping at Jo Goldenberg's famous delicatessen before returning home. Since we didn't get to see each other all that much anymore—I have lived in the United States since 1987—this was also an opportunity for the two of us *to be together.* We were walking along the rue Vieille du Temple, and branching off to the west of there is the rue Sainte-Croix de la Bretonnerie, the heart of what has recently become an American-style gay neighborhood, rainbow flags and all, in the heart of old Paris. To the east, almost facing the rue Sainte-Croix but off by no more than a few yards, begins the rue des Rosiers, *the* cultural metonym for the French Jewish community. My father suddenly pointed to a shop window. "When I lived here," he said, "I used to work in this store. And I had a big crush on a girl who was working across the street." He said this seemingly blind to the fact that the store in question was now called the "Boy Zone" and sold a totally different line of clothing—tight and shiny (you know the kind). All the signs were right there in the window for him to see, but he didn't see them. At that moment he was in a different Marais, at a different time in history. In fact, during our entire stay in the area, my father was completely unaware that the neighborhood was no longer just Jewish but also conspicuously gay. The bathhouse, the S&M store, the bookstore with its unmistakable window display, not to mention the people—none of this was immediately legible to him the way it was to me.

Once I was over my inner hilarity at imagining my father selling revealing lycra underwear to a bunch of gym queens, I started thinking that the gap between us seemed unbridgeable. Although we were walking side by side, my father and I were strolling through two different spaces and two different times—I through the new gay Marais where I would perhaps return that night for fun, and he through the old Jewish Marais where he used to live and work in the 1950s.

But let me backtrack a little.

My father's name was Joseph Gottlieb. Everyone called him Jo. He was born on 17 August 1919, in Sátoraljaújhely, a medium-size regional capital in Hungary near the border with what is now Slovakia. Between nine and ten thousand Jews lived in the city, he once told me—25 to 30 percent of the total population. These figures may not be historically accurate, though.

Before going any farther, I should clarify a few things. In telling my father's life story, I am not relying on objective historical research but on his own recollections, which I gathered in a series of taped interviews. What emerged from these recordings was highly subjective, since it was the sum of what I asked and what he volunteered, that is, what was important to me and what was important to him—all this caught up, of course, in the treacherous dynamics of a personal relationship. What did I want to know from my father? What did he want his son to know? I also paid attention to the way he assigned certain events meaning and relevance in hindsight. As he noted during one of these interviews, "Personal memories are not always personal. One embellishes, one mythifies." This remark can be read at several levels. For one thing, it recognizes that a degree of fictionalizing may sometimes be inseparable from the act of remembering—and indeed, my father made countless references to canonical works of literature (by Balzac and Zola, for example) in order to validate, or simply to convey or underscore, the significance of real events. But this also implies that, once told, personal memories cease to be personal; they become stories with the potential to be shared and thus to form communities. My father knew, of course, that I was interviewing him for a book project, that I was going to share much of this information with unknown readers. Nearing the end of his life, he may also have been concerned with something like a legacy, thinking of the future as well as the past and the present. (And I have to admit that all this—stories, community, and the relation between the two—interests me a lot more than perfect factual truths that may be impossible to recover.) But foremost in his mind, I assume, was the community he and I were forming as we were talking, which was not a given at the outset and remained somewhat problematic until the end.

As my father kept reminding me, other people often told him that he and I were just like each other—looks, character, everything. And he often added: "Let's leave them with their illusions," implying that our sameness was nothing but a fictional construct of a father-son relationship imposed on us by the gaze of outsiders, but by which he and I should not be duped. On the one hand, my father's comment was quite subversive, since what it dismissed as an illusion is for most people today a matter of genetics, which has become, of late, the most powerful authenticator of objective truths. For the time being, at least, it is the only uncontested way to prove that two or more individuals have "a real thing" in common, something like a shared substance. DNA testing to establish paternity is an obvious example. Ignoring genetics means flouting the whole truth system it seeks to legitimate; under a different paradigm it would be called blasphemy. Yet my father's comment, "Let's leave them with their illusions," read like a paradox. Both in its syntax (the first person plural) and in the context of its utterance (the complicit sharing of a private joke) this statement performed into existence the very community it purported to deny: my father and I formed the community of people who knew better than the people who said that we formed a community. Like any good paradox, however, it told us something more— that we did have a community there, albeit one whose claim to existence was in the way it actively assumed the absence, not the presence, of a shared substance. And the fact that my father repeatedly informed me of others' comments about the two of us may have betrayed his frustrated desire to believe that they contained an element of truth. But, as I was saying and as my father's paradoxical comment confirmed, the truth of our relationship was not a given.

Back to the past.

My father's family was quite large. Between the number of children who died in infancy and the difficulty of defining an "extended family," I could not get an exact figure from him. He quit school at age thirteen to become an apprentice with a clockmaker and later a tailor. Despite having received a religious education and learning to speak Yiddish, he was not a very religious man. In fact, the whole family, although Orthodox, was rather integrated, speaking only Hungarian at home. Like the vast majority of Hungary's Jews in those years, my father considered himself Hungarian. What Hungarians considered him was a different story. In his youth, he was repeatedly taunted and assaulted by local peasants, who hit him and even threw stones at him. "I would have liked to be Hungarian first and then Jewish," he said, "but they didn't let me. Screw them!" He decided to leave.

After my father died, our friend Caroline told me a story I had never heard. The night before my father was to leave home there was a big farewell dinner. Sitting next to him was a girl he liked but had been too shy to pursue. All of a sudden, he felt the brush of her leg against his. "If she wants me," he thought, "I'm staying." He leaned back as discreetly as he could and took a glance. What he had felt was the leg of the table. The next day he was gone.

He arrived in Paris in January 1937 with a student visa. He had no intention of becoming a student; he just lied to be let into the country. In any case, he was picked up at the Gare de l'Est by my uncle Albert, who a few years earlier had married my father's older sister Hélène in an arranged match. Hélène had come to France in 1930, and my father had never met his brother-in-law. The couple had settled in Caen, where they sold clothes in outdoor markets. My father joined them there, and although his dream was to run a bookstore, he started working for them. In those years, he made very few trips to Paris, as the business dealt mostly with local wholesalers. It is only after World War II that the Marais played a part in his life.

At the outbreak of the war, moved by a sense of duty as a Jew, and because he "had no reasons not to do it," my father enlisted as a volunteer in the Foreign Legion to fight Hitler. His enrollment in a *régiment de volontaires étrangers* [regiment of foreign volunteers] was the source of "yet another stigma" in addition to being Jewish. On 6 June 1940, he was captured and sent to a POW camp in Silesia. A Jewish friend of his, a *copain* as war buddies were often called, who belonged to the same platoon and knew German, was in charge of registering the new prisoners. Just as my father was about to answer "Jewish" to the question about religion, his friend took the liberty of writing down "None," hence classifying him as a French POW— until the day came when Jewish prisoners arrived and were placed in a separate block. My father felt compelled to visit them on several occasions and was soon noticed by a fellow prisoner, who exposed him as a Jew. He was imprisoned ("in a prison within a prison," he laughed), and a few months later he was sent to a tough disciplinary labor camp before working on a farm, and finally as a tailor for a Volkswagen factory outside Hanover.

It comes a shock to many people that my father wasn't killed when it became known that he was Jewish. In fact, Jews imprisoned in German stalags were protected by international conventions on war prisoners, and Wehrmacht officers, including those running the camps, often were not Nazis themselves. Some even authorized religious observances in the stalags (Priollaud et al., *Images de la mémoire juive*, 230). As for my blond-haired, blue-eyed father, he was often singled out as a perfect Aryan by his initially unsuspecting jailers.

When the Allies bombed the Volkswagen factory after it had started manufacturing parts for V1 rockets, the prisoners were evacuated. They were guarded by dispirited old Poles under German uniform. They were bombed again on the road and took cover in a nearby forest. When it became clear that their captors were mostly interested in their own survival, my father and a few *copains* walked back to the camp, commandeered some trucks and fled toward France, raiding farms for food along the way. Some of the guys were planning to keep the trucks and set up a carrying business in France after the war. They eventually reached Koblenz where they met US troops, French prostitutes, and three thousand forced laborers "of all nationalities." They played poker, won big and lost everything right away, stole bottles of the finest Rhine wines, and—the best memory of all—enjoyed cups of hot, exquisite Nescafé au lait.

Unfortunately, the Americans soon confiscated their trucks and put them on a train to Calais. However, my father and a *copain* managed to take a train to Paris where they arrived on 1 May 1945. All in all, my father concluded with more than a hint of modesty, the war hadn't been too hard on him. If he meant that he was a Jew and yet was not sent to his death, it is true. The only concentration camp he saw was Bergen Belsen, where he would go to get fabric and soles for the Volkswagen factory. But since the camp was also used for tank maneuvers, he said, "we couldn't see anything. It's only after the war that we learned about all that." His "ex-almost-fiancée" (for an arranged marriage that never took place) died in Bergen Belsen.

My father applied for and received French citizenship in 1946. Unlike many returnees, he did not actively seek the company of fellow veterans and prisoners. At one point he belonged to a veterans organization, or *amicale*, but he soon drifted away from it. "I don't live in the past," he told me, "and I don't give a shit about ceremonies and medals and all that stuff." In Paris he once took out to dinner a Hungarian Gentile with whom he had become quite close in the stalag. Szabo was a funny guy then; he kept detailed records of his sexual encounters and told wildly popular stories about them to his fellow prisoners—a masturbatory yet collective survival strategy not so different, after all, from listing all the stations of a Paris metro line or recreating a classic play or poem from memory. Once liberated, Szabo was only the shadow of his captive self. His sense of humor had vanished, and he appeared to my father "as a candle that had been put out." Another friend, who had entertained his fellow prisoners with a mandolin and had always volunteered to help out and alleviate other people's suffering, lost all his generosity of spirit after the war. He became psychologically abusive with the two young nieces he had been forced to raise because their parents hadn't returned.

No doubt thinking of himself, too, my father's interpretation was that, paradoxically, some of these men felt liberated by their captivity because they found themselves free from, say, a dead-end job or their family. Since they no longer had to be fighters or providers, these men among men were also less than men and, it appears, some of them enjoyed it. When they had to shoulder once again the burdens of masculinity, the weight just seemed too crushing. Naturally, it wasn't imprisonment per se that gave them such a feeling of freedom, but the community of *copains*. While my father often described himself as a gregarious man who enjoyed the company of friends (a lot more than family life, I can testify to that), he soon realized that the sense of community he had experienced during the war had been contingent upon external factors that no longer existed: the lack of freedom, of food, of health, and, what ultimately cemented the community—a sense of duty toward strangers. With this duty gone, the *copains* vanished. This does not imply that the community was any less legitimate or valuable because it was ephemeral and defined negatively from the outside, for this is true of all communities.

So the war was over, and that part of our interviews became more difficult, requiring a great deal of tactfulness. I had to ask what I already mostly knew: What about his family? His brother Jacob had been deported and survived. After a brief trip back to Hungary and a visit to France, he moved to Palestine in 1946. Another brother died in a Hungarian-controlled labor camp in Russia. None of the others returned. At least twenty-five relatives had died, probably a great deal more. (One of my father's many brothers, for instance, had ten children.) I have always assumed that, like most Hungarian Jews, they had been rounded up in 1944, taken to Auschwitz, and murdered quickly before the arrival of Soviet troops—very much as in the story Elie Wiesel tells in *Night*. Hoping not to sound like Claude Lanzmann, whose interviews of survivors in *Shoah* often verge on cruelty, I asked my father whether he had any information about where his relatives had been taken. "I don't even know" was the answer. And that was that. If he never asked his brother Jacob and never tried to know exactly what had happened, why should I? I can't remember a time when I did not know that my father's family had been exterminated, but we never really discussed it in factual detail. Now we never will.

Right after the war my father moved back to Caen, but he often returned to Paris on business. He told me he saw very little Jewish life in the Marais at the time. Since the bulk of its population, foreigners for the most part, had been deported and killed, Jews, while still very much present, were not as conspicuous as they had been. My father seldom went to the *Pletzl*, as the neighborhood was nicknamed, after the main square of Jewish villages of Central and Eastern Europe before the war. He never set foot in a synagogue, but he sometimes had lunch in a Yiddish restaurant at the corner of the rue des Rosiers and the rue des Ecouffes, the very heart of the *Pletzl*. He and I ate there a few times. It has become a falafel joint.

But let me jump back to 1998 and the walk we took together in the neighborhood.

It wasn't long before I realized that my father was as aware of the Marais's gayness as I was of its Jewishness, since he later remarked that gay bars were beginning to encroach on both the rue des Rosiers and the rue des Ecouffes. What I had thought hilarious and endearing short-sightedness on his part had been in fact an embarrassing misreading on *my* part. To complicate matters further, he later denied that the episode in front of the Boy Zone had ever occurred. He had never worked on the rue Vieille du Temple, he protested, but on the rue du Roi de Sicile, a few blocks away. Whose memory to trust? Mine or an old man's? I decided not to solve that enigma but to revel instead in the idea that an entire book may have been triggered by a misunderstanding—and it doesn't matter whose really. This case of miscommunication ought to be read as a *mise en abyme* of my whole relationship with my father, which is itself an allegory for my take on the question of community. So that special moment when our lives had seemed to intersect had had no tangible existence, no substance. The site of overlapping between the Jewish father and the queer son had been empty.

When he and I had been walking together in the Marais, had he been in my neighborhood, or I in his? Both, of course, since we had been both together and simultaneously on familiar and unfamiliar territory—and, as it turned out, equally aware of the situation. So what I had first perceived as signs of hopeless disconnection—my father's apparent blindness, my misreading of it, the final misunderstanding—could form the basis for a different type of connectedness, in which common ground could be found only on unfamiliar territory. Our lives *had* intersected that day, even if the site of the intersection had been empty. While such connectedness may have been painful, or at least uncomfortable, he and I had owed it to one another, for not having a relationship at all would simply have been unbearable. If our relationship was a disaster, it was because it could not have been otherwise. If not for disaster, he and I would have had nothing in common. But we could perhaps have been something like *copains*. That may have been our only option—our duty, our burden, our gift to one another.

The real question, then, is the following: If the title of this essay, *My Father and I*, signals a relationship, what is the nature of the community it performs? What "thing" did we have in common? In etymological terms, what *munus* did we share? In his book *Communitas*, Roberto Esposito proposes the following theory. The radical *munus* that forms the etymological core of "community" has three possible meanings: *onus* (burden), *officium* (duty or service), and *donum* (gift). By bringing together the notions of "gift" and "duty," *munus*

is, in sum, the gift that one gives because one must give and *cannot not* give. . . .
Although it stems from a service that was previously received, the *munus* desig-
nates only the gift that one gives, not the one that one receives. It is entirely
guided by the transitive act of giving. It does not in any way involve the stability of a possession—and even less the dynamic of acquisition of a gain—, but
rather a loss, a subtraction, a surrender. It is a "forfeit" or a "debt" it is obliga-
tory to pay. The *munus* is the obligation one has contracted toward the other
and is forced to discharge in an appropriate fashion. (18)

Communis, in its old acceptation, indicates the sharing of a duty or a task.
"As a result," Esposito adds, "*communitas* is a group of people united not by
a 'property,' but precisely by an obligation or by a debt; not by a 'plus,' but
by a 'minus,' by a lack" (19). From this perspective, the community's subjects are thus united not by a "you owe me" but by an "I owe *you*," which
deprives them of their autonomous personhood, expropriates them, and
forces them to alter themselves. As Jean-Luc Nancy puts it in "Conloquium," his preface to Esposito's essay, these are subjects "with no other
support than a rapport" ["sans autre support qu'un rapport" (10)]. What the
members of a community have in common, then, is nothing—a term,
Nancy explains, that should be understood not as the absence of a thing but
as the thing itself that is to be passed on and shared (9). "From this point of
view," Esposito adds, "not only is the community not identifiable with the
res publica, with the common 'thing,' but it is rather the hole in which the
latter continuously threatens to slide. . . . Here is the blinding truth lodged
in the etymological fold of the *communitas*; the public thing is inseparable
from nothingness" (22). I will return to the question of the Republic in a
moment. But at an individual level, the dual awareness of this "nothing" in
common and of the duty to have a community nonetheless is what I call *the
disastrous realization*—meaning both the realization that there is a disaster and
the realization of the community through something like a founding disaster. What my father and I had begun to acknowledge was no longer just the
fault line between us but the fault line within ourselves—the unbridgeable
gap that signals that one always misses the other, much as the rue Sainte-
Croix and the rue des Rosiers miss each other. Not by much, but still. The
short segment of the rue Vieille du Temple that simultaneously connects and
separates the Marais's two main communities may have been, in the end,
the true marker of our relationship. I find it amusing that it is the site where
the rue des Rosiers, the street that, more than any other, has come to symbolize Jewish memory, meets a gay bar called Amnesia.

Once, many years ago, my father told me he thought he had failed and
had been a bad father. He was right: he had. I didn't exactly tell him that,
but I did tell him that *all* fathers fail and that it was probably a good thing.

In fact, failure could make room for another, less comfortable kind of connectedness, one that could not rely on the pre-existent institutional support of the continuous father-son narrative within the heterosexual familial model, but was worth exploring precisely for that reason. (Of course, I didn't put it to him in such a long-winded way. I told him I was glad we were friends.) At any rate, he seemed to find solace in my reply, and I thought I had handled the situation quite well—that is, until I realized what was implied in my father's tricky admission but what he would never say outright. When he stated, "I have failed as a father," he also meant, "You have failed as a son." Again, he was right: I had. From the family's institutional perspective all queer children are failures, since they signify the disruption of filiation. Naturally, or not so naturally, there are many ways for us queers to have children of our own, and my father's disappointment could have been dismissed simply as stemming from an outdated vision of homosexuality. But in my case, such a vision happens to be right. I *am* an old-fashioned, Marlene-Dietrich-identified, end-of-the-line, degenerate pansy whose favorite holiday is Fleet Week in Manhattan. When my father said it saddened him that he would have no grandchildren from me, I resented him for forcing me to bear witness to his genuine heartbreak. And as the son of a Holocaust survivor, I am conscious that such heartbreak may have a far-reaching significance. But there was nothing I could say. Yes, I chose to be a bad son, and as the classic tee-shirt says, "The family tree stops with me."

Grandchildren aside, a queer child always exposes the parents' failed heterosexuality. If homosexuality was invented as that against which the modern family must define itself, then all bonds with the queer child must be severed or redefined as nonfamilial or both, as in "You are no longer my child. Get out of this house!" (I don't know to what extent homophobic parents say these exact words in reality—probably a lot—but they repeatedly do so on television, which indicates some degree of cultural significance.) So when my father cunningly admitted his failure and unveiled mine in the same performative statement, he was doing away with a familiar and familial relationship and ushering in a new, uncharted one at the same time. I wish the English words *fail* and *failure* offered the same semantic possibilities as the French *manquer, manque, manquement*, for they would better convey how such dereliction of duty (*manquement au devoir*) also signifies "lacking" and "missing." My father failed me, he missed out with me, and he missed me. By the same token, he also failed his heterosexuality, he missed out with it, and presumably, he missed it.

In the terms I laid out, failure was the founding disaster of the community we formed. But that failure was more than a symbolic death to the family; it had a lot to do with actual death: death *in* the family and death *of* the family—in the Holocaust, in my father's case. Referring to the genocides that have characterized the history of the twentieth century, Nancy writes:

> The fact that the work of death . . . was carried out in the name of community—sometimes that of a self-constituted people or race, sometimes that of a self-fashioned humanity [respectively fascism and communism]—is precisely what put an end to all possibilities of relying on any *given* of the common being (blood, substance, filiation, essence, origin, nature, consecration, election, organic or mystic identity). (5; original emphasis)

In other words, the given that makes the community is the transcendence that legitimates it. It is both external (since it must be given by an uncontestable authority, such as God or nature) and internalized, or made proper. Each member of a community carries within himself or herself the transcendental justification of the being-in-common: he or she is, for example, a biological entity or made in God's image. Founding community on a given, therefore, entails the destruction of what threatens its legitimacy.

In *Heidegger and "the Jews,"* Jean-François Lyotard shows how the presence of the Jews, who were expected to disappear by themselves with the advent of Christianity, was a constant reminder of the failure, indeed impossibility, of Western culture's closure. Killing in the name of the community indicates a failure to recognize that death is in fact the constitutive core of the community. As Esposito writes, drawing on Georges Bataille's notion of the "community of death," "The *munus* is the individual *nonbeing* of the relation" (33; original emphasis). This is why, I insist, there is no community without disaster, and the awareness of that is inseparable from a work of mourning.

My brother Denis—my mother's son from an earlier marriage—died several years ago. While my brother's accidental death and my father's family's extermination at the hands of the Nazis are two "events" with no common measure, they are both disastrous in their own way. As my father told me after Denis died, "Things will never be the same again in our family." My father and I became closer after that. In a sense, this was not a surprise. The shocking awareness that death, brutal and absurd, can come without a warning often underscores the futility of petty conflicts and resentments. My mother and I, however, started drifting farther apart at the same time. Clearly, my parents did not deal with Denis's death in the same way. It was not because he was my mother's son and not my father's. My father also raised him, loved him, and was devastated by his death. Yet after he died, my mother cut herself off from others by, among other things, repeating over and over again to everyone around her, "You cannot understand what it's like to lose one's child." However, my father's remark that things would never be the same again acknowledged that something had been lost but that something else was to come. "Things will never be *the same* again" implies that things *will* be, but they will be different. These "things" being, in this case, familial relationships, my father was, in effect, mourning the loss of sameness itself, that is, of substance but also of reproduction. Sameness and reproduction did not go away, of course; they just ceased to be compulsory or substantive. That means, essentially, that we were free to escape the normalizing function of the family if we so desired. Or we could, as my mother opted to do, live "as if"—not as if her child hadn't died but as if that didn't entail a radical rethinking of her relations with others, of what it means to be a member of our family. Instead, she has tried to keep her private hell separate from her public expressions of grief. She uses clichés whose main function is to position death-in-the-family precisely *in* the family as a tragic yet normal event that poses no fundamental threat to the system. (I am not judging my mother here. She is doubtless acutely aware that her relations to others are an act. Who is to say that this isn't in the end a more devastating subversion of the family?)

My father's reaction to this event became legible to me thanks to an old joke of his that, as a result, became fully legible too. When I was a kid, a man he used to know back in Hungary came to visit us in France. My father described him as "a new childhood friend." I didn't get it, so he explained: "We used to live in the same neighborhood, we knew each other when we were kids, only we were not close then. We only had common friends." Why they were closer now was obvious: both their families had been killed, their whole world wiped out. The disappearance of their common friends constituted the absent core of their new-old friendship, the *nothing* they now shared. Disasters, in other words, found communities just as surely as they destroy them. Think of the *copains* in the stalag.

My father experienced the inaugural function of disasters with an acute sense of what may be called (pardon the oxymoron) "historical immediacy": soon after World War II, he left France to fight for the creation of Israel. He volunteered in 1948 very much in the same spirit as in 1939—out of duty toward other people and a lack of reasons not to. He also missed the camaraderie he had experienced in World War II. In Hungary, as a teenager, he had been "a little bit" involved in Zionist movements. Not that he needed Israel himself, he said, but some people did. And because Zionist clubs, back then, mostly provided convenient venues for young people of both sexes to socialize, "this was a great way to meet women." So was the sexually permissive new state where he got married (to a woman I've never met) and lived until 1949. That year his sister asked him to come back to France to work with her, which he briefly did. He then moved to Paris in 1950, opening a tailoring business with an associate. The shop was located in the Marais, rue du Roi de Sicile to be exact. But soon both the business and his marriage began to fall apart, and in 1951 he left his wife, who refused to get divorced, and returned to Caen. They remained officially married until 1972, when I was ten years old. Incidentally, this is the reason why I do not carry my father's name. For the first ten years of my life the French Republic considered me a bastard—or, to put it in less campy but perhaps theoretically richer terms, an illegitimate child. The law forbidding an otherwise married father from recognizing a child has since changed. My parents never married, though, and they eventually separated. My mother, a Gentile, was somewhat relieved that my sister and I never attached a Jewish name to hers: "You can never be too careful."

In 1953 my father decided to return to Israel, where, he proclaimed, a person could build an ideal to live for—"se forger un idéal," an expression

Hungarian

POW

suggesting that ideals may stem from lack and thus follow rather than precede one's commitment to the collective. Today, he readily admits that his
"idealism" was just an excuse and that he really left "because [he] was
bored." Anyone who has ever lived in Caen will easily understand his decision. Back in Israel, he worked in a kibbutz for three years, but in 1956, in
order to get out of yet another bad relationship, he came back to Caen.
That year he met my mother, and as far as I know, that was to be his final attempt at coupledom.

When the Suez crisis erupted and a military conflict broke out a few
months after my father had left Israel, he regretted his decision and wished
he had stayed there to help. Not that he liked war particularly, but he liked
Israel because it had provided him with a sense of purpose, of usefulness.

French

Israeli

1960, the normal life

What he remembered most fondly, along with the military lifestyle he loved so much, was his time in the kibbutz where collective life fit what he called his "gregarious instinct." In the kibbutz, work was not rewarded by money, nor sex by family. In those years children were raised collectively by the whole community of adults. Today this radical aspect of kibbutz life has all but disappeared along with its experimental socialism. Back then, though, while labor and pleasure were in abundance, no personal profit was to be derived from them. Promiscuity, both social and sexual, created community— the kibbutz itself, but also a new nationality whose fundamental values were supposed to be simultaneously reflected in and produced by kibbutz life. That promiscuity was what my father loved. By the mid-1950s, however, he just felt too old and useless. When I remarked that he had spent a large portion of his life working for nothing, he replied that he was never interested in working for money, only for and with others. Admittedly, that's not nothing. Or rather, it is, but perhaps in the sense of nothingness-as-duty that Esposito proposes as the foundation of communities.

And this brings me to my next point. Citizenship, in the fullest, nonadministrative sense of the term, was not satisfying to my father; otherwise he would have stayed in Israel to reap the fruit of his labor. And as he acknowledged himself, he was not concerned with this. As much as I enjoyed the romantic fantasy of a legionnaire leaving his country because of a doomed love affair, my first reaction was to dismiss his claim that he had left just in order to get out of a bad relationship. My father was not the Gary Cooper type—it had to have been an excuse. But the two cannot be easily separated. Just as citizenship (in the active, participatory sense) was supposed to be his reward for his service in the Israeli military and in the kibbutz, so were coupledom and family life. In other words, my father failed on both levels: he worked hard but never embraced the institutionalized nation he had helped to build, and he had sex with several women but never successfully adopted the normative heterosexual lifestyle that is supposed to be the outcome of sex acts between people of different sexes. In a sense, my father was faithful to the sexual pioneering spirit of early Israeli society, and his personal failure unveiled that of the Jewish state.

Since heterosexuality is historically entangled in the construction of modern nationhood, its failure is inseparable from the failure of citizenship. This is particularly true for European Jews, whose emancipation was inseparable from the definition of citizenship and the separation of public and private spheres, as well as from questions of gender and sexuality. In his study of Jewish masculinity, *Unheroic Conduct*, Daniel Boyarin proposes to reread in a positive light the traditional feminization of the Jewish male in Western culture. According to Boyarin, the ideal Jewish masculinity found in the Babylonian Talmud was produced in opposition to the Roman masculinist model, which feminized Jewish men because they did not participate in the public sphere, did not carry arms, and devoted their lives to study. While the Romans saw circumcision as a symbolic form of castration, the Jews saw it as oppositional. When the Roman model of heroic, militaristic manhood became the dominant model in European culture, the apparent self-feminization of the Jews allowed them to retain their cultural specificity. In the eighteenth century, when the ideas of the Haskalah, or Jewish Enlightenment, began to spread, the Westernization of European Jews became inseparable from their masculinization. By the second half of the nineteenth century, popular markers of Jewish otherness within Western societies drew on the newly medicalized categories of sexual perversion, as well as on Orientalist imagery, as Sander Gilman has shown in his vast body of work on the subject. With the concurrent inventions of pathological homosexuality and racial anti-Semitism in the nineteenth century, Jews ceased to perceive their self-feminization as oppositional and repudiated it. Theodor Herzl's Zionism, whose tenets actually echo the Emancipation's ideals of integration and citizenship, equated nationhood with manliness and, in essence, diaspora with queerness.

Israel in its infancy tried to separate sex acts between men and women from institutionalized heterosexuality and the capitalist economy it seeks to naturalize. Whether such experiments in sexual socialism resulted in actual openness toward same-sex relations remains to be proved. Think, for example, of the homophobia, not to mention the misogyny, that often accompanied the sexual revolution of the 1960s and '70s. Still, the notion that homosexuality would no longer be defined as deviant is made at least theoretically possible if sexual relations between men and women are divorced from an institutional support from which to deviate. In that sense, I believe that one can find a certain queerness in early Israeli Zionism, and read it as an attempt to retain a diasporic model of identification within the new nation rather than put an end to it. Once the young state had reached adulthood, however, its polymorphous sexuality was eventually abandoned and order prevailed. Israel fulfilled the promise of manhood contained in turn-of-the-century Zionist theories. Jews, back then, felt that they had to prove that they were not degenerate or, at least, that they could regenerate themselves, that is, fulfill the promise of the Emancipation. In France, for example, in the wake of the Dreyfus Affair many Jewish men and boys tended to prove their Frenchness by, in effect, dissociating themselves from the shy, bespectacled captain, whom they publicly supported but who had crystallized so much hatred around his body. The tragic irony, of course, is that Dreyfus's exemplary military career should have been evidence of successful integration. Yet in those years Jewish males started practicing gymnastics, outdoor activities, and other wholesome, masculine occupations designed to assert citizenship and manliness all at once. The super-Jew was born.

What have these manly affairs got to do with me today? Not much. But they do concern my father directly. His decision to leave Hungary was clearly motivated by the rise of anti-Semitic violence which he experienced personally. The choice of France as a final destination, rather than, say, the United States, was motivated by the extraordinary prestige, in many European communities, of the first country to emancipate its Jews. For a secular, modern Jew like my father, who had never been particularly interested in becoming wealthy and successful, France, more than the United States, represented the ideal that Hungary hadn't been able to fulfill. Hungarian anti-Semitism had been a painful betrayal for him, because he thought of himself first and foremost as Hungarian. To him, his Judaism was what Enlightenment principles said it should be. It was a private matter, and citizenship came first, just as Hungarian came before Yiddish. So the promise of France was that of a successful integration after the trauma of disintegration he suffered in Hungary. His joining the French Foreign Legion at the outbreak of World War II was the logical thing to do, even if his primary motivation was to fight Hitler. France officially recognized his sacrifice and gave him citizenship in 1946. In other words, my father's Frenchness was validated by desire to imagine my father as a fearless, gun-toting warrior, and I found his revelation extremely disturbing. I had also grown sensitive to the beauty of the Palestinian boys around me. In retrospect, that one desire was displaced by another makes perfect sense, a Jean Genet kind of sense. So it was with tremendous apprehension that I asked what I had to ask. "Have you ever killed anyone?" His response came as a relief. "Honestly," he said, with a faint smile that could have signaled either embarrassment or awareness of what I wanted to hear, "it's very unlikely, and it wouldn't have been on purpose, because I never aimed at anyone." I was grateful for that reply, whether he was telling the truth or telling me he knew that for me to respect him he had to admit that he was a bad soldier. Either way, my father's confession of inadequacy filled me with intense filial pride, and I felt close to him at that moment. Call it defective male bonding. But what fulfilled this little faggot's expectations could not possibly have satisfied the state of Israel. My father never theorized, aestheticized, and embraced failure the way I do, and he suffered for it, but the fact is that whether Hungarian, French, or Israeli, his successive citizenships never took. Whereas the first two failures are inseparable from the history of European anti-Semitism and are rather typical of many Jews of his generation, the failure of the third raises deeper questions about the nature of citizenship in general. So when, in the late 1980s, he toyed with the idea of emigrating to the United States, I thought, "Why bother?" He must have reached the same conclusion, because he quickly gave up that plan.

Enter the bad son. The son who, by embracing difference, otherness, seemed to negate everything the father aspired to: not assimilation, of course, but the most French and most enlightened and most valued of French Enlightenment values—universalism. How could I be a homosexual? Or to be more truthful to my father's concerns, how could I willingly face homophobia? The parallels between homophobia and anti-Semitism were not lost on him. "I know what it feels like," he once said. I can't help but compare this to another one of his ambiguous remarks about how his own useless life would be validated if one of his descendants found a cure for cancer or something like that. Strangely, the problem with my being so different from him was that I was going to be just like him: useless and unvalidated. My ambivalence toward Enlightenment values, let alone toward Zionism, is nothing more than a reflection of his own failure to embody this ideal, modern citizenship he aspired to but that always eluded him. He probably regarded what he perceived as my failure as a failure on *his* part, as in: "I am a bad father," which the critic may unpack as: "I am a bad Frenchman because I haven't been able to embody the Western masculinist ideal and that's why I have been a bad role model and my son is a homo and yes I will

Father and son

have another scotch on the rocks thank you." If it helps, think of the father figures in the work of Hanif Kureishi, such as "My Son the Fanatic" and, more to the point perhaps, *My Beautiful Laundrette*, and you will get a good idea of what I am talking about—except that my father was not from Pakistan and he was not Muslim, but, like Kureishi's misintegrated fathers, he liked scotch. A lot. And that's what really mattered.

Eventually I became the man that got away. I emigrated. I disintegrated myself. My existence in this family has now taken the form of an absence, or at the very least of a transit. How long am I staying? When am I leaving? When am I coming back? To some extent, it seems that whenever I go "home" my relatives just can't wait for me to leave again so that they can go on missing me. I would be lying if I said I didn't feel the same way. To my two young nieces, whom I briefly see about once a year, I am the *oncle d'Amérique*, or the gay uncle, or both. Needless to say I am projecting here, since all they seem to care at this point in their lives is that I bring them presents on my visits. But the real present may be that of difference and transit, which define my position in the family and make me something like Lyotard's "Jews"—a reminder of the impossibility of closure. In that sense, my departure too shed doubts on my father's integration, just as my homosexuality shed doubts on his heterosexuality. Instead of being the masculine straight man defined by identification with the Republic, I am queer and I disidentified myself.

What has my father transmitted to me, then? Not the stability and safety of integration he was supposed to achieve, but the instability and disintegration he came with in the first place. Not nationhood but diaspora. Not Frenchness but Jewishness. And since the laws of compulsory heterosexuality no longer seemed to apply so stringently to this father-son relationship, I feel authorized to ask: What have I transmitted to him? This: I was talking with my father on the phone one day, and he said: "Oh, funny you should call just now. I was watching TV, and they had this program on transsexuals, and of course I was thinking of you." *Of course?* I took a deep breath and calmly replied, trying to hide my, what was it? disappointment? discouragement? impatience? "Dad . . . you know . . . transsexualism and homosexuality are not necessarily the same thing." "Oh, I know," he said. "What do you think I am? Stupid? It's just that, if it weren't for you, I wouldn't have been interested in that program at all." Just as my father made me Jewish (although I'm not), I seem to have made him queer (although he was not). So there we were. There *we* were: I was writing a book on the Marais while my eighty-four-year-old father was developing an interest in transsexualism. Everything was going to be all right after all.

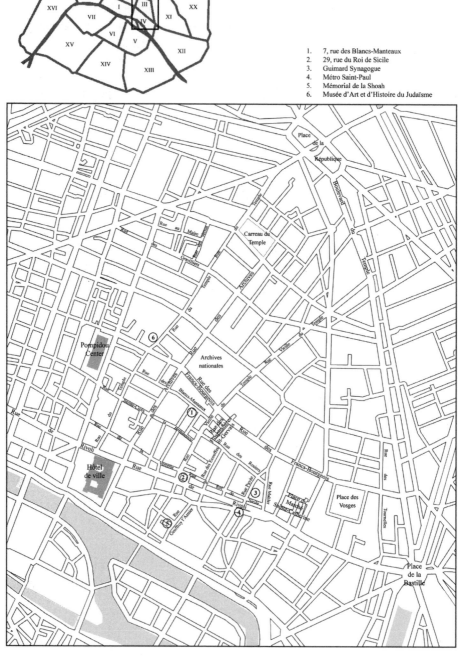

1. 7, rue des Blancs-Manteaux
2. 29, rue du Roi de Sicile
3. Guimard Synagogue
4. Métro Saint-Paul
5. Mémorial de la Shoah
6. Musée d'Art et d'Histoire du Judaïsme

Maps of the Marais

Part I

The Marais

[1]

The Old Neighborhood

It was a marshland. It was a fashionable neighborhood for the aristocracy. It was a dilapidated enclave in the heart of Paris where poor immigrant Jews first settled before moving up in French society—or not. It was later rehabilitated and transformed into a prime real estate area and a magnet for foreign tourists. It is filled with the ghosts of a bloody history: ghosts of aristocrats who were massacred by a revolutionary mob and of the young Dauphin himself; ghosts of Jews taken from their homes before being sent to Auschwitz; ghosts of old people who killed themselves rather than be roughed up and expelled from renovated apartment buildings where they would no longer be able to live; ghosts of Jews who alongside a few others were shot by terrorists inside Jo Goldenberg's deli; ghosts of thousands of young gay men who died of AIDS; ghosts of Chinese sweatshop workers—although, if you believe the rumors, they "never die." It is a living museum of a long-gone Jewish life and, supposedly, a testimony to the success of the French model of social integration. It is a communal home where gay men and women are said to stand in defiance of the French model of social integration. It is a place of freedom and tolerance where people of color and lesbians nevertheless feel unwanted and where young Zionists from the suburbs gather every Sunday and sometimes harass Arabs. It is a hot topic in the press and on television. It is open to the world and open for business. It is a place of tension and contention, a place of great fun and intense boredom, a laboratory for diversity and a clone factory. It is a good place to eat falafels and have sex—but not at the same time and preferably not in that order. It is an open ghetto, a gay and Jewish neighborhood where few gays and Jews actually live. It is a place to be seen and a place of invisibility. It is like a home to me, a place where I feel both safe and out of place and where my father felt comfortable and alienated at the same time. It is a place of nostalgia, innovation, shame, pride, and anxiety, where the local and the global intersect for better and for worse. And for better and for worse, it is a French neighborhood.

AN EXHIBIT AT THE HÔTEL DE VILLE

An exhibit commissioned by the city of Paris and called "From Refuge to Trap: The Jews in the Marais" was held at the Hôtel de Ville (or City Hall) from 12 May to 27 August 2005. In many ways it was a watershed. Located across the street from the traditional boundary of the Marais and set in the official heart of the capital under the high patronage of its Mayor, Bertrand Delanoë, it promised to be an unprecedented recognition of both the history, culture, and contributions of Jews in Paris and, more important perhaps, of the city's role in the deaths of so many of them. Delanoë's foreword to the exhibition's catalog even included a conspicuous reference to the ongoing and thorny question of reparations for Jews whose property was stolen and businesses "aryanized" during the war. Historian Jean-Pierre Azéma was the curator, and rigorous attention was given to the accurate attribution of responsibilities—what exactly was done by the German occupiers, what by the French. In that respect the public display of Vichy Prime Minister Pierre Laval's letter offering to deliver to the German authorities the Jewish children they had not even requested was an event in itself. What may have been the lowest, most despicable point in French history was the spectacular high point of the exhibit. And that may have been the problem.

The exhibit was a disappointment to me. To be sure, it was rich in factual information on the Holocaust as it happened in Paris and, in that sense, it may have fulfilled its much needed didactic purpose. There were displays of yellow stars and identity cards with a special stamp for Jews, incriminating administrative documents, and rare photographs of the French police carrying out arrests. But what immediately struck me was that only one room was devoted to the Jewish presence in the Marais from the Middle Ages to World War II, while nearly all the others focused on the different stages that punctuated the Jews' destruction—exclusionary laws, identification, arrests, deportation and, for a very small number of them, the return from the camps.

The first room of the exhibit included a few medieval engravings and books, some religious objects, a handful of photos of Jews posing proudly in front of their businesses on the rue des Rosiers, and little else. Interviews with three former residents of the Marais were shown in a loop on a video monitor. By comparison, more than a dozen survivors similarly recounted their Holocaust experience in taped interviews. Even the famous synagogue of the rue Pavée designed by Hector Guimard, a unique Art Nouveau masterpiece at once completely Parisian and completely Jewish, was represented by a mere blueprint and a letter. Considering that the temple is closed to visitors, the absence of photos was particularly infuriating. And how could the organizers have neglected the many theaters, newspapers, and groups of all kinds that once made the Marais a vibrant outpost of Yiddish culture stretching over decades and two Parisian arrondissements?

Equally baffling was the section on the return from the camps. One very large photograph was particularly telling. It showed General de Gaulle welcoming a train of returnees from Ravensbrück. The caption described these returnees with the grammatically masculine word, *déportés,* which is odd, given that Ravensbrück is well known as a women's concentration camp (as the presence of visibly female *déportées* on the photo reminded us) and not primarily a death camp for Jews.[1] Germaine Tillion and Charlotte Delbo, among others, have written about it, and the distinction between concentration camps and death camps has long been established. So why revert to the sort of historical confusion that once served to produce the myth of a uniformly heroic France by erasing the specific fate of the Jews? The answer is simple and sad. The exhibit wasn't about the Jews but about France, and its title should have been a dead giveaway.

For one thing, "The Jews in the Marais" seem to be relegated to secondary status, whereas "refuge" and "trap" in the main title foreground France's dual role as emancipator and persecutor of the Jews. A charitable observer could argue that this already constitutes progress after decades of official denial and mythification. Irritated as we might be by the tardiness of it all, better a late recognition than no recognition at all. In all fairness, the exhibit, whose location was a loud and powerful symbol, seemed to cap ten years during which France officially undertook a radical reevaluation of its role in the Holocaust. It was 1995 when a newly elected President Jacques Chirac finally admitted France's share of responsibility in the events, a fact his predecessors, most notably de Gaulle and François Mitterrand, stubbornly refused to acknowledge in the face of overwhelming evidence. A few years after that, new plaques in memory of murdered Jewish children were placed outside Paris's schools and included for the first time the words, "with the active complicity of the Vichy administration." The national railroad company, the SNCF, has even issued a formal apology for the logistical support it gave the Nazis for the deportations. All this may sound obvious to, say, Americans who have made the masochistic (that is, painful and self-serving) display of collective guilt something of a national pastime; it really is a lot for the French. So much in fact that it must arouse suspicion. Given the fact that the exhibit was specifically and explicitly about the Marais and not about France as a whole, the trap in question, the title implies, may have been the neighborhood itself—an urban area largely associated with one minority community and, as such, a violation of the French model of integration which prohibits "nations within the nation." The Jews of the title, after all, are *in* the Marais and not *of* the Marais, occupants of a section of Paris rather than its defining population. The cursory and mostly folkloric treatment the exhibit gave to Jewish communal life in the neighborhood could therefore be explained by a profound reluctance to acknowledge that such a rich minority culture ever existed as it did, not just in the heart of the French capital but as a crucial part of it.

The disturbing implication is that "excessive" cultural visibility, or conspicuousness, may in itself lead to vulnerability and even mortal danger. One may remember that, a few years ago, during the debates around the PACS and the legalization of same-sex couples, one rather surreal argument coming from those opponents, left and right of center, who didn't want to be perceived as homophobes, was that the PACS would create an administrative database that, should fascism return, could effectively be used to round up and exterminate homosexuals. The word they used for database, or files, was *fichier,* and its echoes were unmistakable when controversies around the possible discovery of the infamous *fichier juif* established during the German occupation had recently made headlines.[2] But of course Jews and gays share more than a history of oppression by the Nazis; they also share a neighborhood—the Marais. Add to this the more recent ban on "ostensible" signs of religion in public schools, a ban really aimed at Muslims, and it is easy to recognize the distinctive French Republican discourse on universalism and community: collective invisibility is the only way to have and protect individual freedom. It is this defining principle that was reinforced by the exhibit on the Marais. And while it may have appeared at first to be a sign of recognition of French responsibility in the Holocaust, it had the effect of casting "true" France as the opposite and, logically, the country's less than honorable acts as un-French by definition. That, in essence, was Mitterrand's syllogistic argument: true France is the Republic; Vichy wasn't the Republic; therefore France is not responsible for what Vichy did. The long-awaited recognition, it seems, was no recognition at all and the Marais, more than ever, a contested neighborhood.

Is it its central location? Its architectural wonders? Is it the fact that it is one of the oldest neighborhoods of Paris still standing? Whatever it is, no other part of the city has been so fiercely laid claim to by so many different communities recognizing it as their own. For many traditionalists, the Marais, with its elegant seventeenth-century residences and historical museums, is a testimony to the grandeur of France and to its peculiar genius. For Ashkenazi Jews, it remains the Pletzl, while Jews who came there from North Africa after decolonization call it the Quartier Saint-Paul. Gays and lesbians have made it France's first and, arguably, only modern gay neighborhood. Foreign tourists adore it for its quaint narrow streets and fashionable stores. And then there are the Chinese who have settled in some parts of the Marais as well and who seem to arouse near unanimous suspicion these days.

What specific area actually constitutes the Marais is not so easy to determine and, predictably, different people have had different notions about it. For one thing, a quartier has no legal status in France today; it is neither a borough nor an electoral district, and its boundaries are seldom written in stone, so to speak. For instance, the recent exhibit, and companion book, focused specifically on a section also known as the Quartier Saint-Gervais that is located between the Seine to the south and the rue des Francs-Bourgeois to the north, the rue des Archives to the west and the rue Saint-Paul and rue de Turenne to the east. As such, it is entirely contained within the fourth arrondissement. Inexplicably, it leaves out some of the area's most beautiful aristocratic residences and even the famous place des Vosges, widely considered to be the crown jewel of the Marais and perhaps of Paris itself. The organizers clearly wanted to focus on Jews in the Marais, but the square des Vosges, as people often called it, played an important part in the daily lives of many as a meeting place and playground. In the eighteenth century, large sections of what is now the eleventh arrondissement, including today's rue Oberkampf and boulevard de Belleville, were considered part of the Marais.[3] As for the historic Pletzl, it extended farther east toward the place de la Bastille and well into the third arrondissement, particularly on and around the rue du Temple, all the way to the place de la République—an area known as the Quartier des Gravilliers and now booming with Chinese-owned businesses. The more symbolic Pletzl of today, however, is limited roughly to the rue des Rosiers and a few adjoining streets. But when the Pompidou Center was built along the rue Beaubourg, farther west, its opponents were scandalized that such a huge modern building could be erected "in the heart of the Marais!" The gay area, however, is but a small enclave more or less limited to the rue Sainte-Croix de la Bretonnerie and its immediate surroundings. And don't ask real estate agents; they will stretch the Marais's outer boundaries as far as they possibly can in order to capitalize on the neighborhood's prestige. And, before you know it, you may find yourself living in a dump by the city limits wondering what on earth happened. And they're not the only ones. The farther one strays from the neighborhood's center (within limits, of course), the likelier one is to come across shops with "Marais" in their name. The Marais, it seems, is less a matter of urban topography than of collective affect and socio-historical claims. Naturally, it took centuries to get to this point.

The origin of its name is itself contested. While the area used to be a marshland (*marais* in French), later drained and built as the medieval city began to expand on the right bank, many historians tend to agree that the neighborhood most likely owes its appellation to the vegetable gardens (*cultures maraîchères*) that once were its main activity beside the increasingly busy harbor on the Seine. The name "Marais," specifically applied to the neighborhood, may have appeared either in the 1560s or sometime in the seventeenth century and, in either case, was a direct reference to the gardens located within the domain of the Knights Templar.[4] In the pre-Christian era, the Gauls devoted that part of the right bank to their dead, and it is only when the first churches, Saint-Gervais, then Saint-Paul, were built there, beginning in the fourth century, that the area started to become populated as parishes developed and market gardens appeared. The dead and the living were now neighbors.[5] By the twelfth century, as the Grève harbor developed by what is now the Hôtel de Ville, the Bourg Saint-Gervais had extended its activities to include commerce and crafts, particularly in the textile industry. At that time, the Knights Templar began to occupy a large section of the area. Today's rues du Temple, Vieille-du-Temple, du Faubourg-du-Temple testify to their once powerful presence. More churches, abbeys, and monasteries were built, as well as residences for provincial prelates and nobles increasingly attracted to Paris as it developed into the country's political and intellectual center.[6]

In the 1360s King Charles V established a residence in the Hôtel Saint-Paul, a vast complex of houses and gardens of which there is nothing left today. By the reign of Charles VI the area had become home to princes and nobles, until the English occupation forced the French monarchy out of Paris. The city soon regained its freedom and status, but the old Hôtel Saint-Paul was divided up in lots and sold. Kings didn't abandon the Marais, however, as François I and Henri II started to make the Hôtel des Tournelles their residence, until the latter died there in a jousting accident in 1559 and his widow, Catherine de Médicis, abandoned the place. By the end of the Renaissance and the dawn of the classical era, the Marais had been thoroughly transformed into a vibrant urban area of tremendous economic and social diversity.[7]

Henri IV had big plans for Paris and for the Marais in particular, which he wanted to transform into a modern neighborhood. To a large extent the transformation had already begun under the monarchs of the Renaissance. But it was in the seventeenth century that the Marais was to reach its zenith. The place Royale, renamed place des Vosges since the Revolution, was completed in 1612, two years after Henri IV's assassination. It was an immediate sensation and was soon known simply as "la place."[8] Luxurious residences in the classical style appeared where gardens used to be—they are the great hôtels, now renovated to their original glory—and the neighborhood rapidly became the most elegant and fashionable part of the capital. Theaters and salons opened everywhere and, for a while, it seemed that everyone who was anyone—artists, men and women of letters, the rich and the powerful, the religious and the libertines—lived in the area: Mme de Sévigné, Corneille, Molière, François d'Aubignac, Scarron, Mademoiselle de Scud-

The Marais during the Renaissance: The Hôtel de Sens

Place des Vosges

éry, known as Sappho, and many more either had homes here or made it their playground.[9] The name may have been known before, but this is the time when the neighborhood truly became the Marais, and perhaps no-one embodied its spirit better than Ninon de Lenclos, the great lover of her time and queen of the salon society. In his memoirs of Ninon's life, M. B★★★★★ (Antoine Bret), her contemporary, describes the neighborhood:

> It was mainly in the Marais that the most famous pleasure seekers had established their residence, or at least that was where nearly all of them gathered. In this charming neighborhood, far from the noise and the turmoil that indigence, also called industry, caused inside the city, one was busy only with what could contribute to life's amusement. It was there that those gifted with considerable riches, others with a delicate imagination and an easy, natural wit, and all of them with a disposition for pleasure, enjoyed the happiest of fortunes. There the courtier, the warrior, and the man of letters practiced the sort of placid and good-natured philosophy whose system finds its source in the needs and desires of the human heart.

Musée Carnavalet

[[C'était surtout au Marais que les plus célèbres voluptueux avaient fixé leur séjour, ou du moins c'était là qu'ils se rassemblaient presque tous. Loin du tumulte et du fracas que l'indigence, sous le nom d'industrie, causait au sein de la Ville, on s'occupait, dans ce quartier charmant, de ce qui pouvait contribuer aux agréments de la vie. C'était là que les uns avec une fortune considérable, les autres avec une imagination délicate, un esprit aisé et naturel, tous avec un coeur ami des plaisirs, jouissaient du sort le plus heureux. Le Courtisan, le Guerrier, l'homme de Lettres, y devenaient philosophes, et de cette Philosophie commode et tranquille, dont le système a sa source dans les besoins et les désirs du coeur humain.]][10]

For many, this lovely description could easily apply to the neighborhood today. Roughly a hundred years later, however, Sébastien Mercier described a much different society in the Marais:

Should one have the misfortune to dine there, one will only meet fools; one would search in vain for the amiable men who adorn their ideas with sparkling wit and charming sentiments: a man, sitting in a circle, is but another armchair cluttering the parlor. . . . Should a man of wit accidentally stray among such tedious company and attempt to sparkle, it will be an hour before you see these people emerge from their dull apathy and smile inanely at the fireworks that amaze them; but their card games soon regain the upper hand, and it will be another year before they hear of tomorrow's news.

[Si on a le malheur d'y souper, on n'y rencontre que des sots; et l'on y cherche en vain ces hommes aimables, qui ornent leurs idées du brillant de l'esprit et du charme du sentiment: tel homme assis dans un cercle, est un fauteuil de plus, qui embarrasse un salon. . . . Si cependant un homme d'esprit, égaré par hasard dans ces fastidieuses sociétés, s'avise de faire jaillir quelques étincelles, vous les verrez, au bout d'une heure, sortir de leur lourde apathie, et sourire niaisement au feu qui les étonne; mais les cartes bientôt reprennent le dessus, et ils n'apprendront que dans une année la nouvelle du lendemain.][11]

What had happened? Still home to craftsmen, shopkeepers and bourgeois, the Marais had seen, by the end of the seventeenth century, a steady influx of aristocrats and financiers. After all, part of the appeal of the area was that, while very close to the center of power, it still offered space and relative calm. Not for long, however. By the turn of the eighteenth century, both were becoming scarce. As the neighborhood became more densely populated and under the growing influence of Versailles, both architecturally and as the seat of power, elegant society began to relocate to the western part of the city. The faubourgs Saint-Honoré and Saint-Germain, in particular, offered the rich and powerful the possibility of enjoying larger palaces and gardens,[12] leaving behind the dull, modest and conservative bourgeois that so horrified Mercier. During the Revolution, the Marais found itself in the eye of the storm: its first victim, the warden of the nearby Bastille, was killed there; the royal family was imprisoned in the Temple before being paraded through the neighborhood on their way to the guillotine; and aristocrats, most famously the Princesse de Lamballe, were massacred at a prison on what is now the rue du Roi-de-Sicile. But the party had been over well before that, and by the end of the reign of Louis XIV the Marais had already entered what was to be, for some, a long period of decline, until the Malraux act of 4 August 1962 started the process of renovation of the neighborhood.

In the eighteenth and nineteenth centuries the Marais was but the shadow of its former self. The place grew increasingly filthy, its residents poorer and poorer. Even religious orders began to leave. One by one, the old elegant residences were divided up into smaller, more affordable apartments, their courtyards now housing shops and small factories. The population was densely packed, and epidemics of cholera and tuberculosis repeatedly struck the area. The Marais had become a cesspool.[13]

Still, Beaumarchais lived in the Marais in the eighteenth century and, in the nineteenth, so did the famous actress Rachel, Théophile Gautier and

Victor Hugo who described, in *Choses vues*, the events of yet another revolution, that of 1848, unfolding almost under his windows. (The area had also seen its share of street fighting during the revolution of 1830 and was to see a lot more during the Paris Commune.) But the downward trend could not be reversed. The narrow and crowded streets left untouched by Haussmann's renovation of the city made the Marais look very much like the medieval Paris that the elegant seventeenth-century neighborhood had tried to relegate to a distant past. Novelists such as Gautier, Balzac, and Zola, as well as Eugène Sue and Alphonse Daudet, all depict a dark, decayed, often unwholesome maze, yet one that, with its throngs of street peddlers and artisans of all kinds, was also lively and colorful and would, in turn, also become an object of nostalgia. The presence of Jews often endowed these writings with a distinctive touch of local color, emphasizing even further the dramatic contrast between what the Marais used to be and what it now was. In *L'évangéliste* [The Evangelist], Daudet thus depicts one of the old hôtels:

At that time, like the other princely mansions turned into shops, it sported a lively, industrial physiognomy and, under its large porch, the endless traffic of wagons crisscrossing the vast courtyard ran between the business in Paris and the refineries of Petit-Port . . . while in the large parlor on the ground floor, with its walls made nebulous by mythological tableaux, the old woman sat atop a desk shaped like a pulpit, wearing a hat and gloves but no coat, her parakeet on a perch by her side, and on it supervised the sales and purchases from above the pay-desks and the scales, calling out to some clerk, loudly enough to cover the ruckus of gold and haggling, "Moses, make up your account again . . . you have one grain too many."

[A cette époque, il avait, comme ces demeures princières transformées en maisons de commerce, une physionomie vivante, industrielle, et sous son vaste porche un continuel va-et-vient de fourgons, traversant la cour immense, faisant le service entre la maison de Paris et les affineries de Petit-Port. . . . tandis que dans les vastes salons du rez-de-chaussée aux murs tout vaporeux de peintures mythologiques, la vieille femme juchée sur un bureau à forme de chaire, en taille, en chapeau, strictement gantée, avec le perchoir de sa perruche à côté d'elle, surveillait de haut les guichets, les balances, à l'achat comme à la vente, et criait à quelque commis, dominant le bruit de l'or, les discussions du trafic: "Moïse, refais ton compte . . . tu as dix centigrammes de trop."][14]

Jews had indeed become ubiquitous in the neighborhood by the end of the nineteenth century, as wave after wave of immigrants from the east found it a cheap and convenient place to settle in. But the Jews' presence in the Marais, part myth and part history, is much older.

"LEBN VI GOT IN FRANKRAYKH"

As they did in several other cities in Gaul, the first Jews arrived in Paris, or Lutèce, in the footsteps of Roman armies at the beginning of the Christian era. They settled in the Ile de la Cité.[15] By the sixth century, they had established what could be called a neighborhood around the marketplace where Notre-Dame now stands. They were craftsmen and shopkeepers, for the most part, and a few were doctors. As the city began to outgrow its old limits and spread to the left bank, so did its Jewish inhabitants. By the eleventh century, there were several Jewish neighborhoods in and around the city. Unlike the neighborhoods of today, these had strict boundaries and were even locked at night. In 1182 the Jews were expelled from the kingdom by Philippe Auguste, who reversed his decision in 1198 in the face of unanticipated economic consequences. In the interim, Jewish properties had been confiscated and sold, and the poorer among the returnees had to settle near Les Halles, the market on the right bank, while the richer ones settled in the Marais. This expulsion, followed by a partial return, was the first of many. The 1306 expulsion under Philippe Le Bel saw the end of a rich rabbinical culture that had developed in Paris. Some Jews decided to stay, albeit semi-clandestinely, but they too were expelled in 1311. When they were allowed back in 1315, Louis X expelled the Christians who had taken up residence in the Marais, thus marking the "official" beginning of the Marais as a Jewish neighborhood. But the entire fourteenth century was a long series of expulsions and returns. Each time the Jews lost something— privileges, property, and, for some, their lives, as in the outbreak of anti-Jewish riots of 1380 and 1382. When the Black Death struck, Jews were accused of poisoning the wells. Finally, after Charles VI expelled them from the kingdom yet again in 1394, it would take another three centuries for there to be a Jewish community in Paris again. Interestingly, another religious minority later settled in the Marais in the absence of the Jews— Protestants.

If some Jews still lived in Paris—they never completely disappeared— they did so illegally and outside of any organized community. Such communities had begun to appear in European cities in the tenth century, and one was first officially identified in Paris under Philippe Auguste.[16] In the diaspora, a community had to be strictly organized in order, first of all, for Jewish life to follow rabbinical laws, but also to deal with the Christian (or Muslim, as the case may be) society among which they lived, worked and worshipped. Jews formed assemblies and elected delegates, promulgated edicts and ordinances regarding everything from education and marriage to judicial and financial matters. Community leaders organized tax collections, both for the king and for the sustenance and autonomy of the community itself. Relations between communities were also strictly regulated. These were the communities that vanished after 1394, yet were effectively outlawed by the Emancipation in the name of universal citizenship. Today, what French Jews call a community consists of the congregation of a given synagogue, with at least some members living within walking distance of it in order to be able to get to it on foot on Shabbat. Today still, walking to the synagogue wearing distinctive clothes is one way for Jews to invest urban space.

The earliest presence of Jews in the Marais cannot be dated with precision. Not all of them lived in their own *juiverie* and, in all likelihood, they followed the spread and economic development of the city itself, moving to the right bank when commerce and industry did. When the riots of 1380 broke out, the small Parisian community, in official existence for only twenty years, lived around the Hôtel Saint-Paul, where the king had his residence, as well as on the rue des Rosiers and the street then called rue des Juifs (and renamed rue Ferdinand-Duval after the Dreyfus Affair)—interestingly, what's left of the Pletzl today. But by the thirteenth century, at least, there was already a significant number of Jews in the Marais. This is when the miracle of the bleeding host is said to have taken place.

On Easter Sunday in 1290, as the story goes, a Jewish money-lender named Jonathas demanded that one of his customers pay him with a host. As he proceeded to pierce it with a knife, streams of blood spurted out of it. He then attempted to boil it but the water immediately turned red and the host, now floating in midair, transformed itself into the image of Christ on the cross. News of the miracle soon spread in the neighborhood. Jonathas was arrested, tried, and burned at the stake (this much is historically true) with a copy of the Talmud in his arms. A chapel was erected at 22 rue des Archives, where his house was located. Today, on that very spot, right in the middle of the gay Marais, stands a Protestant church. The edifying story, the like of which is common in one form or another in much European anti-Jewish folklore, was passed on over the centuries and was still memorialized by artifacts and paintings in several churches in the neighborhood as late as 1960.[17] A series of seventeenth-century etchings depicting the story was included in the exhibit at the Hôtel de Ville.

The Marais became conspicuously Jewish again under Louis XIV, when the eastern province of Alsace was incorporated into the kingdom by the Treaty of Westphalia and Paris attracted members of the large Jewish community of Metz. In the eighteenth century, under Louis XV, the Jews of Paris consisted of three distinct groups: the Jews from Metz and other Ashkenazim, who lived in the rue Beaubourg area and made up the bulk of the community; the Portuguese Jews—Sephardim whose ancestors were expelled by the Inquisition and relocated in Bordeaux and Bayonne—who lived on the left bank; and the Jews from Avignon, the oldest community in France, also living on the left bank. All in all, there were no more than 500 to 800 Jews living in Paris on the eve of the French Revolution. After the Emancipation the numbers grew quickly. By 1810 there were about 2,500 Jews in Paris. While they didn't live in specific neighborhoods, there was a sizable Ashkenazi presence in the third and fourth arrondissements of today. In 1820 there were between 6,000 and 7,000 Jews in Paris; in 1831 12,000; in 1857 13,000. Most were coming from eastern France, where the largest and most vibrant communities were still located at the time. The poorer ones lived in the areas of La Roquette and Belleville—still noticeably Jewish to this day—while schools and an orphanage were built in the Marais. By the Second Empire, Jews who numbered 20,000 in 1860 lived more or less everywhere in Paris,[18] but in 1872 40 percent of Parisian Jews lived in the Marais.[19] The annexation of the eastern départements of Alsace and Moselle by Germany after the Franco-Prussian war of 1870 marked a turning point in the history of the Jews in Paris. Many Jews, who wanted to remain French, immigrated to the city, which, for the first time, effectively re-placed Metz as the center of Jewish life in France and became a magnet both for foreign Jews fleeing persecutions at home and for some in the Jewish communities of colonial North Africa. By 1914, at the start of World War I, more than 60,000 Jews lived in Paris. The native community soon found itself outnumbered by foreigners, creating tensions and con-flicts between a largely acculturated French Jewry and the more religious newcomers.

The 1881 assassination of tsar Alexander II triggered an explosion of pogroms and other anti-Semitic disturbances in and around the Russian Empire. Jews began to emigrate from Russia but also from present-day Poland, Romania, and several provinces of the Austro-Hungarian Empire. While many tried to make it to the United States, a few thousand[20] settled in Paris, attracted by its near mythical aura as the birthplace of the Emanci-pation and by its promise of integration and freedom.[21] "Lebn vi Got in Frankraykh" ("To live like God in France"), went a famous Yiddish saying at the time.

Another major pogrom, coupled with the failed Russian revolution of 1905, started the second wave of immigration from Eastern Europe. Some of these immigrants, like their predecessors, were poor, rural, religious, and speakers of Yiddish, but most belonged to the artisanal working class of Russian cities and towns.[22] As for the Jews of the Maghreb, who spoke Judeo-Arabic (as well as French for some), the term "immigration" seems inappropriate since Algerian Jews had been made French citizens by the Crémieux decree of 1870, while those from Morocco and Tunisia were not strictly speaking foreigners but colonial subjects. Their influx did not constitute a wave either, but their steady arrival in Paris between 1870 and the outbreak of World War II was nonetheless culturally significant as a different type of Judaism began to take root in the city. North African Jews who settled in the Marais lived mostly south of the rues de Rivoli and Saint-Antoine, while the Ashkenazim were to the north of it. Between 1908 and 1939, the Jews of the Levant, that is, of the Ottoman Empire, and later Turkey, represented the next wave. Ladino speakers and descendents of the Sephardic Jews expelled from the Iberian Peninsula, they came from prosperous urban communities in Salonika, Istanbul, and Smyrna. In all, about 10,000 of them may have settled in Paris but, unlike their Askenazi counterparts whom they often regarded with elitist contempt, they ignored the Marais, opting instead for the part of the eleventh arrondissement situated around the rues Sedaine and Popincourt that soon became known as Little Istanbul. Throughout the nineteenth century, many foreign Jews also came as students from countries that restricted their access to universities.[23] Soon, the end of World War I brought more trouble to the Jews of Eastern Europe. Violence, growing intolerance and poverty in rural areas, and the aftermath of the October Revolution brought tens of thousands of Jews to Paris from Russia, Romania, Hungary, and especially Poland. This was by far the largest wave of Jewish immigration to France. It too would last until 1939. Finally, several thousand Jews from Germany and Austria, fleeing the threats of Nazism, arrived in Paris between 1933 and 1939.[24] When World War II broke out, 200,000 Jews lived in Paris, the majority of them foreigners.

Before the mass immigrations of 1881 and 1905, the Jewish identity of the Marais had been shaped in large part by the Alsatian Jews, who had lived there since Louis XIV and arrived in larger numbers after 1870. The decision to leave Alsace, now under German rule, testified to the Jews' belief in the French ideals of the Emancipation and their successful integration. They easily found their place in an acculturated and secularized Parisian community. The same, however, cannot be said of the "Russians," as the newcomers were universally known. French Jews saw them as something of an archaic tribe, hopelessly backward, uneducated, and religious to the point of superstition—much, of course, as they had themselves been described at the time of the Emancipation. The press started depicting the Marais as an exotic enclave in the heart of Paris and even as a hotbed of contagious diseases.[25]

At best, the Yiddish-speaking *Ostjuden,* as they were known in Germanic cultures, were seen as an embarrassing lot whose strange clothes and manners attracted unnecessary attention to the community; at worst, that visibility was perceived as a threat to the French Jews' own successful integration. The wave of anti-Semitism that was sweeping other parts of Europe in those years hadn't seriously affected France yet, but when Edouard Drumont's *La France juive* [*Jewish France*] came out in the spring of 1886 and became an immediate bestseller, the respite was over. The Dreyfus Affair would soon engulf the country.

In the mid-1880s most French Jews left the third and fourth arrondissements to relocate to other, slightly more upscale Jewish neighborhoods in the ninth, tenth, and eleventh. This was as much a result of their rejection of foreign Jews than of upward mobility. The once luxurious mansions were becoming ruins, the living conditions plummeting. At that point, just as it would be for the next waves of immigrants, the Marais was first and foremost a hub, a stage in the process of integration into French society. Indeed, by the mid-1890s, French Jews had started to leave traditionally Jewish areas for the *beaux quartiers* of the left bank and the west—the usual topographical translation of Parisian upward mobility. From 1905 to 1907, in the face of the second wave of immigration, the "Russians" of 1881 proceeded to do more or less the same thing. The richest moved westward, while the others settled to the north and east, creating new Jewish neighborhoods at the city's periphery.[26]

Suspicion cut both ways, though.[27] Paris may have been the new Zion to some, but many saw it as Babylon and vehemently resisted their fellow Jews' paternalistic attempts to frenchify them. The newcomers were a little baffled to discover that so many French Jews, who called themselves *Israélites,* were, well, French. They dressed and spoke like French people and didn't even keep kosher! More shocking were the differences in religious traditions in the temples themselves. Ushers in Napoleonic hats? Organ music and a choir? No separation of the sexes? The Consistory—the central Jewish authority created by Napoleon I and responsible for most of these changes (designed to make French Judaism structurally more like the Catholic Church)—soon found itself in the middle of a full-blown conflict. The monumental synagogue of the rue des Tournelles, the biggest in the Marais, with a structure designed by Gustave Eiffel, "belonged" to the Alsatian Jews who refused to turn it over to the immigrants. A new synagogue had to be built, and in 1914 the synagogue of the rue Pavée was opened and dedicated to traditional orthodox rites, albeit amidst Guimard's Art Nouveau architecture and lights, lamps and doorways that echoed the brand new Paris metro.[28] Many small oratories also appeared in private apartments, fulfilling the needs of specific communities, often of people from the same town or in the same line of work, who were capable of putting together a minyan, a quorum of ten men. In time some immigrants did adopt a more secular, more French way of life, while others remained attached to their traditions. Overall, though, the Marais remained a more religious neighborhood than Belleville, for example, where Jews found their place within that neighborhood's politically active, left-leaning working class. If anything, these episodes, and many more to come, are emblematic of the profound heterogeneity of the French Jewish community.

Between the two World Wars, the Marais continued to be a vibrant center of Jewish culture in general and Yiddishkayt in particular under the added influence of the new wave of immigrants—the "Poles," who were Polish in the way that the "Russians" were Russian: mostly, but not only. The Yiddish press, while not new (*Die Zeitung* appeared in 1789), was especially active and numerous.[29] Titles included *Unzer Welt, Unzer Wort, Unzer Shtime, Di Naye Presse, Der Yidisher Arbeter, Der Forverts,* and the main daily newspaper, *Der Parizer Haynt,* among many, many others. All sorts of organizations, often started during the Russian wave,[30] served all sorts of needs. Some were political—Zionist, Bundist, Socialist, Communist—and some religious. Many were mutual aid societies organized around a common home town or trade and known as *Landsmanshaftn,* that played an in-

The synagogue on the rue des Tournelles, built by Gustave Eiffel

The synagogue on the rue
Pavée, built by Hector Guimard

dispensable role in welcoming new immigrants and facilitating their integration into French society, while providing crucial services, such as daycare
and charity, loans and pensions.[31] There were youth groups[32] and burial societies. In what was already a long tradition in the Marais, artisans and
craftsmen continued to flourish, particularly in the textile, shoemaking, and
fur industries,[33] which provided newcomers with a craft easily learned, if
they hadn't come with it, and, as a result, immediate employment and
quicker economic autonomy. These trades also had the tremendous advan-
tage of dividing labor and, therefore, provided more jobs to more people.[34]
The *casquettiers,* or cap-makers, were ubiquitous, a trade already popularized
by the Jews of Alsace. But there were also kosher butchers, cabinet-makers,
and poorer tradesmen, such as ragmen, street peddlers, and dealers in all
sorts of second-hand goods, alongside bookstores and theaters. And naturally, there were all the restaurants and stores where one could find the foods
of the old country.[35] Even though Jews were far from being the majority
in the area, the third and fourth arrondissements were teeming with Jewish
life. The Pletzl may have been named after that little triangle where the rue

Rue des Ecouffes: A typical oratory during Sukkot

Miron meets the rues de Rivoli and Saint-Antoine, by the Saint Paul metro station; or perhaps it was the small square formed by the rue des Hospital-ières Saint-Gervais, in front of the school founded by the Baron de Rothschild to promote integration; or the more secluded place du Marché-Sainte-Catherine maybe. This probably did not extend to the place des Vosges—the Pletzl wasn't *la place*, although two Jewish schools opened there in the early nineteenth century and it, too, became a Jewish site, where children played and adults socialized,[36] and where brawls between Jews and anti-Semites took place.[37] Nobody knows for certain, but whatever the origin of its name may be, the neighborhood known as the "little square" extended over a large chunk of central Paris, and its Jewish population was mostly made up of foreigners.

"From Refuge to Trap" was the title of the 2005 exhibit. When the German occupiers and the Vichy government set the extermination of the Jews of France in motion, they knew just where to go, and neighborhoods identified as Jewish were targeted first. Foreign Jews were the only ones to be marked for arrest—although Vichy denaturalized thousands of people and thus made them deportable. The Marais, known to be heavily populated with foreigners, was hit hard. At the outbreak of World War I, a patriotic

A small synagogue next door

march had been organized on the rue des Rosiers, and the first regiments of foreign volunteers had left from the Pletzl;[38] in World War II, it was decimated. In the Marais, as elsewhere, the extermination of the Jews was conducted in stages. First, there were exclusionary laws and anti-Semitic incidents. Synagogues were burned in the Marais and in other parts of Paris. Then businesses were confiscated and aryanized, a process that, itself, rendered the removal of the Jews inevitable. If a neighborhood was predominantly Jewish and potential customers speakers of Yiddish, how could Aryan businesses survive? This question was asked explicitly during aryanization procedures. One file states, for example, "As long as the Saint-Paul district remains an emblematic neighborhood for Jews, the customers of this business will remain Jewish, and no Aryan will ever be able to make a living here"; and a new restaurant owner complains, "as long as the area is populated with Jews, the customers of this business will be solely Jewish. As a result, no Aryan will be able to make a living here, no Aryan will be able to find his place here and buy such a business."[39] The destruction and renovation of the *îlot 16,* a particularly decrepit and unsanitary section of the Marais located between the rue de Rivoli and the Seine, could begin in earnest. Drawing from a long tradition of metaphors linking the various vermin and diseases that had long plagued the Marais with the poor foreign Jews who lived there, the administrative authorities could now literally clean up the place.[40] Raid after raid soon emptied the neighborhood, culminating with the infamous *rafle du Vel d'Hiv* on 16 and 17 July 1942. When De Gaulle stood at the balcony of the Hôtel de Ville on 25 August 25 1944, a stone's throw from the heart of what was once the Pletzl, and proclaimed Paris liberated, the last convoy of deportees had left the triage camp of Drancy eight days before.[41] Seventy-five thousand Jews of France were deported to death camps; two thousand five hundred survived. The Jewish Marais was dead.

There were about twenty thousand Jews still living in Paris after the Liberation; some, destitute, in the Marais. Returnees from the camps often came to the old Pletzl first, even if they had never lived there. *Griners,* they were called, green, newcomers to the area. But there were no reasons for them to stay very long, and many rapidly took off for America or Palestine.[42] The Marais was still a place of transit, but no longer on the way to integration. A few shops and workrooms began to reopen, if only to ensure day-to-day survival. Some of the people whose businesses and homes were

Traces of the Holocaust

stolen, and who could afford the costly procedure, tried to recover them, while many simply gave up, often in the face of the new occupants' resistance. On 19 April 1945, a brawl broke out, followed by an anti-Semitic demonstration (one of several in the neighborhood) during an attempt to evict an Aryan tenant on the rue des Guillemites.[43] For a while the traditional artisanal trades persisted, but the Marais's Jewish universe was now reduced to the rue des Rosiers and its immediate surroundings, a far cry from the vast area it covered before the war. It is interesting to note that, decades later, this complex intermediate period would be particularly favored by some Jewish writers such as Jean-Claude Grumberg, Robert Bober, and Cyrille Fleischman, to name but a few. Their work emphasizes the hauntedness that characterized the area in those years.[44] These were the days when the Jews of France tried to keep a low profile. The use of Yiddish started to wane and naturalizations increased. So did name changes, interfaith marriages, and conversions. As in the rest of French society, discussions of the Holocaust and the specific fate of the Jews during the war were soon smothered by the new official history, which privileged the memory of political deportations and French heroism. For Jews, however, discretion was the order of the day.

ALL that soon changed when the Sephardim came. I should say, the Jews from North Africa, many of whom were not descendants of the Jews expelled from Spain and Portugal in 1492 but of those who came much earlier with the Phoenicians. But *Séfarades* is what they are universally called in France (that is, if one doesn't seek to specify their country of origin). French colonization facilitated a small but steady influx of North African Jews into metropolitan France during the nineteenth century and the first decades of the twentieth. But the creation of Israel in 1948 made their situation in predominantly Muslim countries increasingly uncomfortable. In the mid 1950s, with the start of the Algerian War and Tunisian and Moroccan independence, the exodus began, until nearly all Jews had left the Maghreb. Many chose to go to Israel, but most, literate French speakers, came to France in what was the largest mass arrival of Jews in the history of the country. By 1970 between 220,000 and 250,000 Jews from North Africa had settled in France.[45] With a total Jewish population now over 500,000 strong, the country boasted the largest community in Europe. This is still the case today.

Needless to say, the Sephardim were greeted by the old French Ashkenazim with a mix of curiosity and apprehension. In colonial days, French Jews coming in contact with North Africans made it their (civilizing?) mission to bring the values of the Emancipation to a population perceived as backward and archaic. They had welcomed European Jews the same way. But by the 1950s French Jews, stunned by the Holocaust, were in no cultural position to impose their values on anyone. If anything, the Sephardim brought with them a promise of renewal to the exhausted French community. Unlike their more integrated Western European counterparts, many had lived in tighter, more homogeneous communities, and even if they were not necessarily more religious, they had a strong sense of ethnic and cultural self-identification that was often untainted by national allegiances. To the more sober Ashkenazim they seemed loud and exuberant and shockingly ostentatious. They spoke French and Judeo-Arabic but of course no Yiddish. They dressed, ate, and worshipped differently. But in the end their energy took over and the two communities blended harmoniously. More important, the Sephardim, who are now the majority, profoundly transformed the Jews of France. By 1967, when the Six-Day War united them in solidarity with Israel, they had become a vibrant and assertive community, still faithful overall to the Republican ideals of the Emancipation, but at once more religious and more self-identified than ever before.[46]

I wrote earlier that, for the Sephardim, the Marais was known as the Quartier Saint-Paul, or just Saint-Paul, after the metro station that serves the neighborhood. The reason for that is simple. Many North Africans landed in Marseille where they would board a train to Paris's Gare de Lyon. From there, they would take metro line 1 and get off at Saint-Paul. They would then cross the rue de Rivoli, walk up the rue Mahler and make a left onto the rue des Rosiers—the obvious place to go first.[47] To be sure, most Sephardim didn't settle in the Marais, since the neighborhood no longer was the center of Jewish life in Paris. Many stayed in the south of France while others opted for different areas of the capital or were settled by the government in the developing suburbs. Yet the old Pletzl was at least symbolically revived by this new blood, and some North Africans, like the Alsatian Jews and other Europeans before them, used it as a springboard for integration. They, too, stayed there for a while, before moving out as they moved up in society. Since the 1980s some immigrants from Israel have made the Marais their destination and the place where, among other things, they serve the best falafel sandwiches one is ever likely to eat.

In the end, the Marais's symbolic power as the site of Jewishness in France owes as much to myth as it does to history. While the presence of Jews in the area is indeed attested since the Middle Ages, it was often tenuous, repeatedly interrupted and transformed, while other parts of the city hosted significant Jewish populations at one time or another. Yet, it is here that the Musée d'art et d'histoire du judaïsme and the Mémorial de la Shoah are located. To trace the Jewish history of the Marais as far back as possible

A kosher bakery and pastry shop

is, for a diasporic community, to seek legitimacy and assert community at the same time.[48] "I am here," Jewish residents seem to say, "because we have always been,"[49] forgetting that this "we" was never cohesive or uncontested and that, therefore, neither is the "I." The sense of community has resulted, in fact, from a long process of sedimentation on the one hand, and the foundational catastrophe that was the Holocaust on the other. Today each new wave of Jewish residents having left traces and people behind, and tragic events having made their marks, the small Pletzl is like a living museum of Jewish history that one visits and revisits, a space defined by its own memory, yet still alive. A survivor—like the Jews themselves.

"THE CHINESE ARE BUYING UP EVERYTHING ANYWAY!"

In 2005 in Paris, several fires broke out in run down buildings and a hotel populated by poor immigrants, some of them undocumented, some of

Posters and advertisements of Jewish interest

them squatters. All the people killed were Africans. The shock was tremendous and, on a smaller scale, not unlike Americans' stunned reaction in the aftermath of hurricane Katrina the same year.[50] How could people (of color) be living in such appalling conditions in this day and age, in a country like ours? One of these buildings was in the Marais, in the third arrondissement. That, too, was a shock, for it didn't square with people's perception of the neighborhood. Weren't the days of the Marais as a poor immigrant hub long gone? Yes and no. Well before gays and lesbians began to arrive in the area, indeed at a time when Jews were still massively living there, parts of the Marais had attracted a group of immigrants seldom discussed in French society and that hardly ever comes to mind in relation to this particular neighborhood—the Chinese.

The first significant wave of Chinese emigration to Europe started in the late nineteenth century and originated in the Zhejiang province, south of Shanghai, when the port of Wenzhou was opened to international trade. During World War I, as French men were mobilized and left their jobs

A Jewish bookstore

vacant, between 100,000 and 140,000 Chinese laborers from Zhejiang province, specifically from the cities of Qingtian and Wenzhou, were recruited, sometimes coerced, to work in France; between 2,500 and 3,000 stayed in the country after their contracts expired.[51] Most of them settled by the Gare de Lyon in the twelfth arrondissement, forming the first bona fide Chinese neighborhood in Paris. In the 1930s the Wenzhou and the Qingtian went their separate ways and the former moved to the third arrondissement, in the Marais, where they mostly specialized in leather goods, like many Jews who lived there at the time. When the Holocaust decimated their Jewish colleagues and employers, the Chinese began to dominate the trade.[52] They lived and worked around the rue du Temple, rue des Vertus, rue au Maire, and rue des Gravilliers, an area their descendents, joined by newcomers, still occupy. To this day, *les Wenzhou,* as they are usually known, constitute the largest Chinese community in France.

After the French defeat of 1954, many ethnic Chinese of Cantonese descent left the newly independent countries of Indochina (Vietnam, Laos, and Cambodia) and took up residence in the sixth arrondissement, on the Left Bank. In the 1970s, when the U.S., too, had to disengage from the area, another wave of ethnic Chinese, the Taizhou, emigrated—the famous boat

A Chinese restaurant in medieval Paris and an unseen gay club across

people. Those who came to France settled in an area of the thirteenth arrondissement, around the place d'Italie, now nicknamed the Triangle de Choisy, where brand new high rises had been snubbed by French people and remained vacant. According to Kristin Ross, Parisians disliked these buildings because they saw them as an "invasion of banlieue architecture into the city proper," which, I would add, made them seem somehow appropriate for outsiders.[53] Today, when French people think of a Paris Chinatown, this is the area they are referring to. Just as the television news crews go to the rue des Rosiers for their yearly report on Rosh Hashanah, they go *dans le treizième* for the Chinese New Year. Following the same avenues of integration as most Jews had before them—namely, entrepreneurship and a strong belief in education—the Taizhou, too, have begun to move out of their neighborhood as they have moved up in society.

In 1978, Deng Xiaoping's new economic policy of openness triggered massive waves of Chinese emigration. Wenzhou became a sort of laboratory where elements of capitalism and free market economics were first introduced in China. The population quickly grew wealthy and began to look for more economic freedom in the West. The 1980s saw the largest wave of Wenzhou immigration in France. The newcomers, mostly successful business people, joined their predecessors in the Marais, but also in other traditionally Jewish neighborhoods: Belleville, where they added yet another element to what may be the most ethnically diverse neighborhood of Paris, and Sedaine-Popincourt, the former Little Istanbul. They primarily work in the professions known as "the three knives": restaurants, the textile industry, and leather goods. They did not, however, go to the *treizième*, where they were not welcome among the more integrated Southern Chinese who looked down on them with disdain. A familiar story. (Incidentally, because the Wenzhou are widely known throughout China as shrewd business people, they are sometimes called "Jews" by their contemptuous compatriots.) Then, in the 1990s, a whole new wave of immigration began to swell the ranks of an increasingly diverse Chinese community in France. With the more recent turn to a market economy and China's growing distance from its communist past, many people who had prospered under the old system found themselves socially adrift and ready to leave. Most of these newcomers are Mandarin speakers from Northeastern China and are often referred to as the Dongbei. It doesn't appear, however, that they will affect Wenzhou predominance anytime soon.

———

REACTIONS to the Wenzhou in the Marais, a blend of anxiety, rumors, and urban legends, have echoed those in the rest of Paris. "The Chinese," some people say, "buy up every retail space that becomes available and quietly take over entire neighborhoods." "Their businesses are entirely controlled by Chinese crime syndicates known as triads, and only shady practices, unfair to their French competitors can explain their extraordinary success." In reality, Chinese business owners often practice the tontine, or *hui* as they call it, which consists of a small number of participants pooling their money and rotating loans until each one has benefited, thus bypassing the need for out-of-community bank loans.[54] "Many live ten in a room in unsanitary conditions and are exploited, even enslaved, by their bosses in illegal sweatshops." To some extent this is true, but this does not, by any stretch of the imagination, represent the Wenzhou experience in Paris as a whole. The need to discharge the debt contracted when they left China does, however, force many into extremely difficult and illegal working conditions sometimes akin to slavery.[55] "And of course they put all sorts of disgusting things in the food they serve in restaurants (dog food, rat meat, excrements, you name it)." These charges are a classic urban legend and have also been leveled against other kinds of ethnic restaurants, notably North African couscous joints when they, too, started to dot cityscapes and were perceived as serious competitors by their French counterparts. These rumors, designed to transform a perceived commercial threat into a far-reaching cultural one, are a slightly more benevolent version of the old ones that accused Jews of using their clothing stores as fronts for white slavery rings. Most intriguing, finally, is the persistent legend that "the Chinese never die." Or rather that, when they do, their corpses mysteriously vanish so that new immigrants can get their papers, since, as everybody knows, "they all look alike."

But beyond the rumors, and perhaps because of them, Chinese entrepreneurs have been under political attack for the way they supposedly transform neighborhoods into sectors of *monoactivité*, the development of a single trade (usually the garment industry) to the exclusion of what is known as *commerces de proximité*, stores such as bakeries, grocery stores, and the like, that fulfill the basic daily needs of the local residents and are perceived as staples of a now endangered French lifestyle. (If the Wenzhou tend to live in the Marais where they work, they don't, however, live in the Sedaine-Popincourt area.) Since the immigrants do not have the right to vote, this issue has been shamelessly used by demagogical politicians tapping into popular fears and anxieties.[56] And in the Marais, where several gay bars have gone bankrupt in recent years, it isn't uncommon to hear things like, "The Chinese are buying up everything anyway!"

A feeling often expressed in the Marais, be it regarding the Quartier des Gravilliers in the third arrondissement to the north or the explosion of Chinese restaurants and fast-food joints on the rue Sainte-Antoine to the south, is one of invasion. The fear is that the Marais could soon become a full-fledged Chinese neighborhood, upsetting the area's delicate balance. In general the Wenzhou, the largest but least integrated of all Chinese communities in Paris, are depicted as living in airtight, autarkic ghettos, refusing to learn French and to integrate. Often the victims of racism in the Marais,[57] they are the latest group to be perceived as fundamentally un-French—because of their foreignness, of course, but mainly because of their specific communal practices. Even the area's Arab residents are more welcome than the Chinese, who, to this day, are still seen as outsiders in the neighborhood, though they first settled there in the 1930s. To a certain degree, all waves of immigrants, perceived rightly or wrongly to be the most recent, have to face the kind of hostility once directed at their predecessors—even, at times, from those who happen to be one of these predecessors. But in the case of the Marais, anti-Chinese sentiments also stem from the area's reinvention as a quaint and idyllic urban village, where markers of a new kind of globalized mass migration can only stand out as misfits and a threat to a time-honored, if largely fantasized, way of life. Few residents seem to recognize, however, that the Chinese, whose commercial activities in the Marais are the very same ones that used to be called *métiers juifs*, or Jewish trades, may be the neighborhood's only chance to maintain the social diversity it has always had and that is now mythified to create its so-called unique charm. As long as the Marais's image remains one of bourgeois balance and moderation opposed to, rather than an active part of, the globalized city where it stands, its Chinese inhabitants risk being eyed with suspicion as too different, too ethnic, too many, and too conspicuous.

In 2007, a series of events increased the visibility of the Chinese in Paris and firmly anchored them at the heart of the debates on illegal immigration, for better and for worse. On 20 March, an undocumented Chinese man was arrested in a Belleville café as he was about to pick up two of his grandchildren from a kindergarten. The police raid was met with immediate protests from parents, teachers, and other neighborhood people of various ethnic groups. A melee ensued, complete with clubs and tear gas, until the man was eventually freed. The event, in all its brutality, was filmed by several persons and was soon found on "YouTube" for all to see. The day before, a Chinese woman had been arrested when picking up her niece from the same school. After parents protested, she was let go. Tragically, on 20 September a fifty-one-year-old undocumented woman from northern China, Liu Chulan, jumped from the second floor of a tenth-arrondissement hotel in order to escape the police, mistakenly believing that they had come for her. She lapsed into a coma and died soon after. The event was all over the news and, just as the hotel fires had, it generated sincere emotion and ambiguous compassion. Not only did the once invisible Chinese manage to unite various immigrant groups and their allies, but they also exposed the violent repression meted out by the French government. How long this newfound sympathy will last, however, is anybody's guess.

Like the Jews before them, the Chinese have been caught up in the double-bind that characterizes the question of the visibility of minority communities in France. They are either too visible or not visible enough. While the universalist culture inherited from the Revolution mandates that minority cultures be privatized and thus rendered invisible, invisibility creates paranoid anxiety in the society at large. In turn, anxiety demands visibility. For example, it is only after European Jews were emancipated that conspiracy theories started to flourish and that biological anti-Semitism sought to establish empirically recognizable racial types.[58] Finally, the resurgence of visibility entails a universalist backlash, and minority communities are once again attacked for their alleged lack of cultural integration and their community-based politics. The Chinese began to be visible to many in France when, in 1996, some of them joined movements fighting for the rights of undocumented immigrants—the famous *sans-papiers*. Today, they are full-fledged participants in the fight for immigrants' rights. In the end, the most common way out of this bind is a mode of visibility acceptable within the parameters of the Republic: folklore, that is, the opportunity to acknowledge cultural difference and to reject it at the same time. This is pretty much the status of the place d'Italie and the rue des Rosiers today, and it is fast becoming the lot of the gay community, starting with gay pride marches whose periodic return parallels Chinese New Year's parades in the French media. What better way to deny relationality than official celebrations of difference?

THE NEW OLD MARAIS

If the symbolic power of the Marais as a historical site of Jewish life was enough to attract North African Jews on their arrival in Paris, the reality of it soon made them look elsewhere. For one thing, the neighborhood no longer provided the sort of infrastructure that had served the Russians and the Poles. Given that the Sephardim were French speakers and relatively familiar with the culture, they had less need for organizations like the old Landsmanshaftn to facilitate their social integration. The booming economy of the 1960s also made it easier for them to work and gain financial autonomy, while the brand new banlieues were still welcoming back then. (The towns of Sarcelles and Créteil became, and still are, homes to large Jewish communities.) But the truth is that the Marais was simply no longer an active center of Jewish life. Soon it would no longer be a cheap place to live, either. The neighborhood's new identity was being shaped by and as a return to a more ancient historical past—its seventeenth-century glory.

The gentrification of the Marais under the auspices of de Gaulle's Minister of Cultural Affairs, author André Malraux, found itself inscribed within a larger political project before it even began. The Fifth Republic was born as a response to the unfolding crisis of decolonization, in the aftermath of the humiliating French downfall in Indochina and in the face of Algeria's struggle for self-determination. With the looming threat of a military coup orchestrated by right-wing generals opposed to Algerian independence, de Gaulle was called back from political exile in 1958. The following year, he and Prime Minister Michel Debré decided to create France's first Ministry of Cultural Affairs. Its purpose was clear: to produce a unified and unifying French culture from the top down in order to crush any further desire to dismantle the Republic from the bottom up, either from without or from

A bilingual call for a march of undocumented immigrants posted in the Marais

within its European borders. In case anyone harbored any lingering doubts about the whole enterprise, the new ministry was soon staffed by colonial cadres left idle by decolonization and eager to apply to metropolitan France what they had learned and practiced in the colonies.[59] It should come as no surprise, then, that once restored to its lost classical splendor the Marais would no longer be so hospitable to cultural pluralism. It is also difficult, I believe, to read the area's gentrification without considering de Gaulle's politics of national reconciliation after the country's liberation and the fall of Vichy. Silencing the Jewish specificity of the Holocaust was a convenient way to skirt the thorny issue of French complicity. The restoration of the Marais as a unifying symbol of France's long-lost glory could serve a similar purpose: with the Jews gone, so would the conspicuous reminders of a less-than-glorious history fade away. Once again, it seems, "a certain idea of France" (to use de Gaulle's famous phrase) would be enacted on the back of the Jews. All this, in essence, constituted the underlying motivations behind the neighborhood's renovation.

For many on the extreme right of the political spectrum, the Marais had never ceased to symbolize the grandeur of classicism and of France itself. To them, the neighborhood's slow descent into urban decay was but an illustration of the decline of French culture since the Revolution—even though it had started earlier. Yvan Christ's introduction to his historical homage to the Marais, published in 1965 at the outset of the neighborhood's renewal phase, best expresses the historical claim laid by conservatives and nationalists. For example:

> Before it, too, died out like the Marais itself, the old monarchy, humiliated, vanquished and powerless, was forcibly returned to the neighborhood it had helped create and where it resided in all its might. Louis XVI, the last king of the Marais, imprisoned in the Temple before marching to his death: such was the dark symbol that fate had devised. It marked the death certificate of the old France and of the regal Marais.
>
> The square that since 17 Ventôse, year VIII, we are legally obligated to call place des Vosges, played an unquestionable role in the evolution of the Marais.
>
> [Avant de s'éteindre comme le Marais lui-même, la vieille monarchie, humiliée, vaincue, impuissante, regagne par force ce Marais qu'elle avait contribué à créer et où elle avait résidé dans toute sa puissance. Louis XVI, dernier roi du Marais, détenu au Temple avant de marcher à la mort: tel est le sombre symbole que le destin avait imaginé. Il marque durement l'acte de décès de l'ancienne France et du Marais royal. (23)
>
> Celle que, depuis le 17 ventôse, an VIII, nous sommes légalement tenus d'appeler la place des Vosges, joua un rôle certain dans l'évolution du Marais. (17)]

But the slightly funny rants of diehard monarchists only thinly veil the violent politics of the extreme right and its anti-Semitism:

> The rebirth of the Marais will be the revenge of the spirit and the triumph of order over anarchy.
>
> This final result will only be obtained thanks to the transfer outside the Marais's boundaries of the small and medium-sized industries that have spread uncontrollably for more than a century and have been the primary reason for the neighborhood's downfall.
>
> [La renaissance du Marais, ce sera la revanche des yeux de l'esprit et, sur l'anarchie, la victoire de l'ordre. (13)
>
> Un tel résultat ne sera finalement obtenu qu'à la condition de transférer hors du périmètre du Marais ces petites et moyennes industries qui, par leur prolifération

> incontrôlée depuis plus d'un siècle, ont été le principal facteur de la déchéance
> du quartier. (30)]

Given that small artisans have populated and defined the Marais since the beginning, and not just for "over a century," the people who must "finally" be the object of a "transfer" are easy to identify. Interestingly, Christ's coffee-table book on the Marais is still easily available and "usually ships within 1–2 business days" if ordered on *Amazon.fr*.

When the renovation of the district began in earnest in 1965, following the 1962 "Loi Malraux" on urban preservation, the whole area still ranked well under the Parisian average for modern conveniences, and its architectural wonders were in a dramatic state of disrepair. The heart of Paris, run down and filthy, was an embarrassment. What followed is now a familiar story that has been taking place in many urban neighborhoods. One by one, the old aristocratic residences would be cleaned up and modernized, many of them turned into museums and government offices, while other buildings of meager value and too run down to be salvaged would be destroyed.

The Marais was becoming beautiful and elegant again—and very, very expensive. Home ownership was encouraged both by government actions and pure market forces, and, after three centuries of absence, the well off began to return to the area.[60] As fashionable boutiques, art galleries, and antique shops sprang up on the rue des Francs-Bourgeois leading to the place des Vosges, more magnificent than ever, scores of inhabitants moved out.

As is always the case with urban gentrification, the poor, the old, and the immigrants were hit the hardest, sometimes literally. This topic is still mentioned sottovoce and anonymously, but people tell stories of psychological pressure, intimidation, suspicious fires and suicides, and violent evictions carried out by government officials and the SAC (Service d'Action Civique, de Gaulle's semi-secret, strong-armed "protection services" that soon descended into right-wing gangsterism and was eventually banned under Mitterrand). Being forcibly removed by right-wing thugs was especially cruel and an added trauma for the Pletzl's old Jewish residents who, by and large, would rather not talk about it at all.[61] Bohemian life—always a sign that a neighborhood is becoming hot—had found a temporary home here, but as the quartier became gradually unaffordable it, too, left the area—always a sign that a neighborhood is no longer so hot. Foreigners still came in droves, though only this time as rich tourists, not as poor immigrants, shopping in the fashion boutiques of the rue des Francs-Bourgeois and the art galleries of the place des Vosges. Today, a neighborhood once celebrated for its social diversity is fast becoming quaint, safe, and homogeneous—a bourgeois paradise.

Well, almost.

A very busy rue des Francs-Bourgeois, lined up with fashionable stores

THE GAY MARAIS

As one would expect, homosexual life in one form or another used to be all over the map—and not always as invisible as one might think. Alongside cafés, restaurants, hotels, bath-houses, and the ubiquitous cruising spots (some, such as the Tuileries Gardens, documented since the reign of Louis XIV), certain neighborhoods were at times relatively welcoming. While "gay neighborhoods" as we know them today are mostly an outcome of the post-Stonewall gay liberation years and American cultural influence, queer people of all sorts often found a home in bohemian and sometimes seedy enclaves more tolerant of queerness—in all senses of the term. Starting around 1880 and up until World War II, Montmartre was one such neighborhood. Home to artists and prostitutes, writers and criminals, and a wide array of shady or fashionable characters, it was notorious for its open homosexual life for both men and women and as a place of interclass mingling. Francis Carco, in *Jésus-la-caille*, and Jean Genet, in *Notre-Dame des Fleurs* [*Our Lady of the Flowers*], described Montmartre's night life, while Jean Cocteau made the famous cabaret Le Boeuf sur le toit his headquarters and René Crevel was a regular at Graff's.[62] On the Left Bank, Montparnasse also had its share of gay and lesbian life in the interwar years. So did the decidedly working class rue de Lappe, by the place de la Bastille. And, yes, there were a few venues in the Marais as well, in the rue des Vertus, for instance, where La Petite Vertu, a gay, transgender, and lesbian bar, is today.[63] Its famous drag balls notwithstanding, all in all Paris wasn't Berlin; there was no liberation movement to speak of, no thriving press, but rather a more haphazard dynamic of social heterogeneity that fostered contacts and encounters across groups and classes.[64]

After the brutal disruption brought about by the German occupation and Vichy (which partially recriminalized homosexuality in France for the first time since the Revolution[65]), the Left Bank neighborhood of Saint-Germain-des-Prés emerged as the new Parisian center of gay and lesbian life. Far more elegant and sophisticated (read: queenier) than Montmartre ever was in its day, Saint-Germain in the 1950s was the capital of jazz and existentialism, and its permissive atmosphere naturally attracted the queer crowd.[66] But like Montmartre it was a sexually, socially, even racially mixed place, and while it, too, had several exclusively gay and lesbian bars, it was not what we would call a gay neighborhood today. That, more or less, was what the rue Sainte-Anne was going to be, the first neighborhood of its kind in Paris.

The area, conveniently located near the Tuileries and the Opera, was not, by any stretch of the imagination, the sort of bohemian or seamy place where queer life used to find shelter and comradeship. Rather nondescript in a bourgeois sort of way and a place of business during the day, the rue Sainte-Anne saw its first gay bars discreetly open in the 1960s. By the following decade, the street and its surroundings offered a variety of gay and lesbian venues catering to all sorts of needs and clienteles—from the backroom bar called Le Bronx to the posh and exclusive Sept.[67] This degree of specialized commercialization concentrated in a specific space was a radical break from the earlier centers of gay life in Paris. But it was still a far cry from what the Marais represents today. The rue Sainte-Anne was schizophrenic, in a sense. Perfectly banal during the day, it only became a gay neighborhood around 10 or 11 at night when the bars, otherwise undetectable, finally opened and a totally different crowd began to roam the streets. The cover charges and the drinks were expensive, the bars and sidewalks full of hustlers. While the area was widely known as a gay enclave and even though celebrities frequented Le Sept, the atmosphere of the rue Sainte-Anne was still semi-clandestine. Its bars, whose doors were equipped with peepholes, were a world away from the more open, more democratic sites of queer visibility that an increasing number of gay Parisians had, by then, seen in New York and San Francisco. The Marais was going to change all that.

The times were ripe. By the late 1970s the gay movement in France, if one wants to call it that, had morphed from the revolutionary discourse of the FHAR (Homosexual Front for Revolutionary Action) to the more pragmatic, rights-oriented politics of the CUARH (Emergency Committee Against the Repression of Homosexuals). Discrimination needed to be fought legally and politically, anti-gay laws inherited from the Vichy era and the early years of the de Gaulle presidency had to be abolished, and a gay-friendly left was poised to gain power. The first Gay Pride march commemorating the New York Stonewall riots of 1969 took place in Paris in 1977 and, with the exception of 1978, became a yearly event after that.[68] More and more gay venues opened—bars, sex clubs, discos—that catered to the needs of an increasingly open and vocal clientele. All in all there seemed to be a cultural push toward more gay visibility, be it social or political. And there was money to be made, too.

Le Village, located in the rue du Plâtre, is usually said to have been the first gay bar to open in the Marais in 1978.[69] We know there had been gay places in the Marais before, however, so what, in hindsight, makes Le Village the first? For one thing, its owners' intention was clearly to open a different kind of place—different from the bars of the rue Sainte-Anne, that is. Le Village was open during the day, did not feel secretive or closeted, charged regular prices for drinks . . . and it was an instant hit. The gentrification of the Marais was far from complete, rents were still reasonable, while the nearby Forum des Halles and Pompidou Center were now attracting larger and larger crowds to the center of Paris. Les Halles had its share of gay bars for a while in the early 1980s, but the Marais possessed the sort of quaint urban charm that often characterizes gay neighborhoods. Think of Greenwich Village, New Orleans's French Quarter, or Miami's South Beach for other examples of what I would call urban camp: the appropriation of neighborhoods whose glory has long faded and whose beauty is legible only in their decrepitude—the Norma Desmonds of neighborhoods, if you like: "We had façades then." Within a few short years, more bars had opened in the area, including Le Central in 1980, Le Swing in 1983 at the corner of the rue des Rosiers and rue Vieille-du-Temple, the threshold of the Pletzl. That same year, the gay bookstore, Les Mots à la bouche, settled on the rue Sainte-Croix-de-la-Bretonnerie. By the mid 1990s, there were dozens of gay and lesbian spots in the Marais—bars, of course, with their distinctive crowds, but also restaurants, a few sex clubs, a (short-lived) bath-house, clothing stores, a pharmacy, a bakery, a travel agency, and so on and so forth, most of them federated under the banner of the SNEG (National Union of Gay Enterprises). Free magazines or rags disseminating ads and community news began to proliferate in these venues.

(*Illico* and *e-m@le* were the main ones, until they ceased publication.) Rainbow flags were everywhere. The Marais had become a full-fledged gay neighborhood and Le Village was, in that sense, its first gay bar.

At first, older residents of the Marais were not too thrilled to see what was happening to their neighborhood. Some of them even organized to fight back, complaining about the potential risks to school children and the unseemly sight of men kissing in the streets. In the 1990s they found a receptive ear in the mayor of the fourth arrondissement, a conservative who fought against the displays of rainbow flags and had the police harass bar owners about every little infraction they could find.[70] This didn't last, though, and the next mayor, a socialist, had more pressing worries, namely the occasional Sunday street brawls between Jewish and Arab youths gangs on the rue des Rosiers. Moreover the 2001 election of the openly gay Bertrand Delanoë across the street at the Hôtel de Ville cleared the air. As for the Jews, they have seldom manifested any hostility toward their new neighbors. The most noteworthy incident turned out to have been a slight case of misreading: members of the Betar, a group of young Jewish activists,

A lesbian bar on the rue Montmorency, now closed

Le Central, one of the oldest gay bars in the Marais

mistook the shaved-head leather men meeting at Le Central for neo-Nazi skinheads and proceeded to raid the bar located by the little kink between the rue des Rosiers and the rue Sainte-Croix. The misunderstanding was soon cleared up and life went on peacefully, with each community sticking more or less to its own area, but moving fluidly between the two. A Lubavitch in a long black coat walking by a group of tank-topped queens isn't an unusual sight in the Marais. The rue Vieille-du-Temple, marking the boundary between the two spheres, is where mutual respect meets sound business decisions.[71] Today, two gay bars stand at each corner of the rue des Rosiers and rue Vieille-du-Temple, while three have opened on the rue des Ecouffes—two lesbian bars and a mixed bar, L'Adonis, owned by two Jewish cousins.[72] By and large, the two communities (assuming they don't overlap, which, of course, they do) seem to be more or less indifferent to each other, and everybody seems to like it that way.

For the first time a Parisian neighborhood was publicly associated with gay life, indeed gay culture, in the minds not only of gay men and lesbians

The boys of the rue Sainte-Croix in front of the gay bookstore Les mots à la bouche

but of the country at large. The rue Sainte-Croix-de-la-Bretonnerie is its main drag and emblem—what the rue des Rosiers is to the Jews. At last, gays were enjoying the sort of social recognition that the French call *pignon sur rue*, literally a gable facing the street. As a headline in *Le Monde* once proclaimed: "Le drapeau gay flotte rue Sainte-Croix de la Bretonnerie."[73] The street, running parallel to the rue de Rivoli, meets the rue Vieille-du-Temple, where several gay bars are located, and intersects with the rue des Archives whose bars overflow onto the sidewalks during happy hour. These three streets, along with the rue du Roi-de-Sicile, make up the heart of the Gay Marais, but the neighborhood extends well beyond them toward Beaubourg and into the third arrondissement, just as the Pletzl did in its heyday. Unlike Jews in the old Pletzl, however, gays do not overwhelmingly live in the neighborhood; now almost fully gentrified, it has become far too expensive for that. The Marais is a center of gay life only insofar as gay life is defined by a network of social interactions taking place in public spaces. Even so, only some of these interactions take place there. With the relative exception of Le Dépôt, known less for the talent of its DJ's than for its

A gay clothing store on the rue Sainte-Croix de la Bretonnerie

Gay 'Amnésia' meets Jewish memory

giant backroom (allegedly the largest in Europe), and Le Tango, a campy 1920s ballroom, the neighborhood doesn't have any late-night dance clubs, so the crowds often start to thin out before the last metro. Other sites of gay socialization are to be found elsewhere as well, such as bath-houses and out-doors cruising spots and ACT UP meetings. But if anything, this signals that urban gay culture now encompasses far more than nighttime entertainment and sexual encounters. If what characterizes the Marais is gay visibility, this doesn't imply that what is now visible is exactly what was once hidden. For one thing, aspects of queer life were often quite visible in the past, as I have explained. But more important, the sort of gay social life openly taking place in the Marais simply did not exist before. The Marais didn't just provide gay culture in France with a public face; it largely created that culture. Simply put, the culture of visibility is not the same as the visibility of a culture. And the Marais is not the same as Montmartre or Saint-Germain.

Another important factor in the emergence of gay culture in France and indirectly of the Marais as its primary site, is the impact of the AIDS epidemic and the new brand of activism that appeared in reaction to it. Gay activism in France had changed over the course of the 1970s, moving away from radical sexual politics aiming at overthrowing the capitalist heterosexual system toward a more integrationist human-rights approach. At the same time, lesbian activists had split from the overall feminist movement. When elected in 1981, Mitterrand kept the promises he had made to gay activists and abolished all discriminatory laws. The police was ordered to stop all harassment of gay people and gay bars. In a speech to the National Assembly, the Minister of Justice, Robert Badinter, even recognized the contributions of homosexuals to French history. (He wasn't very specific, it's true.) Clearly, times had changed. Gay activism more or less disbanded. Activists hadn't yet focused their energy on marriage and parental rights. It was time to party. In the early 1980s, Paris saw an explosion of gay life. Walking in the center of the city at night, it seemed every man around you was gay.[74]

1981 is also the year the first cases of AIDS were described in the press. For a while few paid attention. The socialist government was, somewhat predictably, prudish to the point of silence and utter inaction. Following the typically French belief that a law is all that's needed to solve a social problem, a ban on discrimination against HIV-positive people was soon passed by the National Assembly, but no actual prevention campaign was organized until 1986, under a new conservative government. As I have argued elsewhere, French culture's hostility to the recognition of minority communities left the country unprepared to deal with an epidemic that struck such communities. French gays and lesbians, politically disorganized, were no exceptions and, for a while, they by and large shied away from discourses and actions that would be perceived as stigmatizing.[75] Within a few years HIV infection rates were growing exponentially and the epidemic was out of control. A few organizations appeared (most notably AIDES, founded in 1984 after Michel Foucault's death by his lover Daniel Defert), but they often went to great lengths not to appear specifically gay.

It wasn't until 1989 and the creation of ACT UP-Paris that things started to change. Angry, sexy, and immensely telegenic, ACT UP members did more than electrify the gay community, they embodied it and essentially performed it into existence. As the extent of the AIDS disaster started to register, the organization's ranks began to grow. And so did the sense that being gay meant that you belonged to a collective entity, that you had to be seen and heard. In addition to the success of ACT UP's street actions, Gay Pride marches were a reliable indicator of gay people's newfound sense of community. Some 1,500 people attended the march in 1990; 60,000 did in 1995;[76] 700,000 to 800,000 do now on average, making Paris's *Marche des fiertés* one of the largest events of its kind in the world.

By the mid 1990s, realizing that something new was happening in France, the media were soon all over the Marais. Articles flourished in the press, and television news shows began to feature the neighborhood as the epicenter of everything gay.[77] For a time the coverage was predictably incoherent, hesitating between different registers and genres, and oozing different types of social anxieties. The primary fear was political. The Marais appeared to be an outpost of American cultural domination, bringing with it the perils of identity politics and cultural separatism. The perception was that gay people wanted to be left to themselves, according to an archaic tribal system that was in complete opposition to the universalist model of French citizenship.

Emboldened by their successes on the AIDS front, gay and lesbian activists began to push for the legalization of same-sex couples and the right to parenthood (and more recently for the penalization of homophobia). Never before had the gay community been so politically vocal and so effective in getting legislation passed and changing cultural attitudes. The resulting fear of a gay lobby gave strength to the accusations of *communautarisme*, social separatism. That debate gripped French society for a while in the mid-to-late 1990s but soon receded (or rather shifted its focus to Muslims in the wake of 9/11) thanks to the resounding popular success of the PACS (Civil Solidarity Pact), which offered legal status to all unmarried couples, gay or straight. It seemed that the fear of social disintegration no longer came from the gay community but from the increasingly restless banlieues with their large population of ethnic youths. But for a while television journalists reporting on the Marais adopted the same ethnographic and anthropological

ACT UP poster calling for their annual World AIDS Day march

genres they tend to use, for example, when reporting on immigrant communities or "social problems," staging the courageous reporter as a hero giving the outside world a peek at a strange and mysterious world. Some reports even brought to mind wild-life documentaries, as if they were observing gay people in their natural habitat. What they all forgot to mention, however, was that gay people do not actually live in the Marais—at least not in proportions higher than other parts of Paris;[78] they go there.

Still, as the normalization of homosexuality progressed apace and the fear of separatism got displaced, the media began to depict the gay Marais as a colorful, almost ethnic enclave, home to a festive and essentially harmless community, and as one of the hot nightspots that supposedly contribute to making Paris the world capital of sophisticated fun. Many French tourist guidebooks now make room for the gay Marais (English-language guidebooks often mentioned it years before their French counterparts did) and its lively nightlife, alongside the architectural marvels and the old Pletzl.[79] Needless to say, this more benevolent view rests largely upon a double set of

ACT UP poster: 'The community that we want'

clichés, one about male homosexuality and the other about Paris. It also echoes the sort of folklorization and exoticization processes usually applied to certain ethnic neighborhoods, such as the rue des Rosiers or the thirteenth arrondissement's Asian areas.[80] Like the Pletzl and Chinatown, the gay Marais has now become a cultural metonym for a community that seems to have found its place within the social fabric of the nation. Or rather, the production of this metonym in and by a variety of mainstream discourses has allowed the social reconfiguration of the gay community as no longer threatening, including in its perception by many gays and lesbians themselves.

What a neighborhood like the Marais tells us about the relationship between homosexuality and society is at the core of some gay people's criticism of it—a criticism that points out the political failings of commercial gay culture but doesn't account for its more complex and unexpected effects. The radical activists of the 1970s, such as Guy Hocquenghem and Jean Le Bitoux, who saw homosexuality as a revolutionary challenge to the hetero-phallic order of bourgeois capitalism, favored a more subversive engagement of urban space by homosexuals. A park, where children play during the day (not to mention a myriad other places throughout the city), would become a venue for public sex after dark; a corner bar, frequented by workers and employees on their way to and from work, would fill up with queens at night; and so on. Such oppositional reappropriation and resignification of normal urban spaces could not only map out the limits of heterosexual domination but facilitate interclass and interracial contacts as well. The Marais, however, is seen as propelled primarily by business interests rather than by radical social change. In order to maximize their profits, bars and other venues are conceived in terms of niche markets, often catering to a specific sub-group within urban gay culture and offering exactly what one is looking for. No more wandering, no more flânerie: one knows exactly where to go to find what one wants. Literally territorialized, gay desire has become, in the eyes of the Marais's radical critics, a simple matter of orderly consumption and, therefore, has lost its power of opposition and eliminated all possibility of random encounters and contacts considered to be socially destabilizing. In short, normalized homosexuality eventually becomes normalizing. The Marais, as the primary site of such normalization, has ultimately forced gay people to fit into pre-existing subcategories determined by the market rather than the other way round, thus destroying the self-fashioning creativity that had been a defining force of homosexuality until now.

From that point of view, one should hardly be surprised that gay politics have become primarily concerned with marriage and parental rights and censorious laws against homophobia; or worse, that gay people simply do not care about politics at all, busy as they are with the consumption of easy pleasures.[81] The following anecdote may be very telling. In the fall of 1998, as the National Assembly, now in the hands of the left, was poised to vote the legalization of same-sex couples, many socialist and communist députés failed to show and politicians on the right killed the measure, albeit temporarily. A handful of furious gay activists tried to organize an immediate protest in front of the Socialist Party headquarters. Where did they go to rally up the crowd but the bars of the Marais. It was a Friday evening and not a single person followed them.[82]

It is an undeniable fact that business has always accompanied and sometimes been a major vector of gay liberation in Western societies—if by liberation one understands the acquisition of legitimacy and civil rights and what they imply in matters of daily life. Liberalization may be a more accurate term. Political power is seen to go hand in hand with economic power. In Paris, two central figures in the emergence of a public, more mainstream gay life in the pre-ACT UP years have been businessmen: Fabrice Emaer, the impetus behind the development of the rue Sainte-Anne as the gay neighborhood of its time and owner of Le Palace, the Parisian equivalent of New York's Studio 54; and David Girard, a much maligned former hustler turned gay entrepreneur, who opened several successful bars and bathhouses in the early 1980s and published glossy gay magazines featuring news and naked guys. (Girard died of AIDS, and many people have long suspected that Emaer did too, although there is no evidence of that.) At the time both played a crucial role in Parisian gay life, and their bars and clubs are now remembered equally as forerunners of today's Marais and with fond nostalgia for a more outrageous era in gay culture. Without a doubt, what they offered was responding to an enormous demand, and they contributed more than their fair share to the new gay visibility.

But again, visibility may just be the problem. How can homosexuality be socially visible without being automatically co-opted by a dominant culture that is increasingly a visual one? This is the foundational paradox of recognition: be recognized for who and what you are, and who and what you are will be determined in part by who and what recognizes you. In that case, isn't post-68 gay radicalism, predicated on the act of coming out, also responsible for that evolution? And what the criticism of commercialization also fails to take into account is the fact that public spaces where illicit sex and cross-group contacts take place have not disappeared with the rise of Marais culture and the proliferation of pay-to-play sex clubs and bathhouses. In fact, public cruising spots, while not as numerous as they once were, are routinely used both by self-identified gay men who also frequent gay bars and by the category of people epidemiologists call "men who have sex with men."[83]

In addition, any way we want to think about it, the debate cannot be resolved without taking into consideration the advent of AIDS, which radically changed what it means to be gay by making visibility, and the management of representations and counter-representations, a matter of life and death. By and large, the businesses of the Marais have accompanied and reflected the dominant trends in the dissemination of AIDS information in the gay community and in the country at large: reluctant at first; more proactive at the height of ACT UP's influence; far less so now that the drop in the number of AIDS deaths has once more dulled public awareness and made invisibility a problem again.

In 2003 an AIDS awareness campaign organized by the city's health authorities gave a sense of the problem in an especially eerie way. Posters imitating the ubiquitous "You are here" neighborhood maps that are found all over Paris started popping up, only with the words "You are no longer here." I don't know how successful the campaign turned out to be, but I found it extremely clever. Not only did it suggest that the city was haunted by the ghosts of people who had died of AIDS, but the second-person address had the effect of making *you* a ghost haunting the streets.

At a deeper structural level, it is also worth wondering to what extent the Marais may have also contributed to the kinds of social exclusions that fueled the epidemic. Here lies another thorny question. If business was instrumental in establishing the kind of gay community that was capable of fighting AIDS and defending itself in the face of public indifference, isn't it also the case that adopting capitalism as a social engine can only reproduce the same kinds of exclusions and oppressions that are inherent in that system and were responsible for the spread of AIDS in the first place? Asking oneself who exactly is in the gay Marais and, more to the point, who isn't, may begin to give a measure of the dilemma.

With its growing success, the Marais soon found itself under attack by gay people who felt they didn't have their place in a largely homogeneous neighborhood and the predominantly male, white community it embodied

'You are no longer here': AIDS awareness poster at the threshold of the Marais

and served. The list of criticisms is familiar to anyone who has paid attention to the development of post-Stonewall urban gay enclaves in other Western countries. Lesbian venues, for example, have been vastly outnumbered by their gay male counterparts. For five or six lesbian bars in the Marais at any given time, most of them slightly decentered, there are dozens of bars catering to men. Older men, too, tend to frequent places located at the margins of the neighborhood. Le Bear's Den, a den for bears, is in Les Halles, while the leather crowd tends to favor the bars of the rue Keller, Michel Foucault's old turf near the place de la Bastille, or the various sex clubs scattered throughout the city. A younger, alternative mixed crowd can be found at the Pop In, not far from the trendy Oberkampf area night spots. As for gays of color, they have long complained of discrimination. For many of them, even if they do go there, the Marais does not offer a home or shelter from oppression, and they find themselves twice rejected—as gays by their ethnic community and as non-whites by the gay community—with class differences sometimes an added factor since so many of them live in the poorer banlieues. Too often the main space of visibility provided to men and women of color within gay culture is as exoticized objects of desire. Eventually they, too, have found other sites of socialization in other parts of the city, at the "Black, Blanc, Beur" and "Escualita" [*sic*] dances in Pigalle, for example, and at semiprivate parties for African men and their friends.

In the end, the very exclusions produced by and within commercial Marais culture have resulted in the increased dissemination of different, less homogenizing gay spaces throughout the city and in the decentering of the Marais itself. No other part of Paris can yet claim to be a gay neighborhood, in the sense that the Marais is one, but that may be the whole point. Normalizing as it may be, under attack from all corners of the queer world, the Marais has, in spite of itself, enabled the development of alternative modes of gay life, some new and some that were always there to begin with—visible cultures that have no place in the culture of visibility but have found a certain vitality by problematizing their relation to it. Just as the Pletzl has always been at the same time the emblematic Jewish neighborhood of Paris and one of several, the gay Marais may retain its symbolic force as the center of the gay community and be just one site among others—a diasporic enclave within the diaspora.

It should come as no surprise that through what we must now call its history, the gay Marais has changed. Bars have closed, others have opened. Of course, this is more or less the way all fashionable neighborhoods operate, depending as they do on the whims of fickle followers and the ability to stay at the forefront of all things hip. Some blame rent increases and real estate maneuvers for chasing businesses away and keeping new ones from opening.

[2]

A Queer Ghetto

It works almost like clockwork. Every culture, national or otherwise, peri-odically identifies a threat to its very foundation and core principles. If the danger isn't there—and it seldom is—it must be invented or at least wildly exaggerated. The idea is simple and the phenomenon well known: it is through repeated expulsions of threats that a system reinforces the bound-aries that condition its existence. Since at least the 1990s France has been going through the kind of national anxiety and identity crisis that precipi-tates such reactions. The seemingly unstoppable rise of the extreme right, increased European integration, economic globalization, mass migrations, American cultural domination, etc., have often been perceived or presented either as opposed in essence to the idea of Frenchness or, if left unchecked, as potential threats to the survival of the national culture, or both. The de-bate over *communautarisme* that began to grip France in the mid-1990s al-lowed the country to address all these alleged threats in one fell swoop. The Marais, specifically the gay Marais, played a prominent role in that debate.

THE REPUBLIC AND THE GHETTO

In those years, gays and lesbians had attained an unprecedented degree of visibility in France. AIDS advocacy and activism were in full swing, with ACT Up-Paris at its influential peak; attendance at gay pride parades was doubling every year; there was talk of official recognition of Vichy-era per-secutions of homosexuals; and for the first time the legalization of same-sex couples was within reach. Television and the press were all over the brand new "gay community." Homosexuality, it seemed to them, was no longer just a sexual preference one could either tolerate or find abhorrent, or both, but also a market, a lifestyle, perhaps even a culture. More worrisome, gym queens (and others) were beginning to flex their political muscles too and *that* was the real taboo.

The French republic, in other words, tends to have a problem with community, which it has a hard time distinguishing from essentialized identity. In a universalist nation such as France, where the structuring poles of society are the State at one end and free and equal individuals at the other, intermediate markers of identity—religion, ethnicity, sexuality, national origin, and the like—must be confined to the private sphere and never *ever* serve as the basis for political claims. Indeed, it is thanks to their privatization that such traits are supposed to be protected so that the people who possess them may enjoy individual freedom. This defining principle of modern French citizenship is best illustrated by the debate on the emancipation of the Jews during the French Revolution and nowhere more effectively than in the speech delivered on 23 December 1789 by the count of Clermont-Tonnerre to the National Assembly:[1]

> As a nation, Jews must be denied everything, as individuals, they must be granted everything; they must have our judges alone, theirs must not be acknowledged; legal protection must be denied to the so-called laws of their Judaic corporation; within the state, they must be neither a political body nor an order; they must be individual citizens.
>
> [Il faut refuser tout aux juifs comme nation et accorder tout aux juifs comme individus; il faut méconnaître leurs juges, ils ne doivent avoir que les nôtres; il faut refuser la protection légale au maintien des prétendues lois de leur corporation judaïque; il faut qu'ils ne fassent dans l'Etat ni un corps politique ni un ordre; il faut qu'ils soient individuellement citoyens.][2]

Thus articulated, the emancipation of the Jews has remained ever since the template for how the nation is to deal with its minorities.

To be sure, the process of affirmation of a central political power against its divisive margins was a gradual one that had begun well before the Revolution, at least as early as the seventeenth century when Richelieu sought to establish a powerful monarchy by bringing down regional powers and, with them, regional languages and cultures. In that sense the centralized Jacobin structure of the modern French state has been, to a large extent, a continuation of, rather than a radical break with, the Old Regime.

As a result of the supposedly benevolent privatization of group identities (or their folklorization in the case of regional cultures), political expressions of "community" in France are widely perceived—that is to say, defined—as opposed in nature to individual autonomy and freedom. Unlike "citizenship," the argument goes, "community" does not emerge from the contractual adhesion of individuals to principles but rather from a shared identity over which these individuals have no control. As a result, any society recognizing communities as legitimate political actors would be seen as tribal, that is, as an archaic, pre-Enlightenment mode of social grouping. Or worse. The brand of right-wing nationalism that emerged in the 1890s under the influence of Maurice Barrès was in direct opposition to Enlightenment ideals and to their continuation as expressed in Ernest Renan's "What Is a Nation?" roughly at the same period.[3] Barrès understood the nation as a collective force, a historical organic aggregate, beyond and above the control of individual wills; Renan famously defined it as "a plebiscite renewed everyday" and "the clearly expressed desire and consent to go on living together" (32). In due course, the Barresian concept of group identity as shared essence rather than a product of reason would culminate, and fall, with fascism.[4] To this day, however, and although the outcome of World War II was seen as a victory over fascism, the Barrès-Renan divide still polarizes, in one form or another, many of the debates involving questions of national identity in France. The threat to the system has to be kept active.

In the late 1990s, for example, when opponents of the legalization of same-sex couples, conservative and liberal alike, denounced homosexuality as "the rejection of the Other," their rhetoric was unmistakably identifiable as a direct echo of the terms used to stigmatize Le Pen's neofascist Front National and its anti-immigration platform. In a nutshell, all politicization of community, to the extent that it is understood to be a social manifestation of identity against or before Enlightenment values, is condemned in French culture as barbaric—that is, as archaic and/or fascist and therefore anti-Republican, if not un-French, by definition. Frankly, this hasn't helped the debate.

Because modern Frenchness is dependent upon a strict (yet regularly threatened) separation of private and public spheres, I must clarify exactly what I mean by these terms. The private sphere, as I understand it here, is not limited to domestic spaces and to their more abstract extension that we call privacy; nor is the public sphere simply the sum of what happens outside the home. Indeed, if the two spheres were circumscribed within actual spaces (home and not home), they would be essentially the same in all similar cultures, such as Western democracies. What I mean by private sphere, then, is a set of practices, institutions and relations that the culture defines as distinct from the affairs of the *polis* which, in turn, constitutes what I refer to as the public sphere. Family, love, sex, the body, friendship, illness, ethnicity, religion . . . are thus defined as private matters in French culture and, as such, irrelevant to political affairs. Of course, as feminist and queer some sort of gay bubble, a discrete area where it is possible to live one's homosexuality as a twenty-four-hour lifestyle with little or no contact with the outside world. A journalist writes, "It is an environment closed onto itself, in a situation of marginality. The ghetto acts as a geographical metaphor for the condition of gays"; a Sorbonne professor comments, "No one dares to venture outside his or her tiny territory anymore."[6] Much was made, for example, of the opening of a so-called gay bakery, on the rue Sainte-Croix-de-la-Bretonnerie—really a bakery owned and operated by an openly gay guy and a tad overdecorated. But the implication was that gays wanted to buy, if not gay bread, at least bread from a fellow gay person, and that it was the epitome of separatist nonsense. The same kind of criticism was leveled at the gay pharmacy on the rue du Temple, "La Pharmacie du Village" as it is called. What was hardly ever mentioned, however, was the fact that the pharmacy has for years carried the most complete stock of HIV treatments when many other pharmacies didn't or wouldn't—and still won't—and that it provides gay people with a uniquely safe environment in which to discuss health matters.

And so on and so forth. All in all, the Marais is presented to the general public as a site of socio-demographic homogeneity and cultural uniformity that is at once an ideal terrain for sociologists, anthropologists, and urban ethnographers in search of field work on homosexuality and a manifestation of the separatist urges that are said to threaten the French Republic.[7]

We know that the Marais is primarily a place where gay people *go* and not where they predominantly live, and that it is a central tourist site situated along Paris's busiest metro line where all sorts of people live or work or shop or hang out rather harmoniously. Furthermore, commercially specialized neighborhoods are not a new phenomenon in Paris—or in any big city, for that matter. The Faubourg Saint-Antoine used to be home to cabinetmakers and is now famous for its furniture stores; Pigalle has long been a red-light district; and the Latin Quarter may have a high density of art and repertory movie houses but nobody ever suspected film buffs of harboring secessionist desires. The Marais is one of these neighborhoods, the vitality of which depends on their openness to a constant flow of new customers and users. Why, then, would anyone describe it as a self-contained enclave populated solely by homosexuals who, apparently, must work in gay businesses only and do not even have heterosexual parents, siblings, or friends? This fantasy of (en)closure and full presence is the same fantasy of airtight communities that fueled the AIDS pandemic by positing the possibility that statements such as "not me" and "not here" had any grounding in reality.

I once overheard a young straight woman, walking in the Marais hand in hand with her male companion, exclaim with unfeigned surprise and utter gradually became evident to many that we had to fight for our own survival because nobody else would do it for us. A degree of separatism, the reasoning went, may then be imperative for gays and lesbians to protect ourselves more efficiently against a homophobic society that had so brutally revealed its genocidal undercurrents. The politics of ACT UP-Paris, for example, were premised on the idea that, in order better to fight AIDS, specific gay cultural practices should be embraced and amplified rather than muted as early AIDS groups, such as AIDES, had initially advocated. Just as the re-gaying of AIDS[9] by activists led to more community-based, and therefore more effective, AIDS policies that benefited not just gay men but everyone, so then a gay ghetto would bring about social reforms for the greater good. The PACS would be the obvious example, but one could also include recent debates on adoption, procreation, immigration laws and drug laws, the increased awareness of all sorts of discriminations, and even a fuller reexamination of the Vichy era.[10]

The idea of reclaiming the ghetto also came about as a reaction against another type of condemnation, coming from gay people themselves. Take a quick glance at gay personal ads and profiles on gay websites, listen to conversations, and you will surely notice a widespread tendency to describe oneself as *hors ghetto* (out of the ghetto). The phrase, along with its companions, *hors milieu* and *look hétéro*, signifies that one doesn't wish to associate or, more tellingly, *be associated* with the "gay scene." What the gay scene is supposed to be often remains unspecified, however. Still, *hors ghetto* broadly indicates that one is not any or all of the following: effeminate, shallow, promiscuous, HIV-positive, into drugs, stupid, artificial, vain, mean-spirited, indiscreet, gossipy, obsessive, cold, manipulative, insincere, into weird shit, covered with crabs, and entirely devoid of personality. (I condense.)

A less crude and more political version of the same rejection is also what animates certain gay public personalities who see in all gay neighborhoods, indeed in all collective expressions of gay visibility, a sign of *communautarisme* or *repli identitaire*, that is, the withdrawal of an identity-based community back on itself. (More on *repli* later.) Frédéric Martel, whose book *The Pink and the Black* briefly received the favors of the fickle mainstream media in the mid 1990s, is a typical example of that point of view. In a chapter entitled "Le repli identitaire?" he imagines a communautarian threat to French universalism and equates the gay community with the ghetto:

> A determining factor will be the future positioning of individuals with respect to their membership or nonmembership in the nascent community. Most of the tensions that have cropped up in the homosexual population can be attributed

to two conflicting aims: first, support for the communitarian lifestyle; and, second, the search for a life outside the ghetto. (346)

By taking for granted that the gay community is a ghetto, arguments such as this may conveniently reach the conclusion that membership in a community is an either-or proposition—which is the core fallacy of the ghetto arguments and of the dominant French concept of community in general.

Be it individual or political, some call such gay hostility toward community, a bit reductively in my view, a manifestation of self-hatred. (Well, it *is* self-hatred but, as I will show in the next chapter, that emotion is more complex and richer in possibilities than one might think.) What this hostility actually does is project onto the gay community a coherence and a cohesion it does not have in order to bracket it as a distinct other and to separate oneself from it—"I may be gay but I'm not like that." In that sense, the rhetoric of the ghetto is a disciplining discourse, as Foucault defined it.[11] And that, ultimately, is what is at stake in the disparaging use of the term— no matter who uses it and for what purpose—and precisely the phenomenon I was describing at the outset: a perpetual oscillation between a universalist vision and the invention/rejection of a radical other in response to the anxieties that periodically come to blur that vision. Gay rejections of the ghetto (not reducible to their psychological motivations, yet in relation to them) are merely a manifestation of the tension arising from the perceptions that two identities, French and gay, are in conflict.

The fact is that the "ghetto" is nothing more than a displacement—a metonymic stand-in for homosexuality itself and by extension for community in general. And the dead giveaway, of course, is that the Marais is so obviously not ghetto-like by any stretch of the imagination. The near consensual opinion that it *is* a ghetto is therefore a telltale sign that something significant is at stake in making the Marais signify *in words* something that it is not in reality. A perfect example of such a rhetorical move is to be found in a statement by Joseph Sitruk, "grand rabbin de France" (the elected religious leader of French Jewry) and, interestingly, an advocate of Jewish specificity against the potential danger of assimilation. Asked about his opinion on homosexuality, he replies, "Homosexual unions are a form of withdrawal/closing of the self onto itself [une forme de repli sur soi], an inner ghetto."[12] The word *repli* may translate as "withdrawal," in military terms, but also as "fold" or "crease," simultaneously suggesting a self-imposed disengagement from the national community and the closure of self-sameness. The manifold richness of the metaphor explains the ubiquity of the term *repli* in anti-communautarian rhetoric.

The idea of an inner ghetto echoes the old saying. "You can take the boy out of the ghetto, but you can't take the ghetto out of the boy." But while the latter indicates that a point of departure is never entirely left behind and that inside and outside are in a perpetually reversible relationship to one another (we shall leave aside for now the essentialist concept of origin that the saying implies), Sitruk's remark seeks nothing but to naturalize the idea that homosexuality is defined by the rejection of otherness. To clarify his point, he adds: "My concern and refusal stem from the effortlessness/facileness [facilité] with which some young people forego picking up the human challenge which is to face and overcome the question of otherness. The PACS law 'justifies,' as it were, this attitude" (40). The reasoning may be summed up as follows: (1) all otherness is contained in and represented by sex/gender difference; (2) homosexuality is the negation of sex/gender difference and, logically, of otherness in general; (3) a gay community is, therefore, based on sameness and non-relationality; (4) consequently, its neighborhood is inevitably a ghetto.

The ghetto metaphor is what ties it all together: homosexuality as narcissism and the neighborhood that has come to represent the community that makes unacceptable political claims. The Marais, in other words, can only be self-contained because it emanates from a narcissistic sexuality; and the proof that homosexuality is indeed narcissistic is that it has spawned, so to speak, a ghetto. Gay people who think they are embracing only the second half of the argument unwittingly assume its heterosexist presupposition. As for Sitruk, his condemnation represents a rather standard religious homophobic stance (when asked whether homosexuality is a problem, he begins his answer with, you guessed it, a reference to Leviticus) complemented by the sort of pseudo-psychoanalytic drivel on which many of the anti-PACS universalists drew their arguments. But more important, it demonstrates why the observably false notion of the Marais as ghetto could be so widely accepted as evident and how that came about in the midst of a legal debate that forced the Republic to think about the way it articulates public and private spheres.[13]

That the stigmatization of the Marais occurred alongside the PACS debate is not a coincidence, of course, for both reveal the link between political expressions of community and the dichotomization of the public and the private. Claims of legal recognition could only come from a community that had finally found its footing—at least if they are to have a credible chance of succeeding. The idea of legalizing same-sex couples had been in the air for a long time but was either ignored or mocked. ("The only people who want to get married nowadays are queers and priests," goes the very, very old joke.) So it was because the political drive for the PACS might (and eventually did) succeed that the anxiety about it was so great. The focus on the Marais was crucial in that it gave the threat of dissolution of the public-private divide a visible existence and a recognizable name/concept—the ghetto. Because of its association with Jewish history (clearly, the reference is not to the ghetto as an urban pocket of poverty), the term made it possible to portray gay claims for equal rights as a *repli identitaire* and therefore as a step backward from the Republican ideals that had produced and have been defined by the emancipation of the Jews. By alluding to one of the founding principles of modern France, the figure of the ghetto makes the gay community a symptom of a larger threat—the one posed by "community" in general.

The ghetto, in other words, is read as a sign of a larger cultural trend toward ghettoization and, perforce, a danger to the Republic both at its margin and at its core: on the one hand, the ghetto is a spatial entity that is tightly contained within its boundaries; on the other, it is a cultural notion that blurs the system's inner boundary that separates the private from the public and does so by playing out the implications of a misconception concerning community. What was emblematically played out around the question of homosexuality is true for other markers of social specificity that must be privatized and thus de-othered, such as religion, national origin, etc. Thanks to the twofold rhetorical trick that is the ghetto (a metaphor for the Marais which, in turn, became a metonym for homosexuality), the fusion of spatial and cultural boundaries has resulted in territorializing the antithesis of the Republic within the Republic itself—indeed at the very center of its capital. In sum, the Republic condemns the ghetto (that is, homosexuality) as non-relational (which is what it means to be the antithesis of a universalist republic) at the same time that it produces the ghetto as that with which the Republic, in order to define itself, must have no relation. Who is guilty of *repli identitaire* now?

The consequences are numerous and often unintended. While the strict dichotomization of public and private spheres mandates that homosexuality be understood as a purely individual matter, the ghetto rhetoric recognizes that it is, in fact, indistinguishable from community. And while insisting on seeing a ghetto at its symbolic heart, the Republic unwittingly recognizes that that-with-which-it-must-have-no-relations is really its constituent, that is, something with which it has a foundational yet denied relation. So if the Marais *was* indeed a ghetto, it could easily be liquidated (that's what often happened to actual ghettos) and would therefore pose no genuine threat. But the Marais is *not* a ghetto; it is a neighborhood, and that is a very different thing.

NEIGHBORHOODS AND DIASPORAS

So what *is* a neighborhood? In the second volume of Michel de Certeau's *The Practice of Everyday Life*, Pierre Mayol, drawing in part on the work of Henri Lefebvre, defines it primarily as relational: "*relationships* among objects, more precisely . . . the link that attaches private to public space" (8; original emphasis). It is regulated by what Mayol calls propriety, or *convenance*, a set of collectively accepted norms that tend to abolish individual differences and promote conformity in the neighborhood:

> Propriety is the symbolic management of the public facet of each of us as soon as we enter the street. Propriety is simultaneously the manner in which one is perceived and the means constraining one to remain submitted to it; fundamentally, it requires the avoidance of all dissonance in the game of behaviors and all qualitative disruption in the perception of the social environment. That is why it produces stereotyped behaviors, ready-to-wear social clothes, whose function is to make it possible to recognize anyone, anywhere. (17)

A mode of coercion, propriety is also the price to pay in exchange for recognition and, with it, for all the benefits of communal life. Conformity to proper norms of public behavior is an *obligation* for individuals but, as Mayol points out, the term has two meanings: " 'Obliged' should not only be understood in a repressive sense, but also as something that 'obliges,' which creates obligations, *links* . . . etymologically" (16; original emphasis). The sort of *reconnaissance* one enjoys in one's neighborhood is also, in that sense, what is called in French a *reconnaissance de dette*, an IOU.

Obligation as debt is precisely, for Roberto Esposito, what defines community—and defines it as lack. In other words, each member of a community—here a neighborhood—is obliged to each other member for the benefits of life together. This implies not only that the individual subject is rendered possible by the public subject but, logically, that the two cannot be understood as discrete entities. It is in that sense that the neighborhood represents the site where the private and the public merge to form at once a relation and a restraint, or what could be called a bond (or *lien* in French, which gave us the English "lien" and conveys the original meaning of obligation). Emphasizing what he calls "the organic link to one's lodging" (10), Mayol continues:

> As a result of its everyday use, the neighborhood can be considered as the progressive privatization of public space. It is a practical device whose function is to ensure a continuity between what is the most intimate (the private space of one's lodging) and what is the most unknown (the totality of the city or even, by extension, the rest of the world). (11)

And later:

> Thus, the limit between public and private, which appears to be the founding structure of the neighborhood for the practice of a dweller [usagé], is not only

The mural outside Jo Goldenberg's delicatessen, now gone

a separation, but constitutes a separation that unites: the public and the private are not both disregarded as two exogenous, though coexisting, elements; they are much more, constantly interdependent because, in the neighborhood, one has no meaning without the other. (11–12)

The neighborhood, then, is simultaneously a home and not a home. To be exact, it is home-like, possessing the sort of familiarity the old Yiddish-speaking inhabitants of the Marais called *haymishkeyt*: a blend of recognition, friendliness and solidarity.[14]

What makes the Marais *haymish* for Ashkenazi Jews is, of course, its perceived similarity with the place of origin, whether or not one actually ever knew it. Interviewing French-born witnesses about their feelings toward the street, where they lived in its heyday, Jeanne Brody, in *Rue des Rosiers*, elicits the following answers:

It used to be *heymishkeyt*. There was no other language than Yiddish. Everything was kosher on the rue des Rosiers, rue Pavée. . . . The rue des Rosiers

Chez Marianne

> was the reconstruction of a self-contained Jewish life, with all the authenticity that this implies. . . . It was the old *shtetl*, it felt as good as home. (112–13)

> It used to be completely different; it was a village, a real *shtetl*, the *Pletzl*, in a word! Everybody knew everybody. . . . It used to be *haymish*. (113)

And Brody adds that "for Sephardic Jews 'it was like the *mellah*!' "[15] In other words, what validated or legitimated the Marais as a home in the eyes of Jews is that it was defined in part by its status as evocation, that is, by its relation to something external to it. When the first interviewee, a Frenchman with Lithuanian parents, depicts the Marais of old as both authentic and a reconstruction, one could easily point out the obvious paradox; a reconstruction is, by definition, not authentic. Yet this apparent contradiction in terms is a perfectly valid proposition in the case of diasporic communities, for which each site in the diaspora is simultaneously different from and identical to every other site, while the original origin, so to speak (Zion, for example), is forever irretrievable. In a revealing parallel, Hasia R. Diner notes in *Lower East Side Memories*:

The Musée d'art et d'histoire du judaïsme

> For American-born Jews living on the suburban fringes of America's cities, the
> Lower East Side became their "old world," their *alte heym*. With no towns
> across the Atlantic whose names resonated to them, with no bonds drawing
> them to think about those ancestral places, the Lower East Side emerged as the
> place that all Jews could somehow share as their collective "shtetl," the emblem
> for them all of the places they had left. (170)

One could argue that more recent diasporas, or mass migrations, have a
different, less mythical relationship with their place of origin. Members of
the Chinese community that inhabits areas of the Marais, for instance, could
in theory return to Wenzhou. The city, after all, is still very much there.
Setting aside situations of temporary displacement, I would contend, however, that when populations are compelled to leave their "home" it is because
it has become *uninhabitable* for one reason or another and has therefore ceased
to be the home it once was, making it irretrievable as such.

Diasporic sites, of course, have an ambiguous relationship with the surrounding national culture. In the French context, where the sort of identi-

ties that constitute communities are expected to be private, the question of a community-based neighborhood is an inescapably thorny one. One way to deal with this tension is to folklorize urban space. Today, as the Marais is no longer the outpost of Yiddishkayt or the North African hub it used to be, the remnants of Jewish life serve mostly to testify to a thriving culture that no longer is and, therefore, to the success of the French model of integration. In that sense, to celebrate the neighborhood's Jewish past is really to celebrate French history and to erase Jewish specificity in the act of representing it—which makes the Marais a site of remembrance and of forgetting at the same time.

There are several signs in the Marais that encourage us to read the continuity between Jews and French history. A mural painted by famous deli owner Jo Goldenberg for the bicentennial of the French Revolution celebrated the Emancipation and once graced the outside of his (now closed) restaurant, even if the three chesty women with 1970s hairdos dancing the hora at the center of the piece made it look more like the strangest episode of *Charlie's Angels* ever. The restaurant "Chez Marianne" announces its Frenchness rather clearly by associating its owner's name with the female allegory of (post)revolutionary France. It serves falafels *and* strudels, thus unifying two different Jewish traditions under the same liberty cap. More subtly perhaps, the interior adornments of the Guimard synagogue on the rue Pavée replicate those of the Art Nouveau metro stations for which the architect is most famous, thus emphasizing the building's connection to the fabric of the city at large and, perhaps, encouraging the Jew's inscription in the fabric of the modern nation as well. More recently, when residents and business owners of the rue des Rosiers, inspired by the modern day Astérix, José Bové, successfully foiled the opening of a McDonald's restaurant in the name of the street's unique status in Jewish history, weren't they in fact acting out a very, very French hostility toward globalization and American cultural imperialism? Finally, the installation of the Musée d'art et d'histoire du judaïsme in one of the grand seventeenth-century residences of the Marais's golden age is like the final touch that officially locates the neighborhood's Jewish past within official French history—not to mention the tourist circuit. In other words, what one *reads* in the Jewish Marais is historical continuity—sometimes literally since there are several specialized bookstores there as well. This may sound like a paradox, given that the history of Jews in Western countries is in part one of radical disruptions and displacements, such as expulsions, coerced conversions, emancipation, immigration, extermination, name changes, and so on. Simply put, what (also) produces the continuity of Jewish memory is this pattern of historical discontinuity.

And while remembering is perhaps the most Jewish of all Jewish activities, remembering the Marais is also, for integrated Jews, a sign of Frenchness that superimposes over Jewish history per se the linear narrative structure of modernity-as-progress triggered by Enlightenment thought and the Emancipation. Social specificity, therefore, is showcased, but only inasmuch as it underscores the success of emancipation and integration.

It is no surprise that the responsibility of France in the Holocaust remained largely illegible for a long time, although many signs, most notably commemorative plaques, evoke the events that took place in the neighborhood. Or rather, it *was* legible, but as absence. For example, when the old residents interviewed by Brody keep referring to "before," it prompts the question, "before what?" By contrast, older French Gentiles reminiscing about the past traditionally use the phrase "dans le temps," the English equivalent of which could be "in the old days" but whose literal translation is "in time," thus emphasizing continuity. However, the word used by older Jews reveals discontinuity—without naming the reason for it.

Until recently, Jews deported to the death camps *by* France (albeit indirectly since the French police delivered them to the Germans for deportation) were designated as having patriotically died *for* France. While not exclusively French, such production of official history directly echoes one of Renan's principles: A nation is constituted by remembering what we suffered in common while our collective crimes are better left forgotten.[16] For Jews to have demanded that the Jewish specificity of the Holocaust be recognized in some way would have, therefore, been tantamount to disavowing their own Frenchness. Instead, in the years following the Liberation they decided to lie low.[17]

I explained in the previous chapter that commemorative plaques began to change all over Paris after President Chirac finally recognized France's responsibility in the Holocaust. Typical of the new official attitude, a plaque outside a kindergarten now reads:

In memory of the little children of this kindergarten who were deported between 1942 and 1944 because they were born Jewish, innocent victims of Nazi barbarity with the active complicity of the Vichy government. They were exterminated in the death camps. Let us never forget them.

[A la mémoire des petits enfants de cette école maternelle déportés de 1942 à 1944 parce qu'ils étaient nés juifs, victimes innocentes de la barbarie nazie avec la complicité active du gouvernement de Vichy.

Ils furent exterminés dans les camps de la mort.

Ne les oublions jamais.]

A LA MÉMOIRE DES PETITS ENFANTS
DE CETTE ÉCOLE MATERNELLE
DÉPORTÉS DE 1942 A 1944
PARCE QU'ILS ÉTAIENT NÉS JUIFS,
VICTIMES INNOCENTES
DE LA BARBARIE NAZIE
AVEC LA COMPLICITÉ ACTIVE
DU GOUVERNEMENT DE VICHY.

ILS FURENT EXTERMINÉS
DANS LES CAMPS DE LA MORT.

Le 15 décembre 2001   NE LES OUBLIONS JAMAIS

MAIRIE DE PARIS
DIRECTION DES AFFAIRES SCOLAIRES

An example of the new memorial plaques

The controversy surrounding this official recognition revealed a generational gap within the Jewish community, with older members refusing to equate the collaborationist Vichy regime with France while younger people, more ethnically identified and less integrationist than their elders, demanded such an admission of complicity. Competing plaques, then, echoed competing visions of French history.

Interestingly, younger Jews also tend to favor the official recognition of the "pink triangles," homosexual men deported to concentration camps, while older Jews by and large resist it. As much as it is a sign of the greater openness of younger generations toward homosexuality, this attitude also reveals a greater sympathy for community-based demands if not to jettison at least to rethink and adapt the universalist Republic, including the revision of official history.

There is also one very visible sign of dissent in the Marais, although it is seldom talked about. On Sunday afternoons, dozens, sometimes hundreds of Jewish teenagers, most of them belonging to the more ethnically self-identified North African communities living in the suburbs or in outer neighborhoods of Paris, descend upon the rue des Rosiers to hang out together. Occasionally, violent street fights erupt with groups of young Arabs

Young Jews gathering on the rue des Rosiers on a typical Sunday

also coming from outside the city center. Like most groups of teenagers, these young Jews are loud and conspicuous. They tend to be ardently pro-Israel and anti-Palestinian, and some older boys belong to the Betar, a belligerent Zionist youth group infamous today for beating up Arabs and dovish Jews alike. Disrespectful of the rules of propriety, the kids are largely perceived as outsiders on the rue des Rosiers. Their presence in the neighborhood is a major source of embarrassment for its older Jewish residents who see them as markers of division and disintegration—the opposite, in short, of what the Marais is supposed to signify. Yet for these young people, too, the Marais is a home and a symbol, only one of defiant otherness.

It is interesting to notice that this challenge to the integrationist model finds its source in the suburbs and the poorer peripheral districts of Paris, where many young Arabs of North African origin, who have been made the embodiment of social disintegration, also live. The *banlieues* are home to

tighter, more religious and isolationist Jewish communities as well, as in Sarcelles and Créteil.[18] Disturbance stems from the blurring of urban boundaries, as well as from history and contemporary politics. Those Jews, it seems,
don't belong in the Marais. Moving out of the neighborhood was supposed
to be a sign of integration within French society. However, as the disturbing
return of the urban marginal toward the center indicates, the suburbaniza-
tion of minority communities was more like a disappearing act, a denial that
allowed the center of town to be made the repository of a mythified version
of national history. Here we might (think of the war memorials appearing on
the central square of nearly every French town or village after World War I.)
The periodic intrusions of youth gangs from minority communities figure
something like the return of the tribal past that the universalist project of
modern France was supposed to have overcome, that is, repressed. Similar
accusations of social archaism have been leveled against the gay community
that made the Marais its home.

For queers, however, the home-like quality of a neighborhood is, like the
home itself, fraught with ambivalence. To the extent that "home-like" implicitly means "family-like," conflicts with homosexuality are bound to arise
and test the limits of propriety. Consider this passage from Guillaume Dustan's *Nicolas Pages*, in which the narrator, after telling a story of Portuguese
Jews who used to hide their Jewishness out of fear for their lives, explains his
own need to hide his homosexuality in public places.

> I'm scared of getting killed too, scared of losing an eye or a hand. So I jus'
> hide. . . . Back when I was a kid, in the ninth, everybody liked me. I got big
> smiles from the baker and the grocer and the butcher and the florist. So I ain't
> gonna take no chance and have people give me that You faggot! look. That's
> why I jus' stay home, in my room or else in the ghetto. Well. I should not want
> to appear unseemly.

> [Moi aussi j'ai peur qu'on m'tue, peur de perdre un oeil, la main. Alors
> je m'cache. . . . Quand j'étais p'tit dans le neuvième tout l'monde m'aimait.
> C'était les grands sourires chez l'boulanger, l'fruitier, l'boucher, l'fleuriste.
> Alors j'veux pas risquer la tronche en biais qui veut dire Sale tapiole. C'est pour
> ça que j'reste chez moi, dans ma chambre ou alors dans l'ghetto. Bref. Je ne
> voudrais pas être de mauvais goût. (430)]

Going back to the very activity that, according to Mayol, defines a neighborhood perhaps better than any other—patronizing local businesses—
Dustan reveals the implied violence that underscores breaches of propriety.
Hiding is a matter of bowing to the demands of social norms, a move that is
not only expressed but also textually figured by the more proper French of

the last sentence. If the *commerces de proximité*, as neighborhood stores are known in France, are supposed to be close to people's homes, they effectively make people close to one another.

Conversely, when Chinese business owners are accused of chasing local stores out of neighborhoods, their alleged business practices are often interpreted as a sign that the Chinese do not seek to integrate and blend harmoniously with their surrounding community. More importantly, I believe, such criticism, while stemming from genuine concern, also seeks to nullify these immigrants' possible claim to Frenchness by denying their business enclaves the very status of neighborhoods in the traditional French sense of *quartier*.

But what Mayol described as the price to pay for recognition is also a denial of recognition for queers. This is why Dustan's narrator must rearrange the relation between home and neighborhood. Defining "home" as "in my room or else in the ghetto," the two being interchangeable, Dustan appears to confirm Mayol's point about the neighborhood being an extension of the home. As I will show in the next section, however, Dustan understands the relation between the private and the public the other way round: for queers, it is the home that is an extension of the neighborhood. To put it in larger terms, the community becomes less like a family as the home becomes more like a community—which ultimately confirms, rather than contradicts, Mayol's contention that it is the social that enables the individual and not the opposite.

THE FABULOUS WORLD OF GUILLAUME DUSTAN[19]

Guillaume Dustan arrived on the literary scene preceded by a reputation the French love to call *sulfureuse*. The fuss may sound at first like one of those Parisian nonevents, a controversy without stakes designed to fight vainly the old ennui, as Cole Porter would say, and propel fall season book sales while we're at it. But in 1996 there was something different about Guillaume Dustan, something new and assuredly not boring. For starters, the name was a pseudonym and initially no author photos were circulated. Rumors were rampant in gay Paris. Someone—but who?—was about to publish a warts-and-all[20] autobiographical book about gay life that was an apologia for unprotected sex. The event even made it into the pages of other people's books, as in this transparent passage from a 1997 AIDS-themed novel/memoir by Olivier de Vleeschouwer:

> Stormy discussion last night during a dinner I had considered not attending. People were talking about a forthcoming book cloaked in an aura of scandal. The

author, who is HIV positive and hides behind a penname, was alleged to describe his high-risk sexual practices, more often than not unprotected. Someone ventured the word "daring," which made me react. Some people give the impression that, although their first reflex is one of rejection, they somewhat admire such suicidal and criminal attitudes. I expressed loathing and indignation. . . . And anyway who is this dime store provocateur who would pass off his confessions as sincere but who doesn't have the courage to sign them with his name?

[Discussion houleuse, hier soir, au cours d'un dîner où j'avais hésité à me rendre. On y parlait d'un livre à paraître qu'un parfum de scandale précédait. L'auteur, séropositif, caché derrière un pseudonyme, y décrirait ses pratiques sexuelles à haut risque, le plus souvent sans protection. Quelqu'un a lancé le mot "audace," qui m'a fait réagir. On sent chez certains, derrière un premier réflexe de rejet, une confuse admiration pour ces attitudes suicidaires et criminelles. J'ai dit mon dégoût, exprimé ma révolte. . . . Et quel est ce provocateur de foire qui voudrait faire passer pour sincères des aveux qu'ils ne trouve pas le courage de signer de son nom?][21]

Barebacking (originally understood as the practice of unprotected sex between consenting and fully informed HIV-positive male partners) did become a subject of furious debate in France thanks in part to Dustan. As Christophe Broqua has shown, ACT UP, having lost steam and its sense of direction with the arrival of antiretroviral therapies, was in large part responsible for manufacturing the controversy.[22] Yet, Dustan's first books were far from being the treatises on barebacking they were made out to be. They did mention the practice but without praising it, let alone encouraging it, and there was nothing confessional about them. No, what repelled so many gay men and fascinated some straight readers in Dustan's novels was his unapologetic depiction of urban gay life, equated with Marais culture, as an endless succession of sexual encounters, complete with pornography, extreme practices, and lots and lots of drugs. Dustan, in other words, was giving gay men a bad name by seeming to confirm the worst clichés imaginable about us—namely, cultural separatism and sexual pursuit as death-wish fulfillment. (Don't these people know that a good name can ruin a perfectly bad reputation?)

Other excerpts from the novel quoted above emphasize the extent to which reactions to Dustan often mirror how one thinks about the new, open gay culture on display in the rue Sainte-Croix de la Bretonnerie:

The boys of the Marais stroll about hand in hand along the sidewalks. Their skin is smooth and preciously tanned; they smile for angels who do not see them. They've hung brightly colored flags above the places they patronize. In a different time, pink stars flourished on the chests of men whose shaved heads was not a choice.

[Les garçons du Marais déambulent main dans la main sur les trottoirs. Ils ont la peau lisse et précieusement hâlée, sourient aux anges qui ne les voient pas. Ils ont accroché des drapeaux multicolores au-dessus des lieux qu'ils fréquentent. En un autre temps, l'étoile rose fleurissait sur la poitrine de certains hommes qui n'avaient pas choisi leur crane rasé. (83)]

And later:

The phony Ben Hurs of the Marais may hold hands as much as they like, they may even hook banderillas to the doors of their Western-like saloons and ape the soldiers they never were, I know what dreams they carry around, deep in their pockets full of holes. . . . Such freedom conceals its traps for a long time. Their hands get bloody from caressing ghosts and, ultimately, at the end of one long tunnel of identical nights, they stand and stretch, orphaned, in the middle of a desert.

[Ils peuvent bien se tenir la main, les faux Ben Hur du Marais, accrocher des banderilles aux portes de leurs saloons de western et singer les militaires qu'ils n'ont pas été, je connais les rêves qu'ils promènent au fond de leurs poches trouées. . . . Cette liberté cache longtemps ses pièges. On s'écorche les paumes à caresser des fantômes et, finalement, au bout d'un long tunnel de nuits toutes identiques, on s'étire orphelin au centre d'un désert. (136)]

Beyond the quaint and oh-so-French pomposity of the style and the odd fixation on men holding hands in the street, the passages are rather telling. As the reference to the Nazi deportation of homosexuals indicates, with its historically inaccurate blend of pink triangle and yellow star,[23] to reject Dustan is to reject the ghetto. And few made it clearer than Didier Lestrade, cofounder of ACT UP-Paris and of the gay magazine *Têtu*, safe-sex crusader, and Dustan's archenemy on the barebacking battlefield:

I'm glad that Dustan is popular in the Marais. That he thinks he won because people greet him. He can have the Marais. I've stopped going there: because I find all that ugly and I can't stand even a single rainbow flag . . . because in the end the Marais disgusts me and I can live perfectly well without all that. So fuck them all really. I have a husband and I'm not about to leave him. Dustan lives in a 280 square-foot apartment while I have 1,400 square feet in Versailles where Robespierre once visited.

[Je suis content que Dustan soit populaire dans le Marais. Qu'il ait l'impression d'avoir gagné parce qu'on lui dit bonjour. Je lui donne le Marais. Moi je n'y vais plus: parce que je trouve ça laid et je ne peux plus encaisser un seul rainbow flag . . . parce que finalement, le Marais me dégoûte et je vis très bien sans ça. . . . So fuck them all, really. J'ai un mari et je ne suis pas près de le quitter. Dustan vit dans un 28 m2, moi j'ai un 120 m2 versaillais où Robespierre est passé.][24]

Lestrade uses Dustan's tiny studio apartment as a trope for the cultural and psychological confinement of the ghetto and makes it represent Marais culture as the epitome of immaturity—"I've *stopped* going there"—and emotional failure—"I have a husband." Meanwhile the historical, if incongruous, pairing of Versailles and Robespierre suggests that gay maturity has something to do with choosing Frenchness over queerness, the nation over the community. One may disagree with Lestrade's assessment of the Marais; what is undeniable, however, is that Dustan embraced the ghetto as no-one ever had before.

Guillaume Dustan's first two novels, in particular *Dans ma chambre* [*In My Room*] and *Je sors ce soir* [I'm Stepping Out], were spectacular landmarks in the parallel canon of gay literature in France and the first genuine works of literature to graphically depict aspects of gay culture and sexuality since Renaud Camus' 1979 *Tricks* and early books by Hervé Guibert. Ironic, intelligent, and sharply written in a seemingly effortless dispassionate style, they belonged to what was then called *autofiction*, a genre-bending mix of novel and autobiography increasingly favored by young, mostly female and/or queer authors and whose popularizer and best example arguably remains Guibert.

Dustan's early novels tell the story of Guillaume, a young gay novelist who seems to spend his entire time dancing, fucking, and getting stoned. The critic who (favorably) reviewed *Dans ma chambre* for the daily *Libération*, summarized it as follows: "The plot: the narrator goes in for bigger and bigger dildos." [25] The narrator in question, like the author, is HIV positive at a time when successful combination therapies are just beginning to change the landscape of AIDS in Western countries. Barebacking notwithstanding, the theme of AIDS, however, has remained largely sidestepped by readers and critics alike who have made Guillaume Dustan, for better and for worse, the ultimate chronicler of the new Marais culture. To be sure no other writer had ever portrayed gay life quite that way before—in part because it didn't really exist quite that way before. Once he made his identity public (his real name was William Baranès and he was not, as some had speculated, a well-known figure), Dustan became a frequent guest on television shows where his provocative appearances only cemented his status as a polarizing figure—ultimate rebel or pathetic buffoon, depending on how you felt about him. He eventually created and edited a series of gay and lesbian books for the mainstream publishing house Balland. The output was often mediocre, and the same was sometimes true of Dustan's own increasingly political and experimental but self-indulgent prose. The whole enterprise soon folded. In October 2005, Guillaume Dustan was found dead in his apartment after an "involuntary chemical intoxication." He was forty years old.[26]

I mentioned the fact that AIDS was, and still is, too often downplayed by Dustan's readers. His books, however, are first and foremost about AIDS and, read through the lens of the epidemic, their depiction of the Marais and its culture provides the ground for a model of democratic community that undoes the confining boundaries of public and private spheres. In order to do so Dustan focuses not merely on a culture—the Marais—that is far from being as typical of contemporary homosexuality as the media conveniently and reductively assert, but also on an even narrower subsection of it—the far smaller world of hardcore sexualities. Dustan's cast of characters are men who, when they are not being tied up, can take two fists up the ass as casually as the rest of us enjoy a refreshing Campari and soda on a hot summer day. So if there is to be community (and because of AIDS it has become imperative), it will not be effected through consensual identification but rather by positioning oneself in relation to otherness. Community, Dustan tells us, is a matter of difference, not sameness.

Space plays a central part in that relation, as the titles *Dans ma chambre* and *Je sors ce soir* imply. Dustan often presents the outside, that is to say the world beyond the imaginary boundaries of the ghetto, as a place where queers are at best objects of contempt and at worst in physical danger. It isn't uncommon for gay Parisians to mock those who hold hands on the rue des Archives only to let go when they reach the rue de Rivoli, the outer limit of the gay area, as if that was the height of cowardice or hypocrisy. And some may despise rainbow flags, they do come in handy, since being gay requires the sometimes life-saving ability to understand where you are in order to determine what (not) to do and who (not) to be. More than a concern for safety, such awareness is also an acknowledgment that identity is a function of one's ever-changing relation to space, that is, a metonym for political and ideological context.

After his friend and lover Terrier, for example, attempts yet again to kill himself, Guillaume calls the paramedics. In the ambulance, stoned and admittedly paranoid, he reads homophobia on people's faces: "In the van next to the stretcher I freak, they must think we're a bunch of dirty depraved faggots I think" (*IMR,* 90 [*DMC,* 115]). And at the hospital: "The head nurse, a brunette, looks accusing when she sends me to register my 'friend' " (translation modified [*DMC,* 116]). In contrast, queer spaces provide safety from the dangers of the world, as when Guillaume returns to Paris after a long absence, still alive against all expectations. He gets dressed and goes out clubbing:

> I look around thinking it's really cool to be here again, among my ghetto brothers. Nothing but queers. Nothing but guys I can stare at without any risk

of getting bashed. Even if I look them in the eyes. Nothing but guys who can be expected to enjoy being desired by me. A place where I no longer have to stand on the defensive. A place where I no longer am an animal waiting to be attacked. Paradise.

[Je mate en me disant que c'est cool d'être là à nouveau, parmi mes frères du ghetto. Que des pédés. Que des mecs que je peux regarder sans aucun risque de me faire casser la gueule. Même si c'est dans les yeux. Que des mecs à qui ça fait a priori plaisir que je puisse avoir envie d'eux. Un endroit où je n'ai plus à être sur la défensive. Un endroit où je ne suis plus un animal qui attend qu'on l'attaque. Le paradis. (*JSCS*, 18)]

Considering that Tahiti is the place that Guillaume has just returned from, the description of a dark gay disco as paradise regained is pointedly funny and ironic. But more important is the sentence before. Writing "[a] place where I no longer am an animal" rather than the expected simile "*like* an animal," Dustan suggests that being in the wrong place actually *makes* queers less than human and that it is *humanity* (a universal), as well as homosexuality (a particular), that can be found *concurrently* in queer spaces.

Consider Dustan's use of the word "risk." Associated in dominant AIDS discourses precisely with the narrator's lifestyle and "his high-risk sexual practices" (see Vleeschouwer quotation above), risk, for queers, is shown here to be a defining attribute of the heterosexual world. Indeed the cruelty of life outside the ghetto appears in an early passage of *Dans ma chambre*. One day Guillaume comes across his friend Christophe at a public pool located just outside the Marais.[27] When Christophe announces that he has recently become HIV positive, Guillaume must find a way to express his compassion and solidarity in a space that won't tolerate either that expression or the feelings it conveys:

The last time I saw him was in the water, the pool in Les Halles. When I asked him how he was doing he answered Not so hot. Why not? I asked, and he said I tested positive a month ago and I don't know how it could have happened. Because we were in a public place I couldn't take him in my arms. I caressed him on the sly when we met up at the far end of the pool. (33–34; translation modified)

[La dernière fois que je l'ai vu, c'était dans l'eau à la piscine des Halles. Quand je lui ai demandé Ça va? Il m'a répondu Pas trop fort, j'ai demandé Pourquoi?, il m'a dit J'ai viré séropo depuis un mois je ne sais pas comment ça a pu se passer. Je ne pouvais pas le prendre dans mes bras parce qu'on était dans un endroit public. Je l'ai caressé en douce quand on se retrouvait au bout des longueurs. (48–49)]

The furtiveness of basic human emotions that are forced to remain clandestine appears all the more compelling because of Dustan's unsentimental style. Homophobia, he tells us, permeates the mundane. It is utterly banal. Only the water, a sort of nonspace or in-between, allows for such gestures of friendship. In that sense, and because it tells a story of AIDS, the scene echoes a well-known episode in Camus's *La peste* [*The Plague*], when Rieux and Tarrou, the two main characters, enjoy a night swim in the sea and a brief respite from the plague that ravages the city of Oran:

> He [Rieux] turned around, came alongside his friend and swam with the same rhythm. . . . For few minutes they swam on with equal stokes [sic] and equal strength, alone, far from he world, finally free of the town and the plague. . . . Once they had dressed again they left without saying a word. But their hearts were one, and the memory of that night was sweet for both of them. (197–98)

> [Rieux se retourna, se mit au niveau de son ami, et nagea dans le même rythme. . . . Pendant quelques minutes, ils avancèrent avec la même cadence et la même vigueur, solitaires, loin du monde, libérés enfin de la ville et de la peste. . . . Habillés de nouveau, ils repartirent sans avoir prononcé un mot. Mais ils avaient le même coeur et le souvenir de cette nuit leur était doux. (1427)]

It could be that the reference occurred to Dustan because the scene of male friendship, mixed with nudity and its feeling of illegitimacy, once moved him as a queer kid and stayed with him after that—just as it moved me and stayed with me, allowing me, in due course, to decipher it here. Ultimately, however, the queerest reading may not be the possible appropriation of Camus's canonical novel for the purpose of queer self-awareness (we do that sort of stuff all the time), but to suggest the universal potential of Dustan's denunciation of homophobia.

For Dustan, being in a nonqueer, that is, public and supposedly universal space entails either dehumanization through homophobia or the masking of queerness through passing. Sartre's argument about the Jews being fully human at home because it is the only place where they are not Jewish is an interesting one in that it is so counterintuitive, at least in a French context. We saw how Sartre seeks to demonstrate that it is the public sphere that produces the minoritized groups which it then excludes and confines to the home or its symbolic equivalents, whereas the private sphere is where the individual members of these groups may enjoy their full humanity. However, the distinction does not hold. Furthermore, the argument is premised on the assumption that group identification is necessarily dehumanizing because it is always the effect of a rejection.[28] In that sense, Sartre simultaneously criticizes and confirms a dominant paradigm of French culture. What Dustan proposes, to the contrary, is that communal spaces are where the universal and the particular are revealed to be continuous rather than distinct.

At first glance, though, Dustan's chronicles of Marais life appear to illustrate just the sort of *repli* I was talking about earlier—albeit in the interests of safety as much as for the enjoyment of a uniform communal lifestyle that has little or no relation with the outside world. As if to acknowledge that homosexuality is truly the private (and narcissistic) matter it is said to be, the title of the first novel announces to the readers that they should expect juicy revelations about the narrator's intimacy—and that of a few other people, too. As Ross Chambers and Patricia Meyer Spacks have noted, the close relationship between the novel, gossip, and community is an old one.[29] This implies, then, that once it is revealed and exposed for all to read intimacy is no longer so intimate. So, as if to shatter both the illusion of the novel and that of intimacy itself, Dustan starts off with an episode during which Guillaume actually has to relinquish his room because his boyfriend keeps having sex in it with another man. "I left Quentin the bedroom" (3 [11]) is the opening sentence of the novel. From the onset, the readers are warned not to expect the private to be so private nor the personal to be so personal. (To be sure, the first chapter is ironically titled "Good Intentions," and, as everyone knows, good intentions are mentioned only when they haven't been or will not be lived up to.) Expelled from a room that was never really his own to begin with, Guillaume will soon extend it far beyond the actual four walls that surround his bed and redefine it so as to encompass all the spaces where sex happens, that is, the ghetto itself:

> We're doing fine in the ghetto. There's a lot of people. More people all the time. Queers who start fucking all the time and no longer go as often as before into the normal world. Apart from the job, in general, and seeing the family, everything can be done without going out of the ghetto. (55–56).

> [On est bien dans le ghetto. Il y a du monde. Il y en a tout le temps plus. Des pédés qui se mettent à baiser tout le temps et à ne plus aller aussi souvent qu'avant dans le monde normal. A part bosser, en général, et voir sa famille, tout peut se faire sans sortir du ghetto." (75)]

And because Marais culture, as Dustan understands it, is first and foremost centered on sex, the bedroom and the neighborhood ultimately become one and the same to form Guillaume's fabulous world, a world within which the boundary between inside and outside has all but dissolved:

> I live in a fabulous world where everybody has slept with everybody. The map of this world if found in the community magazines that I read assiduously. Bars. Clubs. Restaurants. Bathhouses. Minitel. Party lines. Cruising spots. And all the telephone numbers and addresses and first names that go with them. In this

world everyone has fucked at least five hundred other guys, in large part the same ones for that matter. The guys who go out. (*IMR* 52; translation modified)

[Je vis dans un monde merveilleux où tout le monde a couché avec tout le monde. La carte s'en trouve dans les revues communautaires que je lis assidûment. Bars. Boîtes. Restaurants. Saunas. Minitel. Rézo. Lieux de drague. Et tous les numéros de téléphone et les adresses et les prénoms qui vont avec. Dans ce monde chacun a baisé avec au moins cinq cents mecs, en bonne partie les mêmes d'ailleurs. Les mecs qui sortent. (*DMC* 70)]

Personal addresses and phone numbers and names are thus sites on the map (or items on a menu perhaps since *carte* has several meanings?) just as public places are. Sex, both a private and a social activity by definition, binds a community of "guys who go out." Domestic spaces and public sites have merged and become a world where one shops for sexual gratification; individual fulfillment has apparently become the tie that binds groups, displacing self-denial and the greater good.

The first problem with that reading (homosexuality as narcissism and community as ghetto) is that sex, according to Guillaume Dustan, is not quite the personal pursuit we assume it to be in the modern era, but rather a collective matter *to begin with*. In his novels it isn't the individual who projects his own sexual pursuit onto the outside and (mis)shapes the collective accordingly—at least not initially; it is the community that enables the sexual individual. Sex, in other words, is public before it is private. And central to that view is the question of technique. In *Nicolas Pages*, Dustan puts it bluntly:

The great argument: there are no such things as a good fuck or a bad fuck, there are only guys who click or who don't. Not quite. When a guy plays with my nipples without knowing what he's doing, or vaguely sucks me, that's no temperament, that's a lack of know-how. . . . The reason I'm one of the best cocksuckers in Paris is that I know how.

[Le grand argument: il n'y a pas de bons et de mauvais coups, il n'y a que des mecs qui s'accordent ou pas. Eh bien non. Le mec qui me fait les seins n'importe comment, qui me suçote, ce n'est pas un tempérament, c'est un manque de savoir-faire. . . . si je suis un des meilleurs suceurs de Paris, c'est que je sais y faire. (249)]

The failsafe recipe for the perfect blowjob follows. Similarly, in *Dans ma chambre*, Guillaume tells in great detail how he fucks a guy (who remains unnamed in the entire scene). The reader knows immediately that what he or she is about to read is not the intimate story of a specific sexual encounter but a demonstration of how to do things right *technically*: "First is the hold. . . . Then there's the arch of the back. . . . And then there is the shove" (35–36).

["D'abord l'empoignage. . . . Après il y a le cambrage. . . . Et puis il y a le poussage" (50–51).] In fact, the whole event is introduced as a repetition of previous instances. The long paragraph begins with "I fuck him exactly the way Quentin used to fuck me" (35 [50]) and ends with "Like Quentin used to do with me" (36 [52]; translation modified) ["Comme Quentin dans le temps avec moi" (52)], emphasizing that good sex is a matter of repetition or imitation [*comme* in the French text], not of originality or personality. In between Guillaume mentions not only what he is actually doing but what he *can* or better yet *may* do according to the Marais's rules of *convenances*:

"I can/may fuck him with my arms extended." (35; translation modified)

["je peux le baiser bras tendus." (51)]

"I can/may also hold him by his lower back" (translation modified).

["Je peux aussi le tenir dans le dos au niveau des reins."]

"I can/may also hold him by wrapping my arms around his thighs or his legs." (36; translation modified)

["Je peux aussi le tenir en croisant les bras autour de ses cuisses ou de ses jambes."]

Soon, the individual subject "je" turns into the impersonal and therefore collective "on." For Dustan, the bourgeois privatization of sex is, in essence, antidemocratic. While horrifyingly depersonalized for some readers, Guillaume's specific sexual encounter has become for others something with the potential to be appropriated and imitated.

Throughout the novel sex is often measured by what it looks like, that is, by its conformity to or deviation from a pre-existing image. Sometimes the narrator has sex in front of a mirror. "What I see in the mirror is world class, it pleases me, it reassures me, it flatters me" (18 [31]). And later, a scene is so right that he thinks, "Someone should film this" (my translation) ["Il faudrait filmer" (81)]. It isn't so much that he is expressing the desire to keep a memento of the event, as one would of a skiing trip or the kid's bar mitzvah, in order to watch it *in the future*. Rather the urge to film comes out of his satisfaction to know that the encounter is already a representation and, in this case, the proper reproduction of a *past* model. And in Dustan's world that model is porn, as in a scene in which he describes a particularly successful ejaculation and concludes: "I explode in a geyser and it's like a super-fine porn movie" (39 [54]); or when he masturbates to a video and defines himself in relation to the porn star he watches on the screen: "I jerked off watching Eric Manchester pack in the action, doing what he knows how to do, tricks I know how to do" (24 [38]).

Porn stars, in other words, are the ultimate reference and validation. Stéphane, for example, knows that he has mastered the technique of anal sex when his performance matches that of a legendary actor:

> After, he tells me he's beginning to understand what anal sex is all about. I tell him that out of the thousand guys I've fucked with there are four or five, OK a dozen maybe, who know how to do what he has done to me. There is also Chad Douglas, but he's exclusively on cassette. (16; translation modified)
>
> [Il me dit après qu'il commence à comprendre ce que c'est qu'enculer. Je lui dis que sur les mille mecs avec qui j'ai baisé il y en a quatre ou cinq, enfin une dizaine qui savent faire ce qu'il m'a fait. Il y a aussi Chad Douglas, mais c'est sur k7 uniquement. (28)]

Again, this could be dismissed as further proof that Guillaume and his friends lead a pathetically artificial existence that erases them as individuals and transforms them into interchangeable ghetto clones or lifeless sex robots. Remember the passage from Vleeschouwer's book I quoted earlier and in which he ridiculed "the phony Ben Hurs of the Marais" and criticized gay men who "ape the soldiers they never were"—as if there ever existed a *real* Ben Hur and if military life was not defined by its conformity to a model. What Dustan proposes, in essence, is that sex works *only* as simulacrum. To imitate porn and its exaggerated masculine types is to copy what is already a copy and becomes a de facto model.

A guy once told me he didn't like porn because "gay men don't have sex like that in real life." I said, "True," but I thought, "Ain't that a shame . . ." One underlying assumption of the romantic view of sex and selfhood (that is, sex as either affirmation of the self—love—or its sublime erasure—orgasm as *petite mort* or little death) is that pornography is a distorted representation that simultaneously falls short of normal sex and is in grotesque excess of it. However, for Dustan, who not only wishes "real life" was more like porn but actually *makes* it so, it is too often normal sex that, alas! fails to represent porn adequately; as in the following passage:

> When I had my hand almost in his ass, he started saying Oh yeah oh man, your hand in my ass, oh yeah I like that, kind of as if he was dubbing a porn movie. I checked his dick. He wasn't hard. It made me sick. On top of it he wanted to see me again." (84; translation modified)
>
> ["Quand j'ai eu la main presque dans son cul, il s'est mis à dire Oh, oui, c'est bon ta main dans mon cul, oh, oui, j'aime ça, à peu près comme s'il doublait un film porno. J'ai regardé sa bite. Il ne bandait pas. Ça m'a dégoûté. En plus il voulait me revoir." (108–109)]

And how could Guillaume possibly want to reconnect with someone who makes sex feel like poorly dubbed porn? The failure of the encounter, then, resides less in the fact that the sex was lousy in itself than in the guy's inability to reproduce the porn model well enough. That, in effect, is what made the sex lousy.

One could argue that Dustan does little more than acknowledge what is a well-documented fact—that porn plays an important and complex role in many gay men's lives. For many, porn is the first "contact" with gay sexuality, and such is probably increasingly the case in our Internet era. Yet beyond this initial moment and later instances when porn may act as substitute for the real thing, unavailable for whatever reason, it continues, like masturbation, to play a part when it is no longer "needed"—an earlier stage that stubbornly refuses to disappear.[30] It is, tellingly, in urban areas where gay sex is easiest to find that video stores stock the widest selection of porn movies. Today, like it or not (deny it or not), porn has become a de facto component of gay male culture and an instrument of self-identification *as gay*. *Têtu*, the principal gay magazine in France, has its "Porno" rubric alongside beauty products and great homosexuals who made history. In its pages porn flicks are reviewed next to regular movies, books, and records. And in *Dans ma chambre*, for example, Guillaume calls some of his dildos simply by the name of the porn star after whose penis they were modeled. (While actual penises are sometimes described as if they were dildos: "mine $7 \times 5\frac{1}{2}$, his 9×6" [9/20].)

Once, he looks for just the right music for Stéphane to use a dildo on him: "I look around for something repetitive but not cold" (19 [32]). Repetitive but not cold. Gay porn, like dildos, is not used as a substitute for the "real" thing; it *is* the real thing. Or to be exact it is just as real (and unreal) as actual sex. Porn, therefore, is something like a supplement in the Derridean sense of the term—in this case, an originary coconstituent of male homosexuality. If repetition doesn't feel cold it may be because it is experienced more as a return than as a departure; but a return to an origin that is revealed to be always already a representation, that is, a departure from a "real" but nonexistent original. (After mentioning porn star Chad Douglas, Guillaume immediately adds, "I only hope that in real life he's not dead" [16 [28].) Furthermore, the queer experience of porn being essentially one of imitation, it is always collective. Simply stated, what Dustan tells us is that homosexuality does not exist apart from community and that porn is not an instrument designed to attain personal fulfillment but rather a form of that community.

But Dustan starts small—the private, the intimate; in fact not just his room but, in a dizzying chapter of *Dans ma chambre*, a small closet in his room. This is the chapter that starts with the sentence, "I live in a fabulous world

where everybody has slept with everybody" followed by the list of the
places and people that make up the community, in this case the Marais:

> There are the guys who are more into bars. More into clubs. More into bars
> and clubs. More into bathhouses. More into party lines. More into Minitel.
> More into dark hair. More into blond. More built. More into rough sex. More
> vanilla. There's a selection. A wide selection. (52; translation modified)

> [Les mecs sont plutôt bars. Plutôt boîtes. Plutôt bars-boîtes. Plutôt sauna. Plutôt
> rézo. Plutôt minitel. Plutôts bruns. Plutôt blonds. Plutôt musclés. Plutôt hard.
> Plutôt baise classique. On a le choix. Beaucoup de choix. (70)]

The opening paragraph ends with a mention of a man who owns a lot of sex
toys and gear, which "he shares generously with quite a lot of people" (53)
["dont il fait profiter assez largement" (71)]. Emphasizing the link between
these objects and community, the following paragraph begins with "Like I do"
["Comme moi"]. Guillaume goes on to describe as meticulously as they are
organized the variety of sex toys he keeps in his closet—dildos, of course, but
also leather and latex garments and BDSM gear. A sample of a very long list:

> Under that there are didlos and butt-plugs arranged by size on two shelves: two
> fat butt-plugs and four small ones, four two-headed dildos, eight ordinary dil-
> dos. Under that, the smaller material hanging on nails: five different pairs of
> nipple clamps, some clothespins, a parachute for the balls, a dog collar, two
> hoods, one in leather, one in latex, six cockrings, in steel or leather, regular or
> with built-in ball-squeezers, two dick sheaths (a regular one in adjustable
> leather and one with spike tips pointing in, a little too much this one), a riding
> crop, a flogger . . . (53; translation modified)

> [En dessous il y a les godes et les plugs, rangés par taille sur deux étagères: deux
> gros plugs, quatre petits, quatre godes doubles, huit godes simples. En dessous il
> y a le petit matériel, accroché à des clous: cinq paires de pinces à seins dif-
> férentes, des pinces à linge, un parachute pour les couilles, un collier de chien,
> deux cagoules, une en cuir, une en latex, six cockrings, en acier, en cuir, sim-
> ples ou avec serre-couilles incorporé, deux étuis à bite, un simple en cuir
> ajustable et un à pointes épatées, ça c'est un peu folklorique, une cravache, un
> martinet . . . (71)]

The list goes on and on, all the way to "my German army boots" (54 [72];
translation modified). With dry irony, the narrator adds, "I've kept only
this. The bare essential." He then moves on to list the accessories to these
accessories:

> I have within arm's reach everything I need. Alcohol. Hash. Acid. X. Coke.
> Weed. Poppers. Sex mags. Sex tapes. A Polaroid camera. (Translation modified)

[J'ai à portée de la main tout ce qu'il faut pour m'en servir. De l'alcool. Du shit. De l'acide. De l'exta. De la coke. De l'herbe. Du poppers. Des revues de cul. Des k7 de cul. Un polaroïd.]

Accessories, then, cease to be just that if they, too, require their own set of accessories. To be sure, referring to objects from the first list, Dustan goes on: "Certain elements are more useful than others. I love them all. They are like parts of me. . . . But it is also their duty to serve the body" (54 [72–73]). Simultaneously distinct from and part of the body, the sex toys enjoy, like porn, the dual status of the supplement. Logically, the same may be said of the body itself. All that's missing is the people as accessories to the accessories to the accessories.

After cataloguing objects and defining them as constituents of the body rather than alien to it, Dustan eventually returns to actual people:

All the queers I know work out. If not, they swim. They are, almost all of them, HIV-positive. It's amazing how long they last. They still go out. They still fuck. Plenty of them get crap like meningitis, diarrhea, a case of shingles or KS, or PCP. And then they're all right. (55; translation modified)

[Tous les pédés que je fréquente font de la muscu. Sinon ils font de la natation. Ils sont presque tous séropositifs. C'est fou ce qu'ils durent. Ils sortent toujours. Ils baisent toujours. Il y en a plein qui font des trucs, des méningites, des diarrhées, un zona, un kaposi, une pneumocystose. Et puis ça va. (74)]

What is striking in this passage is the fact that people are presented solely in terms of their bodies. But more important, these bodies are always in relation to something other than themselves that exceeds and diminishes them—bodybuilding, swimming, and opportunistic infections. The body as such, untouched and unaffected, appears to be unpresentable as well. And the same goes for the actual human beings for whom they stand (again in a relation of supplementation): they *still* go out and they *still* have sex. In other words, they form a community since going out and having sex is what makes the community (in the performative sense). But of course, to be *still here* is not the same thing as to be *here*; to survive is not the same thing as to live. To be still here is an excess of or supplement to life ("It's amazing how long they last"), but it is also a deficiency or lack of life. As a reminder that death and absence are defining components of the community, Dustan immediately adds, "The ones that get a CMV or other more freaky crap haven't usually been seen around for some time. They aren't talked about" (55 [74]; translation modified). And when he notes, "People don't die a lot apparently," it isn't quite the same as saying that people *live*. Think also of the earlier reference to a possibly dead porn star. As Ross Chambers has noted about that passage, "it is also entirely possible that 'en vrai' he may be dead, and that he is therefore a ghost; and if so, those who imitate him in real life are survivors headed for the same fate, and thus already in a sense ghosts themselves."[31] If the title of Dustan's chapter, "People are still having sex," essentially means "community" (as confirmed by the opening sentence, "I live in a fabulous world where everybody has slept with everybody," and everything that follows), that community is defined as never fully present to itself.

The next paragraph opens up the definition of the ghetto beyond the Marais to encompass its international manifestations and what is in essence its diasporic dimension:

> There aren't ghettos everywhere. There's the center of Paris. There's London, Amsterdam, Berlin, New York, San Francisco, Los Angeles, Sydney. In the summer there's Ibiza, Sitges, Fire Island, Mykonos, Majorca. Sex is the centerpiece. Everything revolves around it." (56; translation modified)

> [Il n'y a pas de ghettos partout. Il y a Paris centre. Il y a Londres, Amsterdam, Berlin, New York, San Francisco, Los Angeles, Sydney. L'été, il y a Ibiza, Sitges, Fire Island, Mykonos, Majorque. Le sexe est la chose centrale. Tout tourne autour." (75).]

These various locations are, in a sense, avatars of one another—different embodiments of the same thing, reproductions of the same model in the diasporic sense. When Guillaume notes that, "I prefer to go to London on vacation too rather than discover Budapest" (55 [74]), he presents travels as a means to be simultaneously outside (the Marais) and inside (the ghetto). These different places may be spread out all over the planet but they have the same gravitational center—sex, that is, community. The chapter can then seamlessly return to Guillaume's bedroom, where, in the closing passage, the narrator masturbates to a six-square-meter collage of pictures of penises and concludes, "I live in a world where plenty of things I thought impossible are possible" (57) ["Je vis dans un monde où plein de choses que je pensais impossibles sont possibles" (76)]. This closing, then, is an opening—to and of the world and its possibilities. Essentially a relation of simultaneous continuity and discontinuity, the nature of the ghetto is such that Guillaume's bedroom—indeed his bedroom *closet*—contains it in its entirety. The same goes for any other site in the global, diasporic ghetto where people, places, substances, and accessories (all stylistically presented in similar lists so as to emphasize their kinship) are supplements of one another—equal and interchangeable embodiments of community. The private, in a word, is inseparable from the collective.

But if pretty much everyone has slept with everyone else, Guillaume doesn't fail to emphasize that nearly everyone he knows is also HIV positive (32 [47]), thus inscribing the private not only as an effect of community but also within a global pandemic. Dustan's understanding of space in terms of risk and safety does not imply a mere reversal by which the Marais would provide shelter from the dangers of the outside. If anything, Guillaume's very life in the ghetto is a constant reminder of the threat of AIDS—not to mention drug overdose and suicide. At the end of *Dans ma chambre* he brings a trick home, as he had done so many times before. But the whole hook up is a disaster, and he soon walks the guy to the door. He closes it. The man he had invited in, dressed in black from head to toes down to his underwear, was like an image of death. Increasingly attracted to the idea of unprotected sex, Guillaume decides it is time for him to leave town:

> I thought This man in black is a sign. If I stay here I'm going to die. I'm going to finish up putting up my semen in everybody's ass and having the same thing done to me. The truth is there's nothing I want to do any more but that. Actually it's already well under way. (119)

> ["J'ai pensé Ce mec en noir c'était un signe. Si je reste ici je vais mourir. Je vais finir par mettre du sperme dans le cul de tout le monde et par me faire faire pareil. La vérité, c'est qu'il n'y a plus que ça que j'ai envie de faire. D'ailleurs c'est déjà bien parti." (152)]

He soon accepts a job overseas and prepares his departure. The final chapter of the novel is tellingly titled "Exit." But exit from where exactly? Survival defines community as simultaneous presence and absence. Yet as the passing mention of those who have vanished from the scene indicates, absence is itself but a ghostly presence. In other words, spatial articulation is not, as anti-ghetto rhetoric would have us believe, a matter of distinction between *here* and *not here* but rather a temporal relation between *still here* and *no longer here*, such that *still here* implies partial absence, and *no longer here* signifies partial presence. If so many things previously thought to be impossible are made possible, it is because the so-called ghetto, as community neighborhood, has connected what was supposed to be disconnected—the individual and the collective, homosexuality and humanity.

PART II

The Queerness
of Community

[3]

Things Past

Am I the only one who thinks that *Remembrance of Things Past* wasn't such a bad English title for Proust's *A la recherche du temps perdu* after all? Not so much because of its Shakespearian reference, but because Proust's novel is essentially about, well, things of the past—chief among them, I believe, Jewishness and queerness and, beyond, survival in general. Using each as a metaphor for the other, Proust repeatedly describes queers as Jews and Jews as queers. A cunning rhetorical trick, if there ever was one, it simultaneously makes sense and obscures meaning, since each category he summons to clarify the other is really characterized by its resistance to stable identification, something that also imparts on each group a deep sense of social out-of-placeness.[1] For tactical reasons, Proust may use the essentializing lexicon of race to depict and analyze the socially marginal, he nonetheless conceives their identity as the outcome of social forces and cultural practices, as in the following passages about inverts:

> [L]ike the Jews again . . . brought into the company of their own kind by the ostracism to which they are subjected, the opprobrium into which they have fallen, having finally been invested, by a persecution similar to that of Israel, with the physical and moral characteristics of a race. (4:22)

> [comme les Juifs encore . . . rassemblés à leurs pareils par l'ostracisme qui les frappe, l'opprobre où ils sont tombés, ayant fini par prendre, par une persécution semblable à celle d'Israël, les caractères physiques et moraux d'une race. (3:18)]

And later:

> forming a freemasonry far more extensive, more effective and less suspected
> than that of the Lodges, for it rests upon an identity of tastes, needs, habits,
> dangers, apprenticeship, knowledge, traffic, vocabulary, and one in which even
> members who do not wish to know one another recognize one another im-
> mediately by natural or conventional, involuntary or deliberate signs. (4:23)
>
> [formant une franc-maçonnerie bien plus étendue, plus efficace et moins
> soupçonnée que celle des loges, car elle repose sur une identité de goûts, de be-
> soins, d'habitudes, de dangers, d'apprentissage, de savoir, de trafic, de glossaire,
> et dans laquelle les membres mêmes qui souhaitent de ne pas se connaître, aus-
> sitôt se reconnaissent à des signes naturels ou de convention, involontaires ou
> voulus. (3:18–19)]

The idea that identity is externally produced and results from negative identification may be said to foreshadow Sartre's essay on the Jews,[2] but to some
of Proust's contemporaries, it surely echoed the theories of Max Nordau
and Cesare Lombroso, two (Jewish) theorists of degeneracy who attributed
the perceived mental and physical decay of the Jews to centuries of oppression.

Either way, the Jews and queers of the novel don't stand for stable categories in themselves but, rather, work as irritants to a power system increasingly reliant on the pathologization of deviance and obsessed with
taxonomy as guarantor of social order.[3] This is especially the case when it
comes to the class system, so central to Proust's novel, that queers and Jews
inhabit or mimic or piggyback on so as to quietly unsettle its bourgeois
claims to naturalness. Jewish characters, most notably Swann and Bloch,
sometimes pass as Gentiles, while in the parallel universe of inverts,

> the ambassador is a bosom friend of the felon, the prince, with a certain inso-
> lent aplomb born of his aristocratic breeding which the timorous bourgeois
> lacks, on leaving the duchess's party goes off to confer in private with the ruf-
> fian; a reprobate section of the human collectivity, but an important one, sus-
> pected where it does not exist, flaunting itself, insolent and immune, where its
> existence is never guessed; numbering its adherents everywhere, among the
> people, in the army, in the church, in prison, on the throne; living, in short, at
> least to a great extent, in an affectionate and perilous intimacy with the men of
> the other race, provoking them, playing with them by speaking of its vice as of
> something alien to it. (4:23–24)
>
> [l'ambassadeur est ami du forçat; le prince, avec une certaine liberté d'allures
> que donne l'éducation aristocratique et qu'un petit bourgeois tremblant n'au-
> rait pas, en sortant de chez la duchesse s'en va conférer avec l'apache; partie
> réprouvée de la collectivité humaine, mais partie importante, soupçonnée là où

elle n'est pas, étalée, insolente, impunie là où elle n'est pas devinée; comptant des adhérents partout, dans le peuple, dans l'armée, dans le temple, au bagne, sur le trône; vivant enfin, du moins un grand nombre, dans l'intimité caressante et dangeureuse avec les hommes de l'autre race, les provoquant, jouant avec eux à parler de son vice comme s'il n'était pas le sien. (3:19)]

If disciplinary discourses of identity seek to assign a specific, if negative, social place to Jews and queers—to reterritorialize them, in the terminology of Gilles Deleuze and Félix Guattari—Proust's characters appear to be far more elusive and occupy multiple, ever-changing positions. While acknowledging that their place is precisely to be out of place, they make a game of the whole system. But Jews and queers, tellingly described as "Oriental" in Proust's world, are not just out of place in synchronic relations but also diachronically. And this is what I would like to talk about.

In his essay "Proust in the Tearoom," Jarrod Hayes reminds us that, in French slang, a whole set of expressions pertaining to having tea, such as *prendre le thé*, used to be codes for homosexual acts. He goes on to argue that the famous scene of the *petite madeleine*, so steeped in sensual pleasure, could be reclaimed, along with sundry other tea-related passages, for a queer reading of the entire novel: "The most celebrated passage where the narrator takes tea is the madeleine episode. If in the rest of the novel *prendre le thé* can mean 'to have homosex,' the madeleine cannot be spared this possibility" (1000). As a result, Hayes stops just short of suggesting, homosexuality may be identified with all things past: "The possibility that taking tea is a code for homosex infects not just the most sacred of Proustian passages (the description of the madeleine) but the entire system of Proustian memory; thus the paradise gained from taking tea might, in fact, be Sodom" (993). And he concludes, "*La recherche* implicates the relation of past to present in the relation of homosexual to heterosexual. Resurrected, a homosexual past haunts a heterosexual present" (1003).

Indeed, a disruption of temporality is obliquely hinted at in the madeleine episode, when the narrator observes, "An exquisite pleasure had invaded my senses, something isolated, detached, with no suggestion of its origin" (1:60 [1:44]). With the cause located in the present—in the physical sensation of the madeleine blending with the tea in the narrator's mouth—and the effect being the reemergence of the past, Proust's sentence illustrates something akin to the Nietzschean inversion of the causal relationship and questions the very notion of origin. And that, ultimately, is what's at stake in Proust's multiple references to Zion and Sodom—usually in the same breath.

Symbolically associated *with* their city of origin—hence their figurative orientalism, a redundancy of course—Israelites and sodomites nonetheless always already function in diasporic, that is, relational, terms. As Jean-Luc Nancy tells us in *Being Singular Plural*: "We do not gain access; that is, we do not penetrate the origin; we do not identify with it. More precisely, we do not identify ourselves in it or as it, but *with* it, in a sense that must be elucidated here and is nothing other than the meaning of originary coexistence" (10–11; original emphasis). Proust's Jews and "inverts" reject the illusory wholeness and self-presence that is at once embodied (in the past) by the lost origin and envisioned (in the future) by a possible return to it, in favor of the pure relationality of the here and now. Think of the chance encounter between Charlus the aristocrat and Jupien the former waistcoat-maker that famously opens *Sodom and Gomorrha*. The two have never met yet instantly "recognize" each other—as fellow queers, that is—and before you know it, they're fucking. To many, this spectacular piece of high literature is *also* instantly recognizable. Charlus and Jupien's dance of seduction is Proust's rendition of the old backward glance with which we meet strangers on the street and strangers meet us. More recently, Daniel Mendelsohn in *The Elusive Embrace* described one of his own sexual encounters as follows:

> It was a classic cruise, with its own *predictable* choreography. After exchanging looks, we went on walking a few steps; then each turned round to make sure that the other was watching; then we both walked a few more steps; and finally turned round and walked back toward each other, with protectively ironic grins. (11; my emphasis)

As most of us know, this sort of opportunity must be seized upon immediately lest it disappears for good. It is, in other words, without a future. It is about the present moment, but it is also about the past in the sense that recognition and predictability necessarily presuppose a previous instance. I am tempted to see the backward glance of gay street cruising not merely as a movement in space but as a look to the past as well.[4] After all, it evokes Lot's wife Ildeth who disobeyed the angels' injunction, looked back at Sodom, the home her family was leaving behind, and was changed into a pillar of salt.[5] Sodom is also what Proust would call this past, a name that, for him, conjures ancient times but also signifies community in the (diasporic) present. Sure enough, as soon as they are finished with sex, Charlus and Jupien begin exchanging notes, as it were, about who "is" (queer like them) among the regular visitors of the Guermantes residence where the two men have just met. Community, it appears, was present all along in the random, anonymous sexual encounter of two strangers and their sex act a corporeal indexing of it.

But just as the open, public space that is the city becomes the stage for a spectacle of queerness invisible to those who are not in the know, community piggybacks on the social and undermines it simultaneously, as in this

brief exchange between the two characters, after the backward glances and
before the sex. Charlus,

> deciding to precipitate matters, asked the tailor for a light, but at once ob-
> served: 'I ask you for a light, but I see I've left my cigars at home.' The laws of
> hospitality prevailed over the rules of coquetry. 'Come inside, you shall have
> everything you wish,' said the tailor. (4:9)

> [décidé à brusquer les choses, demanda du feu au giletier, mais observa aussitôt:
> 'Je vous demande du feu, mais je vois que j'ai oublié mes cigares.' Les lois de
> l'hospitalité l'emportèrent sur les règles de la coquetterie. 'Entrez, on vous don-
> nera tout ce que vous voudrez,' dit le giletier." (3:8)]

Not unlike Mendelsohn's "protectively ironic grins," language (that is to say,
the social) is used here to signify something other than what it states. "The
laws of hospitality" may be read as another reference to Sodom. But more
intriguing is the fact that Charlus asks for a match he doesn't need in order
to light a cigar he doesn't have—or perhaps does, in fact, have; it doesn't
matter, that's the point—and Jupien is eager to provide. Sometimes, after all,
a cigar is *not* just a cigar. In this brief exchange, language is not merely a
means of establishing contact (what Roman Jakobson calls its phatic function) because contact has already occurred in nonverbal fashion; it is a more
disruptive mode of inhabiting the social in order to make it serve another,
hidden mode of sociality.

Before moving on to a more detailed depiction of the homosexual un-
derworld that is just being revealed to narrator and readers alike and will
occupy nearly the entire second half of the novel (the Charlus-Jupien encounter occurs right at the halfway point), Proust writes:

> I have thought it as well to utter here a provisional warning against the lamen-
> table error of proposing (just as people have encouraged a Zionist movement)
> to create a Sodomist movement and to rebuild Sodom. For, no sooner had they
> arrived there than the Sodomites would leave the town so as not to have the
> appearance of belonging to it, would take wives, keep mistresses in other cities
> where they would find, incidentally, every diversion that appealed to them . . .
> In other words, everything would go on very much as it does today in London,
> Berlin, Rome, Petrograd or Paris. (4:43–44)

> [On a voulu provisoirement prévenir l'erreur funeste qui consisterait, de même
> qu'on a encouragé un mouvement sioniste, à créer un mouvement sodomiste
> et à rebâtir Sodome. Or, à peine arrivés, les sodomistes quitteraient la ville pour
> ne pas avoir l'air d'en être, prendraient femme, entretiendraient des maîtresses
> dans d'autres cités où ils trouveraient d'ailleurs toutes les distractions conven-
> ables . . . C'est dire que tout se passerait en somme comme à Londres, à Berlin,
> à Rome, à Pétrograd ou à Paris. (3:33)]

This astute observation illustrates what I like to call the Groucho principle after Groucho Marx's famous joke: "I couldn't belong to a club that would have me as a member." To give credit where credit is due, though, long before he knew who Groucho Marx was my uncle Jacob used to say, "I couldn't marry a woman who would have me as a husband." Fate having made my uncle Jacob far less famous than his imitator, I decided it would be more convenient to stick to "the Groucho principle" here. However, I couldn't pass up the opportunity to redress an injustice—or to remind readers that Proust was Jewish too. The joke may be a clever summary of the logic of association and disassociation that characterizes all communities. It also captures the very nature of diasporas: to be in several places at once, that is to say, to be in no place at all.

But diaspora, as we know, isn't just a way of being in space; it is also a way of being in time. My earlier remark about the fundamental queerness of diasporic Jews may be read as an echo and an entailment of Proust's understanding of queers as fundamentally diasporic. With a reborn Sodom/Zion now decentered by its being on an equal footing with any other city in the diaspora, Jews and queers may still be creatures of the past but they are not bound by it. They are, rather, free-floating in an eternal present. This is particularly true of Proust's "inverts," whose archaism all but abolishes time itself.

> In this respect the race of inverts, who readily link themselves with the ancient East or the golden age of Greece, might be traced back further still, to those experimental epochs in which there existed neither dioecious plants nor monosexual animals, to that initial hermaphroditism of which certain rudiments of male organs in the anatomy of women and of female organs in that of men seem still to preserve the trace. (4:40)

> [Par là les invertis, qui se rattachent volontiers à l'antique Orient ou à l'âge d'or de la Grèce, remonteraient plus haut encore, à ces époques d'essai où n'existaient ni les fleurs dioïques ni les animaux unisexués, à cet hermaphrodisme initial dont quelques rudiments d'organes mâles dans l'anatomie de la femme et d'organes femelles dans l'anatomie de l'homme semblent conserver la trace. (3:31)]

Again, and this is almost always the case whenever Proust talks about homosexuality, these remarks could be read—and *were* read at the time—either as echoes of dominant scientific discourses of the period or, then and now, as artful disruptions masquerading as disciplinary knowledge. Such contrary legibility endows the author himself (and in turn some of his readers, no doubt) with the very qualities he assigns to his Jewish and queer characters and is what made him both a "serious," acceptable author to his contemporaries and a radical precursor in the eyes of later sexual revolutionaries such as Guy Hocquenghem and the like.[6] (I shall linger on Hocquenghem in a bit and at greater length in chapter 5.) As for the remaining traces of the other sex, they further underscore the impossibility of self-sameness and, therefore, of any system that rests on strict categorizations. That, in short, is Proust's queerness.

Guillaume Dustan, another queer Jew, once defined homosexuality as having your cake and eating it too.[7] His purpose may have been to explain why marriage and promiscuity shouldn't be mutually exclusive and why the former may not have to be as normalizing as we think, but the deeper implication is that heteronormativity—indeed *all* normativity—may rest on an either-or fallacy. Here Dustan touches on something that is as fundamental in terms of time as the Groucho principle is in terms of space, the two aphorisms, one queer and one Jewish, nicely complementing each other. The expression "to have your cake and eat it too" describes the illogical concurrence of two different moments—a queer statement, in both senses of the term, and what *La recherche* is all about, I believe. On the other hand, proponents of "gayness," a form of identity politics predicated on essentializing distinctions, may find very little grist for their mill in a novel so concerned with proposing what is, in effect, the sort of radical undoing of identity we now recognize, thanks to the early work of Jacques Derrida and its continuation in that of Judith Butler, as the deconstruction of difference—what I call "queerness." The foundational instability revealed in the opening pages of *Sodom and Gomorrha* grounds, so to speak, my thinking of community and traverses much of what follows.

JEWS, QUEERS, AND ARCHAISM

In the Western imaginary, Jews were, for a very long time, considered creatures of the past. Stubborn survivors of an ancient religion that was supposed to have been superseded by Christianity, they were generally portrayed as hopelessly mired in archaic rites and traditions and impervious to all manners of change and progress. When Enlightenment rationalism began to challenge Christian hegemony, and even though many Jewish thinkers embraced the new philosophy as consistent with the fundamental tenets of Judaism, Jews were again designated as a sectarian and irrational counterforce to the universalizing movement of history. Voltaire's infamous diatribes come to mind. During the revolutionary years, the emancipators of the Jews, most prominently the Abbé Grégoire, presented their project as one of spiritual and social regeneration of what was to them a backward, superstitious people. In that the Jews' regeneration was intended to result in their ultimate disappearance, Grégoire and the others implied that the former were inherently and hopelessly archaic. Later, with the triumph of the nation-state, Jews were once more singled out for their presumed multinational allegiances, making them, tellingly enough, very much like the obsolete aristocratic ruling class of the discarded old regimes. (Proust's aristocrats, stubborn survivors of a bygone era and a defunct social system, may be more closely related to the Jews than they'd like to think and their rabid anti-Dreyfus positions during the Affair an expression of denial in the face of their own irrelevance.) Furthermore, as we have seen earlier, integrated Jews themselves regarded with similar contempt the often rural and more religious immigrant newcomers of the late nineteenth century onward. The old Ashkenazi condescension toward North African Jewries pertained to a similar attitude.

As can be expected, the Marais has featured prominently among these representations. Restif de la Bretonne wrote in the late eighteenth century:

> I entered the garden of the Hôtel Soubise. I thought I had walked into the abode of innocence and candor . . . these were all the Jewish shopkeepers celebrating Saturday . . . From what I could see and hear, it seemed to me that innocence and patriarchal ways still reign among them.

> [J'entrai dans le jardin de l'hôtel Soubise. Je me crus dans le séjour de l'innocence et de la candeur . . . c'étaient tous les juifs bas-mercantiers qui célébraient le samedi . . . Par ce que je vis et ce que j'entendis, il me semblait que l'innocence et les moeurs patriarcales règnent encore parmi eux.][8]

Léon Daudet in 1930:

> The district of the Lycée Charlemagne was and still is, I believe, a veritable ghetto, where at every step one encounters shades of Rembrandt . . . Voices have a strange resonance because of the narrowness of the alleys. Each one, when the cold has stopped, composes a series of engravings or small pictures that could be advantageously displayed in the museums of The Hague or Amsterdam.

> [Ce quartier du Lycée Charlemagne était et est encore, je crois, un véritable ghetto, où l'on rencontre à chaque pas des aspects à la Rembrandt . . . Les voix ont une résonance étrange, en raison de l'étroitesse des ruelles. Chacune de celles-ci, quand le froid a cessé, se décompose en une série d'estampes et de tableautins, qui pourraient figurer avec avantage au musée de La Haye ou d'Amsterdam.][9]

Most famously, in his 1939 collection of picturesque vignettes, *Le piéton de Paris*, Léon-Paul Fargue describes the Eternal Jew in the heart of Paris. The section, entitled "Ghetto de Paris," is very often lauded in later works on the Marais for its painted-from-life depiction of Parisian Jewish life on the eve of its destruction. Few commentators, however, bother to notice its anti-Semitic clichés:

> Old Jews, the like of whom one only meets in Bydgoszcz, Zlatana or Milowek, slip among the books at night. It is surprising to see them in Paris, wearing Russian overcoats that sweep the floor, with curly side-whiskers, oily hair and shaky hands. Those Jews, freer in France than anywhere else, have the most brazen contempt for Western garb. Bustling and musing, they come and go through the ghetto's mud, wearing small caps with short visors, wrapped in jet-black, rag-like coats and mournful frocks.
>
> [De vieux Juifs, comme on n'en rencontre qu'à Bydgoszcz, Zlatana ou Milowek, se faufilent le soir entre les livres. On s'étonne de les voir à Paris, vêtus de touloupes qui balayent le sol, le favori roulé, le cheveu huileux, la main tremblante. Ceux-là, plus libres en France que partout ailleurs, méprisent hardiment le costume chrétien. Affairés et rêveurs, ils vont et viennent dans la boue du ghetto, coiffés de petites toques à courte visière, enveloppés, enhaillonnés de longues redingotes aile de corbeau, de lévites funèbres. (101)]

As for the women:

> Rigged out in wigs of silk or horsehair, made up, often tattooed, sickly, fat, frightfully ugly, mysterious women raise and lower their wide eyelids upon the sort of news items that can only attract the wrath of Israel upon this small plot of Jewish land in France. Now and then, however, one may catch sight of a stunning beauty among a magma of old flesh. Genuine gazelles, with cheeks like fragrant wax, daughters of Scheherazade, sultanas with eagle eyes, who make the passer-by dream.
>
> [Affublées de perruques de soie ou de crin, maquillées, souvent tatouées, maladives, grasses, laides à faire peur, des femmes énigmatiques soulèvent et abaissent leurs paupières larges sur ces faits-divers qui ne peuvent qu'appeler sur ce lopin de terre juive en France les foudres d'Israël. On aperçoit pourtant par intervalles, dans un magma de vieilles chairs, quelque beauté fulgurante. De vraies gazelles aux joues de cire parfumée, des filles de Shéhérazade, des Sultanes aux yeux d'aiglonne et qui font rêver le passant. (102)]

Today the rue des Rosiers has become once again a timeless locus of Jewish cultural stillness—only it's called memory these days, and it usually stays clear of Fargue's Orientalist clichés. The Holocaust memorial plaques, for example, whose function is the same paradoxical one as all similar memorials, are there to emphasize that the past should in fact remain safely in the past, as if the injunction "Never again!" were to apply to Jewish expressions of community as well as to their extermination. To be sure, the connection between the Marais and the Holocaust is somewhat perversely underscored by the repeated reminders (often coming from critics of the gay Marais) that the massive presence of Jews in a single neighborhood had facilitated the whole enterprise. But the general unease that greets the unruly presence of young Jews every Sunday on the rue des Rosiers reveals the stubborn refusal of things past to stay where they must. And how else should we read the justification put forward by many of today's Jewish residents of the Marais when speaking to interviewers—*I* am here because *we* have always been here?

A cursory look at the last two thousand years would suffice, of course, to demonstrate that Jews have in fact accompanied and participated in the history of Europe from its inception, and that Jewish cultural isolation, when it happened, was more often than not an effect of discrimination rather than its cause. I don't wish to dwell on this here; the facts are well known. I do want, however, to insist on the strange yet logical corollary to the Jews' archaism—their modernity.

The French antirevolutionary forces that began shaping right-wing nationalism in the closing decades of the nineteenth century didn't just recycle the old stereotypes; they produced their own as well. For modern anti-Semites, Jews are all at once archaic and the epitome of modernity. They are held directly responsible for the spread of materialism, Kantian universalist values, and abstract notions of the human self that have brutally disrupted the long, slow sedimentation of national cultures and thrown Western civilization into recurring, almost viral, bouts of identity crisis met with nationalist "fever," to use Maurice Barrès's favorite metaphor. From that point of view, the Jews are not only obsolete remnants of the pre-Christian era, they are also urban creatures par excellence, both the symbols and the cause of everything that supposedly went wrong with the advent of modernity. Edouard Drumont, in his immensely successful 1886 anti-Semitic opus, *La France juive*, put it thus: "The only one who benefited from the Revolution is the Jew. Everything comes from the Jew; everything comes back to the Jew" (vi).

However, Drumont's remark encapsulates the unique status of the Jews as the West's favorite Other. Archaic for the proponents of modernity, hypermodern for its opponents, the Jews, it seems, are systematically depicted as that against which to define oneself—rhetorical and physical foils, in a sense. But more importantly, the implication is that the circularity that places the Jews at the beginning and the end of what becomes *literally* a revolutionary process ultimately emphasizes their cultural motionlessness and sterility, making them the antithesis of the linear movement of culture we often call history. They are at the vanguard and yet are incapable of creation. The Jews, in short, are social tautologies.

And so are homosexuals. They, too, have been constructed, in post-Enlightenment France, as the epitome of urban life in contradistinction to the more wholesome provinces that are the supposed repositories of the true national identity. Consider the following from Emile Zola's friend Georges Saint-Paul, a.k.a. Dr Laupts, in his treatise on sexual inversion. Just think of it in light of the contemporary American red state versus blue state distinction:

> In France . . . other than in the cosmopolitan environments of major cities (Paris, Marseille) . . . or resort towns (Vichy, Nice) . . . environments that are probably very similar to all cosmopolitan environments around the world, homosexuality is quite exceptional.

> [En France . . . mis à part les milieux cosmopolites des grandes villes (Paris, Marseille) . . . ou des villes de saison (Vichy, Nice) . . . milieux qui doivent par bien des côtés ressembler aux milieux cosmopolites de tous les pays du monde, l'homosexualité est tout à fait exceptionnelle. (420)]

Then and now queers, particularly males as always, constitute a contingent of urban trend-setters who exist in relation to mainstream culture but in perpetual *décalage* from it.[10] And in bourgeois culture, which is by definition suspicious of immoderation, this functions as a form of social marginalization and policing. Today homosexuality may have morphed into gay identity, the result is the same: one imitates the better to discard—much as, for example, white Americans have looted African American musical heritage and, at the other end of the infamous bell curve, Asian-Americans have been called "the model minority."

Yet queers, too, are creatures of the past, except that in their case the past is to be found less in history books than in the darker recesses of the psyche. As Hocquenghem remarks, "The only acceptable form of homosexual temporality is that which is directed towards the past, to the Greeks or Sodom. . . . Homosexuality is seen as a regressive neurosis, totally drawn towards the past" (93–94 [114]). Just as Jews were expected to vanish with the advent of Christianity but haven't, so are homosexuals the archaic relics of an earlier, immature stage of sexual indeterminacy to be relinquished with its fulfillment into mature, reproductive heterosexuality, but whose traces linger on, according to Proust. In coarser versions now mostly fallen in disrepute thanks to the Nazis, this was called degeneracy.[11] This sort of psychoanalytical orthodoxy made a spectacular comeback during the debates around the legalization of same-sex couples in France, when homosexuality and its de facto legal recognition with the PACS were almost unanimously denounced by PACS opponents on all political sides as a negation of otherness, with otherness understood here solely as sexual difference—*the* difference on which the social supposedly rests in its entirety. The left's dire warnings of threats to the "symbolic order"[12] were adopted almost verbatim by the most reactionary right-wingers, such as Christine Boutin, who, during an intervention in the National Assembly, asked in righteous indignation: "What is homosexuality, therefore, if not the impossibility to reach the other in his or her sexual difference? And what is the impossibility to accept difference if not an expression of exclusion?"[13]

In the previous chapter, I discussed a very similar comment by chief rabbi Joseph Sitruk. In a spirit of ecumenical fairness I must now add a little something by the Conference of French Bishops: "Are we sufficiently aware to what extent the quest for the similar or the identical at all costs is in itself a source of exclusions?"[14] and by the Union of French Muslim Families: "We are perturbed by this bill. It will further curb the integration of four million Muslims into French society."[15] I have argued that this sort of rhetoric, with "exclusion" and "integration" as its most resonant key words, has the immediate effect of lumping all political expressions of homosexuality with the extreme-right, particularly with Jean-Marie Le Pen's Front National, *the* cultural signifier of all that is opposed to French republicanism.[16] Whence the coherence of all mainstream anti-PACS arguments, no matter how opposed their champions may be in other political matters: homosexuality goes against the idea of perfectibility and the natural progress of society. Left unchecked, it means the end of the social. Just as the risk of generalized *enjuivement*, or "jewification," peppers anti-Semitic discourses, so does the equally absurd fear that "if everybody was gay"—which, apparently, would be the outcome of any attempt to grant equal rights to gay men and women—it would mean the end of human civilization. Call this "The Protocol of the Elders of Sodom" if you like.

I confess that I find the thought titillating. If there was any chance that my getting married would shake the foundations of the symbolic order, I'd be frantically looking for something borrowed and something blue. Alas! I fear it isn't in the cards. It does make sense, however, that groups of people who have been systematically defined as either archaic or obsolescent or both would, in some crucial aspects of their daily lives and social interactions, experience time in a particular way—one that, like Proustian time perhaps, is dual in nature in that it brings into contact, rather than distinguishes, time lost and time regained. Pushed to its logical conclusion, such experience would give us a glimpse at alternatives to modernity's dominant conception of linear time and to the social system it seeks to ground.

For Lee Edelman, queer negativity in the form (so to speak) of the death drive figures, within society, the abolition of the social itself:

As the constancy of a pressure both alien and internal to the logic of the Symbolic, as the inarticulable surplus that dismantles the subject from within, the death drive names what the queer, in the order of the social, is called forth to figure: the negativity opposed to every form of social viability.[17]

As for Guy Hocquenghem, turning to Proust in his 1972 *Homosexual Desire*, he rightly read the first encounter between Charlus and Jupien as a prime example of an asocial connection—miraculous in its randomness, resistant to disciplinary interpretation (94 [81]), and utterly devoid of social usefulness (95 [81]). A major influence on Edelman's more recent work, Hocquenghem similarly advocated a generalized return to the pre-oedipal, pre-personhood stage of undifferentiated desire as a means to short-circuit the capitalist illusion of social progress and betterment. He saw this backward turn as a move away from and against bourgeois capitalism, whose social structure seeks to perpetuate itself thanks to the internalization of heterosexuality in each individual psyche. This is indeed a clever scheme—modernity's, I mean. In the way that the old monarchies grounded their legitimacy in divine right, that is, in the past as immemorial, uncontestable origin, modern societies would be doing the same thing by turning to the future. This would explain why heterosexuality, or what Edelman terms "reproductive futurism," was invented. One could argue, of course, that both the old and the new regimes place some degree of emphasis on the idea of origin, but they do it in very different ways. While all social systems must presumably anchor themselves to some transcendent authority in order to ensure their own perpetuation, it is imperative that Nature, unlike God, be dominated and overcome, that is to say, left behind. What characterizes modern societies' relation to their origin, then, is a simultaneous dynamic of embrace and rejection. The father must be socially honored *and* symbolically killed.

———

It has now become clear, I hope, that my interest in forms of archaism and in their potential to inspire alternative modes of sociality extends beyond the two test cases that are Jewishness and queerness (not to mention the Marais). My concerns, in fact, encompass all "things" past that, stubbornly and often inexplicably, are *still here* when they were not expected to be, thus disrupting experiences of the present and expectations of the future. Survival, understood as a failure to die, is, in a word, the central question here—survival of people, of practices, of origins, of affects. In chapter 5, I will turn to the question of group friendship and link it to the dual notion of survival and failure, and to the relation between community and time. Here I would like to consider what it feels like to embrace what is no more and yet still is. This odd concomitance—the past not systematically understood as separate from the present but as concurrent with it, both past and part of the present—is the lot of the Jews and the queers and of all those defined as archaic. But conceived as a tool of social policing and isolation, social archaism, I want to argue, may also be reclaimed for the purpose of community. One specific example would be camp, a male homosexual mode of collective reading that involves, among other things, the survival, reappropriation, and quoting of obsolete forms, styles and genres in order to invoke community, while engaging oppressive norms that never cease to determine us. Beside camp that for historical reasons is uniquely homosexual, very much the same could be said of the numerous variations of self-deprecating "ethnic" humor often practiced by members of minoritized groups, such as, say, Groucho Marx and Uncle Jacob. What links all these brands of humor, I believe, is the recognition and ambivalent embrace of collective failure—that is, of failure as a form of community.[18] For now, however, I shall look in some detail at two instances of affects that have been explicitly defined as negative and used as tools of social exclusion but in which archaism, once reclaimed, subserves communitarian impulses. These affects are self-hatred and shame.

SELF-HATRED AND AUTHENTICITY

Self-hating homosexuals, it seems, are the worst people on earth. The worst! Take a look at the news in the United States. A Republican mayor who vocally opposes equal rights for gay people gets caught soliciting gay sex in an Internet chat room. Another gay Republican, who served for years as an advisor to anti-gay rights lawmakers, acknowledges that he had married his male partner of forty years. Former president Bill Clinton immediately diagnosed him as suffering from "self-loathing," or what is often called "internalized homophobia." Commenting on these stories and a few others, the media often remind us that Roy Cohn, whose infamy has again reared its ugly head thanks to Tony Kushner's AIDS play *Angels in America* and its subsequent film version, has become the repellent poster child for schizophrenic gay (and Jewish) self-hatred. Beyond the fact that it is rather irritating to see homosexuality subjected once more to discourses of mental health, I must say that I smell a rat. We used to be too proud; now it seems we're not proud enough. And why are gay Republicans so despised by everyone? They're Republicans. What else does one need? Why this excess, this supplement of contempt? What sort of lack or denial does it unwittingly point to?

But I may have chosen the wrong example. If I want to suggest that the hatred of self-hatred may be as destructive as self-hatred itself, I should perhaps pick another, more vulnerable segment of the population that has also been accused of internalized homophobia. As most people should know by now, the rates of HIV and AIDS are much higher among African Americans than any other American demographics. As one should also know, next to nothing is being done about it. Remember the televised vice-presidential debate in 2004, when PBS journalist Gwen Ifill told the candidates that black women were the most vulnerable to HIV in the United States? Republican Dick Cheney bluntly admitted he had no idea, while Democrat John Edwards pretended that he did but fooled no one. Something that *has been* attracting public attention, however, is the phenomenon referred to as the Down Low, or DL—black men who secretly have sex with other men but live an otherwise heterosexual life and sometimes transmit HIV and AIDS to their often unsuspecting female partners. Black men "on the DL" are portrayed in the mainstream media, as well as in a large segment of the gay community, as the epitome of internalized homophobia and its destructive effects. The solution, they (and we) are told, is self-acceptance—a more "advanced" stage of gayness that is commonly found among (guess who?) white, middle-class men.[19]

In a 2003 cover article for *The New York Times* magazine entitled "Double Lives on the Down Low," Benoit Denizet-Lewis, a white man, begins by positing that the gay community and the black community are discrete entities. Lamenting the silence that still surrounds HIV/AIDS among African Americans, he notes, "We don't hear much about this aspect of the epidemic, mostly because the two communities most directly affected by it—the black and gay communities—have spent the better part of two decades eyeing each other through a haze of denial or studied disinterest"; and he immediately portrays the former as dangerously backward on the question of homosexuality: "For African-Americans, facing and addressing the black AIDS crisis would require talking honestly and compassionately about homosexuality—and that has proved remarkably difficult, whether it be in black churches, in black organizations or on inner-city playgrounds" (30). African American social institutions, it would appear, breed dishonesty and cruelty.

In the course of his investigation, our reporter meets several black men who refuse to identify as gay or even bisexual, while secretly having sex with other men. One of them is a young stripper named Jigga: "Jigga says he has sex with both men and women, but he doesn't label himself as bisexual. 'I'm just freaky,' he says with a smile" (33). The author then returns to Jigga in the closing paragraphs of the article.

He tells me a lot has changed *since the first time I met him*. He's in law school *now* . . . And while he is *still* on the DL . . . he has a *serious* boyfriend who is also on the DL.

Four months ago, having a *serious* boyfriend would have been inconceivable to him. "I think I love this dude," he tells me as we walk to the car.

. . .

Recently, Jigga told his parents that he's interested in both guys and girls. "I was drunk when I told them," he says. "But I'm glad I did. They've been really cool about it."

. . .

Jigga is proof that being on the DL isn't necessarily a lifelong identity. He seems considerably more comfortable with his sexuality than he was *the first time I met him*, and I suspect that *soon enough*, he may be openly gay in all facets of his life. (53; all emphases are mine)

Notice the numerous markers of time indicating progress toward gay identity, as well as the repetition of the adjective "serious" that underscore a process of maturation bringing together career prospects, love, and reconciliation with family—presumably, given the context, the family as institution as well as Jigga's own. Implied by the entire article is the idea that the reckless endangerment of black women by HIV-positive black men who cannot "verbalize," that is, confess and normalize their homosexuality, is the logical outcome of the latter's self-hatred and backwardness manifested in their refusal to identify the way we expect them to. It was no surprise, then, that a letter to the editor published by the magazine two weeks later expressed sadness over "these unfortunate young men filled with self-loathing," while concluding, "No wonder there's no decrease in rape, domestic violence and other crimes." Another reader deplores, "While the obvious internalized homophobia of those featured in the article was disturbing, the blatant misogyny was even worse."[20]

There is no doubt that the harm done to black women is very real and that the Down Low controversy has to be read in the dual context of the AIDS crisis and, to some extent, the question of black masculinity. The problem, however, is fundamentally of a different nature. On the one hand, there is no valid reason why heterosexual couples shouldn't be held to the same safety standards as gay men when it comes to sexual practices. On the other, the situation of women around the world is often such that many of them cannot exercise full control over their sex lives. Either way, the problem lies with (hetero)sexism and not with blackness. Moreover, secretive homosexual activity, under other names and enabled by different cultural modalities, is not a new phenomenon and has by no means been limited to black men. What has contributed to the Down Low's emergence in the public eye is the disproportionate rate of HIV infection in the African American community and the common practice of blaming HIV/AIDS on those affected by it. (In that respect, black women haven't been spared either.) More to the point of this essay, though, I want to emphasize how the epidemic has foregrounded the question of gay visibility. AIDS has played a crucial role in the appearance of a gay community in France and in the development of the Marais, for example. On the one hand, visibility has been paramount to AIDS people's fight for survival; on the other, it sought to address a general fear of the lurking virus and the need to *see* the danger, often by making carriers metonyms for the infectious agent itself.

Alongside the Down Low but beginning before its appearance on the mainstream cultural radar, the question of public sex—a term I use to encompass all manners of sex-oriented homosexual contact in public settings—is also connected to the question of visibility. To the bafflement of many, random street encounters have not gone away with accrued tolerance and the development of visible spaces of gay sociability. True, street cruising tends to be more prevalent in cities with few or no such places. I have found walking the streets of Lima and Santiago de Chile as cruel on my neck as it was sweet to my heart. But the episode Mendelsohn recounts took place in New York's Chelsea, while I have experienced similar meetings in the Marais and in the East Village. More puzzling even, in public spaces traditionally used for anonymous sex between men, such as city parks and riverbanks, there is still plenty of fun to be had in this day and age. It is undeniable that many men who frequent such places are, for whatever reason—age, social class, religion, national origin, personal choice . . . —closeted. But it is equally true that many are not or not completely ("out" and "closeted" are not dichotomous in real life). In Paris, for example, some men alternate without missing a beat between the bars of the Marais and the older, labyrinthine section of the Père Lachaise cemetery—the part that echoes, in its contrast with the wider alleys that surround it, the Marais's own relation with Haussmannized Paris.

In a way that would make Proust very proud, it isn't only public sex that has survived the increasing normalization of homosexuality, but also the uncanny ability of those so inclined to identify the right places. For example, I was walking across the courtyard of the Louvre one afternoon, when I noticed the presence of a maze made of tall hedges. I had never seen it before, but I knew right away, so I stopped and paid attention just to make sure. It was barely a couple of minutes before I saw a Marais-style gay guy make his way into the labyrinth. When I followed (in order simply to confirm my finding, of course), I discovered, among other things, several posters put up by AIDES, the HIV/AIDS advocacy group. Bingo![21] On a related note, my friend Krysztof told me that before going to school in Strasbourg, a city he had never visited and where he didn't know anyone, he studied a map, pointed a finger at a specific location and exclaimed, "C'est là!" A visit soon confirmed that "it" was indeed "there."

Several hypotheses have been offered to account for the resilience of such places when or where there seems to be little need for them. Could it be the eroticism of danger and the appeal of the illicit? That loses its charm amazingly fast. Or perhaps the unique opportunity to have interracial, intergenerational and interclass contacts that are not easily available elsewhere?[22] Say what you want about the proliferation of commercial sex venues, they do allow for such contacts. I won't contribute to the list of explanations that have been proposed, let alone attempt to have the last word on the question. I want briefly to bring up the crackdown on men's room gay sex at the University of Michigan. Although it happened before I moved to Ann Arbor in 1995, people I met were still talking about it. Interestingly, it wasn't the administration alone that decided to reduce the size of the stalls' doors and to put up signs warning students that public sex is illegal. The culprit was, in fact, the gay center on campus. Its argument was that public sex was not only illegal and a public health hazard but also, and more typical of a gay perspective on the question, that young, closeted students were still in a self-hating phase that put them at great psychological and physical risk. Coming out was the solution to the "problem" of public sex, as though the correlation between public sex and self-hatred was self-evident. Mainstream gay rhetoric on the issue is in fact concerned with self-realization, which I understand to mean the realization not just of oneself but of *the* self. The problem of public (or random or anonymous) sex, in the mainstream understanding, is that it is *impersonal* and that impersonality is, from a psychological perspective, a self-destructive throwback. The idea that impersonality may serve as the basis for community is lost on those who conceive of community as a gathering of pre-established selves rather than as the condition for singularity.

The rhetoric of civilizing progress that has framed the Down Low phenomenon in the media and the talk of maturity that condemns it as well as public sex are akin to the readiness of many gay activists to condemn gay Republicans. They too seem stuck at a certain stage of their evolution toward gay self-realization. Like homophobia itself, self-loathing is widely taken to be a sign of immaturity, or even archaism. Think, one of the two poor Wyoming kids who killed Matthew Shepherd was "revealed" to be a self-hating homosexual on a TV news show, as if that explained everything. And what about the sexual abuse of young boys by Catholic priests whose church stubbornly adheres to antiquated rules and forbids its clergy to embrace a healthy, and legal, heterosexual lifestyle? Worse, Mohammed Atta, the mastermind of the 9/11 attacks, was also suspected by probing American journalists of being a repressed homosexual who fanatically embraced a faith more backward even than Roman Catholicism and committed acts of unspeakable barbarity. And if that wasn't bad enough, a recent biography of Hitler claims that he too. . . . [23] So what do we have? Men who give AIDS to their innocent girlfriends? The perpetrator of the most notorious hate-crime in recent American history? Pedophiles? Terrorists? Hitler? Republicans? I told you, self-hating homosexuals are the worst people on earth. The worst!

I smell a rat. Is the hatred of gay self-hatred in the gay mainstream and among some straight liberals—that is, the demand that we love ourselves as homosexuals—the newest manifestation of *externalized* homophobia? In part, yes. Foucault had already warned us in the mid-1970s that the act of coming out—the injunction to self-identify—was suspiciously tied to the Victorian era's disciplinary logic of confession.[24] Also in the mid-seventies, in a dramatic about-face Pier Paolo Pasolini denounced the sexual revolution he had just celebrated in a series of films, as a new modality of power, more insidious and more effective than outright repression could ever dream of being. But there's something else, I think. A bigger rat.

A story:

Once upon a time, when I was a graduate student in an American university, I made extra money by tutoring people in French. (I was already too old for more lucrative ventures.) One of my students was a gay flight attendant. We were both out to one another—somehow he had heard I was openly gay and, as I said, he was a flight attendant. At the end of the year, he gave me a sweet card in which he'd written, "Thank you for being yourself." By that, of course, he meant "Thank you for being open to me about being gay." Although I had never been thanked for being myself before (the pressure was more often to try to be someone else), I was able to understand what the note meant because I was familiar enough with the idea that to be out, not to hide one's homosexuality, is to be oneself, finally—to have gotten rid of the mask and to show one's real self to oneself and to the whole wide world.

I see two main problems with this. The first is that what my student meant was, "Thank you for being like me." But how, I wonder, can I be both my true self and the same as someone else? What sounds like a contradiction in terms is in fact a familiar proposition for all members of minoritized groups, since our selves are made possible only through collective identification, on the one hand, and, on the other, through negotiations with the parameters of an identity imposed on us by the system that produces these identities as marginal or external. This has two direct consequences. The first is that the gay self (in this case) is always already collective—one cannot be gay alone but only gay *like* or, more accurately, *with* someone else. This implies that to be an out homosexual is precisely *not* to be oneself, but rather to be engaged in a relation that always already externalizes "me" from "myself." The second is that even understood as plural, the gay self cannot lay claim to stability, since the process of negotiation with the identity-producing system is a never-ending one. A system is never fixed; it keeps shifting its contours, or margins, in order to ensure its own survival in the face of challenge. This is why it is perfectly conceivable, indeed probable, to have a society one day that will grant complete legal equality to gay people *and* be constitutively homophobic at the same time. This is the inevitable snag met by rights-oriented gay politics. For an analogy, think of the situation of women in today's Western democracies, where the coexistence of equal rights and sexism is the norm and not a temporary stage in the process called perfectibility.

To rephrase: The proposition that "being gay" = "being oneself" presupposes a coincidence between singularity and identity that is impossible, because there exists no self outside the relational. The self *is* the relational. It never comes purely from me or purely from the system. It is an effect, or to be exact, a plurality of effects, of a relation that it does not precede—not even as an idea. Even when I come out to myself, as the phrase goes, it is a relational process since, as the very syntax suggests, I have to split myself in two so that one part of myself may stand in as my own interlocutor. In other words, in order to be myself, I must also posit myself as other than myself. Is this a temporary, tactical move? I believe, rather, that it is foundational. In effect, coming out to oneself is the moment when one realizes that the self exists only in and as self-alienation—not as subject but as object. One can look at oneself but never *be* oneself. If, as Hegel posits, all knowledge is a product of mediation and therefore makes the object of knowledge paradoxically unknowable, the *recognition* that one is gay takes place without *knowing* it first—in the same way that Charlus and Jupien recognized each other even though they did not know each other. In French, *reconnaissance* precedes *connaissance*. That said, many of us will go on to live our gay lives in complete denial of that originary self-alienation—until feelings of shame and self-hatred pop up again, and they always do, out of the blue, when we thought that stuff was safely behind us. Well, that stuff never is safely behind us, because if it were we wouldn't be where we are now.

A scene in André Téchiné's movie *Les roseaux sauvages [Wild Reeds]*, in which the young protagonist struggling with his budding homosexuality looks at himself in the mirror and repeats endlessly, "I'm a homo, I'm a homo, I'm a homo . . ." ["Je suis pédé, je suis pédé, je suis pédé . . ."], illustrates my point. Being out may be a joy; *coming* out isn't. Being out may give us the comforting assurance of self-acceptance; coming out, because we must often do it several times in the course of a lifetime, to different people, in different situations, and for different purposes determined by changing personal and cultural circumstances, reminds us that we were, logically, not that out in the first place and that we never can be. Unless one is at the very threshold of death and one knows it, there will always be more people and situations and circumstances. To put it in more abstract terms, if I may, the situational production of meaning ensures that successive iterations of identity never perform the same thing. Coming out forces us periodically to confront the fact that the assurance of identity—what I termed "gayness" earlier—is but an illusion that rests on the denial of the paradox of (self-) knowledge—the paradox I call "queerness."

In an earlier movie, *J'embrasse pas [I don't kiss]*, Téchiné filmed a mirror scene nearly identical to the one in *Les roseaux sauvages*, except with a street hustler telling himself, "You're shit, you're shit, you're shit" ["T'es une merde . . ."] while slapping his own face. The sequential appearance of the two movies, and more specifically of the two scenes, may seem at first to represent something like linear progress. First self-hating rejection—"You're shit"—followed by painful acceptance—"I'm a homo." (Keep in mind that the story of *Les roseaux sauvages* takes place in the early 1960s, when the word *pédé* had yet to be widely reclaimed against its original insulting meaning.) The juxtaposition of these two scenes, however, suggests that the two statements cannot be so easily separated, each mirror scene being, as it were, a reflection of the other. Viewed specularly, "You're shit" and "I'm a homo" blend in the end into two other statements, one a falsely reassuring rejection of homosexuality—"You're a homo"; the other its disturbing acceptance—"I'm shit." When Bill Clinton and others who know what's good for us urge us to come out already, as if that was the most natural thing in the world, that is what they want us to say out loud—"I'm shit." That statement, I contend, is the founding scene of what is no longer identity but community—self-acceptance and self loathing *at the same time*, self-acceptance *as* self-loathing. The discomfort that Téchiné's second coming out scene gives us, queer viewers (I find it unbearable and certainly more painful to watch than the first scene), comes not from our acknowledgment of what we once were but of what we still are and will always be—self-hating homos.

The second problem with my student's well-intentioned note has to do with the question of authenticity, specifically in terms of language and selfhood. The self is spoken,[25] in the sense that the *I* is always already a *we*. But the self isn't in what is said; it is in the act of making contact—Roman Jakobson's phatic function of language once more—that is to say, it is relational, or communal. In fact, one could argue that a given culture recognizes as a self what it collectively, albeit not always unanimously, agrees it is, thus making the self not a precondition of the collective but rather an outcome of it. The contradiction within French universalist theory, which posits the communal as archaic and the individual as modern, rests in the illusion that the individual exists before the community, as the fundamental and unchanging nature of the human—a nature modernity claims merely to have discovered. (Modernity loves discoveries; they mask the processes by which truths are culturally produced and thus naturalize culture.) The universalist trick is to make the supposedly preexistent individual not archaic but, rather, timeless and spaceless—while claiming at the same time that it is specifically modern and French, therefore excluding those who don't share this view toward the realm of radical, incompatible otherness. Writing in the context of the Muslim headscarf controversies, Joan Scott observes:

> The basis for French republican theory is the autonomous individual who exists prior to his or her choices of lifestyles, values, and politics; these are but external expressions of a fixed inner self, a self which by definition cannot relinquish its autonomy. Critics of this theory point out that the individual is not entirely autonomous, because s/he operates within a set of normative parameters that define individuality (and Frenchness) and that rule out other options . . . the notion of the individual existing prior to external influence masks its status as a cultural belief. (127–28)

My point is that homosexual linguistic and cultural practices do not come out of an identity that would preexist them. Homosexuality has no first instance. (Nothing does.) Rather, our "identity" comes out of our linguistic and cultural practices, much as cause follows effect and the past survives alongside the present. The act of coming out is widely understood and experienced as liberating because it signals authenticity. But how could authenticity be liberating? Isn't it, instead, an additional self-imposed constraint? And a particularly frustrating one to boot? Here lies the problem with the notion of gay authenticity: it is supposed to be a progress and therefore a vision of the future, but it is always caught up in an ideology of origin—that is, of conformity to a preexistent model—making the future a mere reproduction of the past—an *authentic* replica. Etymologically even, authenticity, whose root gave us "author" and "authority," suggests a link to reproduction understood as procreation and, by extension, familialism. Not very queer, is it?

So if coming out is a liberating experience, (and it is, of course it is), it's because I'm finally *not* myself. I am *like* (and "like" here must be understood, as is the case with all tropes, as predicated upon difference, not sameness), that is to say, I am *with*. Put somewhat differently, I am with a proud flight attendant but also in a relationship of community with a poor, self-hating Wyoming gay-basher. "I'm shit," remember? I mean, we're not only supposed to stick to our authentic self for fear of closet-like alienation, but the original we are supposed to be identical to has never even existed. Seen as a product of discourse in the Foucauldian sense rather than adherence to an original referent, authenticity has a name: it's called a construct. Understood as such, and only then, authenticity, should one wish to retain the term at all, may provide us with a very useful tool for community formation, whereas attempts to recapture it as origin lead to the erasure of the relational—a murderous, even genocidal, proposition.[26] So please don't thank me for being myself. I assure you I'm not.

With that in mind, let's return to the urgent reality of the AIDS crisis. Several years through the pandemic, many activists and some public health officials finally recognized that the most effective way to act against it was to take into consideration the specific cultural values and practices of the communities that have been most affected, for example gay men, and enable these communities to carry out self-targeting prevention. But for certain categories of people an effective information and prevention campaign could not be based on the notion of community as shared identity. That, in essence, was the French problem. The French concept of universal citizenship made it nearly impossible for gay men to feel collectively concerned by AIDS *as gay men* because, for the most part, they didn't think of themselves that way. To this day sexuality is, in French culture, first and foremost understood as a practice, not as an identity.[27] It took ACT UP's rhetoric to complicate that mode of thinking by tactically assuming the stance of essentialist identity politics to create more effectively a discursive position— "*pédé*," fag—that may be temporarily occupied by anyone for the purpose of community-based political action that benefits *all*. Thus, when Emmanuelle Cosse, an HIV-negative straight woman, became president of ACT UP-Paris, she made a point of calling herself "une pédée." (I'll venture the far less clever "girl fag" as a possible translation.) And in the United States and elsewhere, what about men who engage in sex with other men but do not identify as gay or even bisexual? For a long time, they fell through the cracks of dominant HIV/AIDS prevention discourses, which can roughly be articulated as follows when it comes to sexual transmission: If you're gay, you're vulnerable because you're gay; if you're heterosexual, you're vulnerable because "Everybody can get AIDS." This familiar minoritizing statement cannot effectively reach people who are not gay but who also accept the fact that their sexual behavior is not "everybody's" either.

For practical purposes, the category "men who have sex with men" was thus named. Does that mean that we have therefore created another identity? If we have, we've only displaced the problem. Who else is going to be the next forgotten, *unidentified* group?

I want to argue, rather, that the category "men who have sex with men" exists outside the gay-straight binary and, more important, may provide a much-needed alternative to it and to the cultural dilemma of identity and universalism. Naming the category "men who have sex with men" *acknowledges* the existence of a community where there was no articulated awareness of it as such. This is what has made it an effective tool against HIV/AIDS. It makes collective self-enabling possible. It allows people to live. The same could be said of the Down Low. What many decry as a reckless lack of self-identification, of internalized homophobia, may in fact be the basis for community—a community without identity. After all, why should one expect minoritized groups to embrace a notion of the (mature, evolved) self that has, by and large, been designed to exclude them and is still waved about for the same purpose?[28] Not that men "on the DL" flout identity in general, at least on the (visible) surface. After all, they often make a point of wearing "thuggish" fashions or other markers of black masculinity—a very loud point, in fact, that inevitably raises the specter of denial. Just as Proust's Charlus proudly displays his virile character and his membership in the aristocracy while enjoying a secret life that undermines both gender and social systems, so do hypermasculine DL black men cast a doubt on the identities they appear to embrace. The author of the Down Low piece in the *Times* unwittingly acknowledges that whereas identity is in doubt community isn't, as he describes "an organized, underground subculture largely made up of black men who otherwise live straight lives" (30). And the most effective way to arm such a community for the purposes of HIV/AIDS prevention would be to embrace its perceived failure to adopt the dominant concepts of selfhood and gayness as a radical rejection of these concepts and as a template for a different kind of social dynamics. This is the question of group friendship. In that sense, it becomes possible to reconsider the Down Low as a means of effective prevention rather than a danger.

Don't get me wrong, though. I know that self-hatred can be a powerfully destructive force driving some people to depression, suicide, violence against themselves and others, or just plain unhappiness. But that's precisely why we must change our approach to it, and this is where a rethinking of self-hatred could come in handy. So here's what I propose. The hatred of self-hatred is homophobic because it stigmatizes such feelings as "just a phase" on the way to full, mature self-identification—a direct reprise of the rhetorical construction of homosexuality I described in the previous section of this chapter.

Self-hatred thus gets defined, not *like*—difference—but *as*—sameness—homosexuality itself. Logically, then, the gay haters of gay self-haters are . . . gay self-haters. This is no mere reversal, however. I am not implying that the haters are really the hated, which would be but another assertion of authenticity. On the contrary, what this shows is that homosexuality can never be separated from self-hatred. Pretending that it can is exactly the sort of denial I was talking about—the rat that I smelled. So if the expression "to come *out*" implies that homophobia, simultaneously internalized and confining, is like a ghetto, for example, I hasten to say: you can take the boy out of homophobia, but you can't take homophobia out of the boy.

Some, just *some*, men on the DL, for example, may very well be in denial of their homosexuality, but by the same token their gay critics are in denial of their own self-hatred. What if self-hatred was not really about hating oneself but about hating *the self*, that is, a certain concept of the self that covers up its defining relationality in favor of the myth of originary identity and self-sameness? Self-hatred is an alienating experience, of course. (Come to think of it, though, no more so than self-love which is simply the denial/confirmation of self-alienation, as comically self-absorbed queens like to remind us). But I am not only advocating what in French is termed *faire avec*, to make do, but also, after Nancy (and Heidegger), *être avec*, an ontological relationality. In that sense, my questions go beyond homosexuality to address what it means to "be" (if that is indeed the right verb) a minoritized self in general and, in the end, just a self.

Consider the disastrous founding statement of the minoritized self: "I hate myself." Its first effect is to split the self in two—a subject that hates—"I"—and the object of that hatred. But it also entails that I hate myself for hating myself. The subject, then, is itself split into a hating subject and a hated object, which in turn entails that I hate myself for hating myself for hating myself. And so on and so forth *ad vitam æternam*. The minoritized I is never fully present to itself because it envisions the self as always already other than itself—an *I* that is necessarily a *we*. But what I called earlier "community without identity" is an unacceptable proposition to many. Assimilationists want us to identify with the hating subject and erase the object of our hatred; identity-lovers tell us that we must sever our ties to the hating self and love what we used to hate. I say, let's just hate our selves and love the alien, the other, the queer in us. Anyway, can I ever cease to be a self-hating faggot? No more, I should think, than my father could ever stop being a Holocaust survivor and orphan or my mother a penniless twenty-two-year-old pregnant widow with a little boy of two and who now mourns a dead son. The painful presence of the past is what constitutes the founding disasters that will be the topic of the next chapter. But in the meantime:

I admit it took me completely by surprise, although in retrospect I realize I should have seen it coming. I was in Paris, and my friends Nico and Guillaume had taken me to see a cabaret act in a small, intimate basement venue in Ménilmontant. The singer, named Michel Hermon, was performing songs from his new CD entitled *Dietrich Hotel*. Accompanied by a pianist, he sang numbers from Marlene Dietrich's film and stage repertoire, as well as other songs evocative of the decadent atmosphere of Berlin and Paris in the 1920s. The show was lovely and I enjoyed it very much.

Hermon's entrance, however, was a different matter altogether. My friends and I were at a table near the back of the room, conveniently sitting a few feet away from the bar. The place went dark, and Hermon's low, husky voice was heard singing Lou Reed's "Berlin"—this was going to be great. Slowly, he made his way down the stairs and appeared at the door wearing— what else?—a black swallow-tail suit like the one Marlene wears in the famous scene from *Morocco*, the one where she kisses a woman on the lips, the one that Guillaume Dustan so campily and movingly references in the opening of *Je sors ce soir*, his second AIDS novel. Hermon is now near the middle of the room, and "Berlin" seamlessly gives way to "Black Market," an original Frederick Hollander song from Billy Wilder's *A Foreign Affair* and a camp masterpiece. I just love this song. Genuine Marlene *and* a pure gem of self-irony, it is, in other words, quintessential Dietrich. I'm in heaven. But instead of making his way to the little stage, the bald, middle-aged, made-up singer starts swishing toward the bar behind me and soon lies down on top of it in an exaggeratedly lascivious pose. Naturally, the spotlight is now right on me, and so are the eyes of everyone in the audience. Nico and Guillaume are trying very hard not to laugh. I'm in hell.

Most people would think of this merely as a slight embarrassment, like being called on stage by a magician or something. And what's there to be embarrassed about anyway since, after all, people were not really looking at me, right? Wrong. They *were* looking at me. You see, liking Marlene Dietrich is quite different from liking, say, macaroni and cheese. Nobody wants to *be* macaroni and cheese. But when you're a teenage gay boy you want to be Marlene Dietrich. At least *I* did, and identifying with a glamorous screen legend was at once a self-affirming gesture and a feeling of self-denying shame. If queer kids are directly or indirectly pressured to be someone else, I'm not so sure it is Marlene Dietrich our censors have in mind. But I can't think of a more fabulous way for boys and girls alike (since Marlene's queer appeal crosses gender lines) to obey and disobey the injunction in one single move—to be someone else all right, but the wrong person. This mode of identification represents, in a way, a failure to understand the injunction, as if instead of trying *to be* someone else, queer kids tried *being* someone else. The attempt to normalize, innocently transformed into an experiment with the abnormal, reveals, in the end, the founding failure that is self-realization as self-alienation and suggests that queer lives are a matter of troping.

Back in my teenage years, the relation between the fantasy of performing "Black Market" in a roomful of drunken sailors and that of being fucked up the ass was already clear to me. In fact, both fantasies alternately "took place" behind closed doors in my bedroom. Admitting to the former was, for whoever could read it, tantamount to admitting to the latter, and, as a youth, I often proclaimed my love for Marlene as a coded, that is, at once timid and provocative form of coming out. It was both an empowering and a shameful gesture inasmuch as it simultaneously announced and silenced what it stood for. In other words, it needed to be read. And this is precisely what I felt was happening at the Hermon concert. The audience was looking through me and could see my adolescent fantasy of myself, my secret shame embodied—my very big faggotry wallowing on the bar like some cheap harlot and finally exposed for all to see. I'm overdoing it a little, of course, because I no longer feel so victimized by my shame, for better or for worse. Yet this episode of the kind of social embarrassment often generated by someone else's shamelessness brought back that shame to my memory in an unexpectedly vivid way. Years later I remembered my shame, and what more spectacular way is there to remember shame than to feel it again, to reawaken a past you thought was safely behind you, to experience all of a sudden the shocking fragility of years of so-called progress? And can such a memory possibly be a good thing? I think it can.

The idea of reclaiming shame has recently become a topic of inquiry among queers, theorists and otherwise. In New York, San Francisco, and other American cities, Gay Shame celebrations have been organized in opposition to the increasingly normative and commercialized gay pride parades and against the emergence of a conservative gay agenda. Following in the footsteps of Queer Nation, a short-lived group that attacked what its members saw as the exclusionary bourgeois values of established urban gay communities in the early 1990s, Gay Shame activists and scholars are reclaiming practices and identities that had previously been abjected not only by the dominant heterosexual culture but by many gay people as well. Public and anonymous sex, gender indeterminacy, promiscuity, and other markers of nonconformity may be reclaimed as alternatives to more mainstream values such as marriage or the right to wear uniforms for real. My purpose here is not to determine whether shame is better than pride or *queer* better than *gay*. I have my opinion on the matter, of course. It is fairly simple, and

it goes something like this: Pride, because it is predicated on its dichotomous opposition to shame, always reasserts what it repudiates. Moreover,
pride produces an additional level of shame—it makes us ashamed of our
shame. No matter how you look at it, shame, it seems, just won't stay away.
So what interests me more is to raise the question of what kind of community might be grounded in feelings of shame.

Consider again the performance by Michel Hermon. The shame I re-
membered/experienced as a result signaled that I felt exposed, that my corporeal self was but a representation while my truest, most private self was
being revealed by Hermon's allegorical performance of it, and that it was
worthy of shame. As Elspeth Probyn writes, "What shames me may not
shame you. But whatever it is that shames you will be something important
to you, an essential part of yourself."[29] But that authentic, supposedly essential part of myself took the form of another man wearing what was in effect
double drag—a man dressed as a woman dressed as a man. The true self I
felt was exposed that night does not so much come from identification with
a real but forbidden object—the other sex—as from a spiral of pure representation. Unlike gay pride's discourse of authenticity, urging us to come
out and be our true selves, this shameful mode of identification forsakes all
claims to authenticity and reveals naturalness as yet another artifice. The system of norms and values that defined me as shameful in the name of truth
and nature is thus deprived of the very terrain that grounds its legitimacy.
The fact that my shame was experienced through, and because of, a collapse
of the private and the public, of the self and the collective, is why it can be
so politically powerful. Shame is located at the precise boundary defining
the normal and the abnormal. Such feelings, of course, are supposed to be
manifestations of internalized social policing, warning signs that give us a
foretaste of what it would be like to be completely desocialized and, as a result, make us want to rush for safety to the side of the normal. But what if
we don't? What if shame relived, the persistence of one's lonely past alongside the present, could be a factor in community formation?

In his essay "Mario Montez, For Shame," Douglas Crimp draws on the
works of Eve Kosofsky Sedgwick and Michael Warner in order to study
shame's "capacity for articulating collectivities of the shamed" (66). Starting
with Sedgwick's observation that one can be flooded by someone else's
shame, Crimp writes:

> In taking on the shame, I do not share in the other's identity. I simply adopt the
> other's vulnerability to being shamed. In this operation, most importantly, the
> other's difference is preserved; it is not claimed as my own. In taking on or tak-
> ing up his or her shame, I am not attempting to vanquish his or her otherness.

I put myself in the place of the other only insofar as I recognize that I too am prone to shame. (65)

I am reminded of my father's comment about how his own experience with anti-Semitism allowed him to know what homophobia *feels like*. Crimp goes on to quote Warner: "Queer scenes are the true *salon des refusés*, where the most heterogeneous people are brought into great intimacy by their common experience of being despised and rejected in a world of norms" (Crimp, 66; Warner, 35–36). As Warner, Sedgwick, and Crimp all notice, heterogeneity, that is to say singularity (not to be confused with essentializing identity), is at the core of any collectivity to be constituted by shame. Crimp, referring to Mario Montez, the Puerto Rican drag queen whose interview in a film by Andy Warhol is the focus of his piece, concludes, "I am thus not 'like' Mario, but the distinctiveness that is revealed in Mario invades me . . . and my own distinctiveness is revealed simultaneously. I, too, feel exposed" (67).

This brings back to my memory a disturbing experience I had many years ago. That day, the first installment of the miniseries *Holocaust* premiered on French TV as part of a then famous weekly broadcast called "Les dossiers de l'écran." The format was always the same: a movie was shown in prime time, usually one with a serious social or historical theme, and followed by a live debate with a panel of guests, during which viewers could call in their questions. On this particular evening, one of the panelists was a survivor who had been deported to a concentration camp for his activities in the Resistance. He was not a Jew. Predictably, given the subject matter of the movie, most of the debate dealt with the extermination of the Jews. Less predictably, the old hero of the Resistance burst into a sudden rant. I quote, and translate, from memory: "Enough with the Jews! All you people seem to care about is the Jews, the Jews, the Jews! What about all the others who were deported by the Nazis? Can't we talk about them too?" An embarrassed silence fell upon the set—and that's putting it mildly. As for me, I was instantly overwhelmed, flooded, as Sedgwick would put it, by that familiar physical sensation of shame—a sensation that is recurring as I'm writing this. For a reason I could not possibly fathom then, I had witnessed the public embarrassment of an anti-Semite and made it my own. For all I knew, the old asshole may not even have felt embarrassed at all—assholes rarely do; that's one of their defining features, in fact—but somebody had to, and that somebody was me. As it turned out, it wasn't just me. The next day I saw my father who, before I said anything, told me of his own similar reaction to that dreadful scene. My father, a Holocaust survivor whose family had been exterminated, had taken the public embarrassment of an anti-Semite upon himself and, just as I had myself, had done so by drawing on his own experience of having been ashamed in the past.

The embarrassment we both felt as a result of that previous instance of shame was not really alleviated by the fact that my father and I had shared the experience. Today still it is unbearable, and it isn't just the shame that floods me but an extraordinary sense of sadness. Yet at that moment, somehow, my father and I knew that we had something fundamental in common. Even though that something was not a thing at all but a dark hole, a stupor, an unspeakable nothingness, it was a vehicle for a feeling of community, and one that didn't just bring the two of us together specifically, as father and son, but also all and any others who, surely, had felt the same way we had. Most disturbingly, it brought us into this strange closeness with a Jew-hating idiot who may not even have been aware of his own shame.[30] How different is this from the sadness I feel toward the poor kid who killed Matthew Shepard and was subsequently exposed for his alleged secret homosexuality? Not very different at all. In both cases I had witnessed another human being's public humiliation and at that moment, as uncomfortable as it was, I was somehow *with* them.

That moment of community as experienced through shame first feels, however, like complete isolation. As Sedgwick writes:

> One of the strangest features of shame (but, I would argue, the most theoretically significant) is the way bad treatment of someone else, bad treatment *by* someone else, someone else's embarrassment, stigma, debility, blame or pain, seemingly having nothing to do with me, can so readily flood me—assuming that I'm a shame-prone person—with this sensation whose very suffusiveness seems to delineate my precise, individual outlines in the most isolating way imaginable. (Crimp, 65; Sedgwick, 14; original emphasis)

"I, too, feel exposed," Crimp wrote—just as I felt exposed by the spotlight that shone on me at the concert. That episode feels far more comical now than the one I just related, obviously, but at that very moment, when shame, brutal and inarticulate, completely overwhelmed me, I felt no sense of community whatsoever with the two gay friends who were with me that night, or with the other queens who comprised much of the audience, let alone with the singer who shamelessly embodied that rejected part of myself. I just felt separated from everyone else, gay or straight. In other words, as Sedgwick points out, the moment of shame is one of isolation, not communion; it registers on the mind as hyperindividualizing in a way that makes you feel, if not fully understand, that one's sense of self is dependent on the social. Yet this extreme singularity does enable the collective. As I said, I am both over my shame and not over it at all, since I remembered it by reliving it with exactly the same intensity and pain. Strictly speaking, it may not even be a matter of remembering since, by shining a spotlight on one's singularity, feelings of shame temporarily remove you from the social, and without the social there can be no memory. Shame, like queerness and Jewishness, is a thing *of* the past that stubbornly refuses to stay *in* the past.

The third and final volume of Charlotte Delbo's testimony concerning Auschwitz and Ravensbrück is entitled *Mesure de nos jours [The Measure of Our Days]*. It deals with the period that followed the liberation of the camps, a context that allows me to probe the question of survival, both literal and theoretical, that is occupying me here beyond the exemplary starting points that are Jewishness and queerness. (Delbo, like most of her companions whose stories she tells, was deported for her activities in the French Resistance. She was not Jewish.) The book contains an episode that underscores the link between shame, the past, and the nature of community.

Years after their return from the camps, the narrator and two of her women companions who were there with her, are gathered around the body of Germaine, another friend, who has just died. Charlotte feels doubly sad because, in spite of the promise she made at their liberation, she had never visited Germaine until the latter was dying. Germaine, who had helped and nurtured Charlotte like a mother at a time of absolute distress, is now dead. Just as she kisses her friend goodbye, Charlotte suddenly feels as though she is being transported back to the camp on the particular day when she and two other women were saying goodbye to their friend Sylviane:

> I leaned forward over Germaine's hand resting on the white sheet and kissed it. I would have liked to give her back all the sweetness she had given me. At that moment, when I touched her hand with my lips, I was seized with terror. I could see Carmen and Lulu on the other side of the bed, and wondered whether I'd get a grip on myself. It was no longer Germaine laid out upon a white bed but Sylviane lying on rotting boards. The three of us stood at the foot of those boards, Lulu, Carmen, and myself. We had come to see Sylviane. (312)

> [Je me suis penchée sur la main de Germaine qui reposait sur le drap blanc et je l'ai embrassée. J'aurais voulu lui rendre toute la douceur qu'elle m'avait donnée. C'est à ce moment, au moment où je posais mes lèvres sur sa main, que j'ai été saisie de terreur. Je voyais Carmen et Lulu qui étaient là, de l'autre côté du lit et je me demandais si je parviendrais à me dominer. Devant moi, ce n'était plus Germaine qui était allongée sur un lit blanc, c'était Sylviane qui était couchée sur des planches pourries. Nous étions toutes les trois au pied de ces planches, Lulu, Carmen et moi, et c'était Sylviane que nous venions voir. (143)]

What follows this passage is a description of Sylviane's dying moments and her friends' final farewell to her. The reason this sudden reemergence of the past is triggered by the physical contact of the kiss is that, back in Auschwitz that day, Carmen had asked Charlotte to kiss Sylviane goodbye, just as Carmen and Lulu had done. Charlotte, however, felt so revulsed by her friend's filthy, emaciated body that she could only manage a reluctant kiss under what she presumed to be the judging gaze of the other two:

> Carmen said, "Kiss her too." Just like that. "Kiss her," as though it were the most natural thing in the world to kiss a dying woman whose mouth is covered with mortal dribble. I leaned over Sylviane's face. Her burning blue eyes looked at me, becoming larger and larger, more and more blue, deeper and deeper as I leaned over them. I wanted to flee, run far away from this bay of skeletons, these tiers covered by skeletons, far from the stench of death and rot. I leaned over Sylviane's burning blue stare, wishing I had the nerve to cheat in the presence of Carmen and Lulu. But since I didn't, I kissed Sylviane with my mouth almost closed, wondering, as I felt my whole being contract with revulsion, if this was satisfactory in my comrades' eyes. (314–15)

> [Carmen a dit: "Embrasse-la, toi aussi." Simplement. "Embrasse-là [sic]," comme si c'était tout naturel d'embrasser une mourante qui a la bouche salie de bave mortelle . . . j'aurais voulu fuir, courir loin de cette travée de squelettes, de ces étages de squelettes, loin de cette odeur de mort et de pourri. Je me penchais sur le regard bleu brûlant de Sylviane et j'aurais voulu avoir le courage de tricher devant Carmen et Lulu, mais je n'ai pas eu ce courage et j'ai embrassé Sylviane en ouvrant à peine la bouche, en me demandant si cela suffisait aux yeux de Carmen et de Lulu, et je me sentais toute contractée de répugnance. (148)]

Delbo concludes the scene with a startling direct address to us, her readers: "Have you ever felt deeply ashamed in your life?" In the paragraph immediately following this question, she returns to the present: "One mustn't feel shame, nor have regrets, for these are useless feelings. Now it was Germaine who was here, not Sylviane."

The answer to the first question is both obvious and unsettling. Delbo's address, inasmuch as it is directed at those who are indeed prone to shame, hardly requires an answer. Yes, of course we have felt shame in our lives. But how could, say, my shame, my silly shame at the concert, possibly compare to Charlotte's in Auschwitz? The notion is revolting. Yet, because her question is intended for readers who are not concentration camp survivors, Delbo's injunction that we recognize her feeling by drawing on the memory of our own shame brings us into contact with her while forcing us to acknowledge the gap between us and her. Recognition, in this context, is to be understood in its double meaning of familiarity and acknowledgment, the former allowing the latter.

As for the second question, a disingenuous dismissal of shame as a useless emotion, it is immediately answered: Charlotte's shame has brought back

Sylviane, Carmen, and Lulu. The past has superseded the present, so much so that Delbo makes a conspicuous point of never naming the two women who were actually with her at Germaine's deathbed, referring to them simply as "l'une" and "l'autre," the one and the other. She explains:

> I know that the two others who were with me on that day, the day Germaine died, were neither Carmen nor Lulu. It's only *because Lulu, Carmen, and I were together* to bid farewell to Sylviane that I confuse them with those who were really with me when Germaine died. One of them, who was neither Carmen nor Lulu, waved to Maurice . . . (315; my emphasis)

> [Je sais que les deux autres qui étaient avec moi ce jour-là, le jour où Germaine est morte, n'étaient ni Carmen ni Lulu. C'est uniquement *parce que nous étions ensemble, Lulu, Carmen et moi*, pour dire adieu à Sylviane que je les confonds avec celles qui étaient réellement avec moi quand Germaine est morte. L'une d'elles, qui n'était ni Carmen ni Lulu mais une autre, a fait signe à Maurice . . . (149–50; my emphasis)]

The community ("parce que nous étions ensemble") formed around the dead friend at Auschwitz, that is to say, around death itself, has been brought back to life by the physical sensation of shame, a sensation that connected "then" and "now" and essentially gutted the present of its presence. Carmen and Lulu did in fact survive, but their uncanny reappearance around Sylviane, coupled with the erasure of the other two companions, endows all four, or five if we count Charlotte, with the ghostly power to stand for those who never returned. The dead and the survivors have become one and the same; all are revenants.

Indeed, there are other points of contact between past and present throughout the whole episode. There are descriptions of Germaine's and Sylviane's beauty in death, as well as mentions of their hair. More important, both women had the same piercing blue eyes, which Delbo recalls repeatedly. Sylviane's blue eyes are the one detail that allows the women to tell her apart from the countless, otherwise indistinguishable living skeletons in the bunk beds around them—a community of the dead. As for Germaine's eyes, now closed, they remain so piercing that they seem to shine through her eyelids:

> Maurice had closed her eyes, yet the memory I kept of those luminous eyes, eyes the blue of light, full of kindness itself, were it possible to separate kindness from all support, confining it to a pure look, my recollection of these eyes was so precise that I felt their look and saw their light shining from under the eyelids Germaine's husband had lowered a moment ago. (309)

> [Maurice lui avait fermé les yeux mais le souvenir que j'avais de ses yeux lumineux, ses yeux d'un bleu de lumière, au regard qui était celui de la bonté

même, si on pouvait détacher la bonté de tout support et la contenir dans un regard pur, mon souvenir de ses yeux était si exact que je sentais leur regard et voyais leur lumière sous les paupières que le mari de Germaine, faisant douce sa main d'ouvrier, avait abaissées un instant plus tôt. (137)]

And a bit later, she mentions "eyes so blue that, for us, their blueness continued to shine from under the eyelids" (309 [138]).

When Sylviane's eyes are mentioned at the moment of her death, it is as if goodness had indeed been detached from one body in the present and transported back to another in the past. The women are helpless to do anything for their dying friend in Auschwitz, and Charlotte wonders,

> What can one say to a twenty-year-old girl who's dying when you cannot even ask her if she'd like to have something since there's nothing to bring? Sylviane was dying and her eyes, the blue of precious stones, would be extinguished. (313)
>
> [Que dire à une jeune fille de vingt ans qui meurt quand on ne peut même pas lui demander si elle a envie de quelque chose puisqu'on n'aurait rien à lui apporter? Sylviane mourait et ses yeux bleus comme des pierres précieuses s'éteindraient. (145)]

Community, Delbo implies, is not about bringing something to others; it cannot be instrumentalized. Rather it is enacted by being *transported* (and I am using this term in full awareness of the connotations it possesses in the context of the camps) back to the past better to awaken the ghosts and allow them to occupy their rightful place among us in the present. A more accurate description, then, would be to talk about the past being transported into the present since Charlotte never lost touch with the present and what she experienced was in no way a regression. Shame, that painful moment of isolation, is also a connector; it erases the distance between past and present and keeps the dead alive to remind us that the safety we try to find in our sense of self is but a lure.

As the story tells us, getting over one's shame is not a process to be completed; otherwise, I couldn't have recognized Charlotte('s). Indeed, if I feel shame today it isn't because I'm not completely over it *yet*. If that were the case I would probably feel less and less ashamed each time and, at worst, a bit nostalgic about that long-gone piece of my life. Instead, the very physicality of that intense emotion, its Proustian suddenness and sense of immediacy, suggests that I am in contact, in touch, with a self that I no longer am yet still am. As Gloria Gaynor famously put it in her 1970s disco version of *La cage aux folles*'s gay anthem, I am what I am. But I am also what I am no longer—which doesn't sound quite right for a gay anthem, but I guess that's why I write scholarship, not musicals. If, as Michael Warner proposes, communities of the shamed are defined by intimacy between heterogeneous people, they are also constituted by people who, in a sense, are not even similar to themselves and who embrace that disconnectedness from an unknowable self. This is where queer and gay overlap but diverge.

In the gay rhetoric of pride, the speech act of coming out is akin to a birth; it inaugurates a new self. Think of ACT UP's slogan "I am out, therefore I am." In this view, the gap between our past and current selves is not one that may be bridged by a kind of developmental or evolutionary continuity. At least symbolically it is supposed to be a radical repudiation, a personal Stonewall, as if the foundational, emancipatory moment of the modern gay movement was to be internalized by each gay individual in a move that will from now on attach the self to the collective. Much of this could be embraced by a queer analysis, but whereas the rhetoric of pride demands that our two selves be forever disconnected, queerness reconnects them without erasing their discrepancy. This is what remembering our shame is all about. It isn't nostalgia for the closet, which would amount to a simple reversal of pride's dichotomy and would lead to the same aporia. The recent development of scholarly interest in the pre-Stonewall era, for example, is often less a matter of archeology than a search for viable forms of queerness as usable alternatives to standardized, and standard-enforcing, gayness. Indeed, the gay rhetoric of pride has always depended on its ability to produce an archaic past against which to define itself, either by ignoring the fact that communities, whether urban or not, all white or not, male, female or mixed, did exist before Stonewall; or by denying these communities' usefulness to articulate current cultural modalities. As D. A. Miller suggests in *Place for Us [Essay on the Broadway Musical]*, the "gay identity to which we have entrusted our own politics, ethics, sex lives . . . stands in an essentially reductive relation to the desire on which it is based" (132).[31] Reclaiming our shame today may finally do justice to the elusiveness and complexity that homosexual desire had for us yesterday, before we even knew what it was, and before we could harness it to an identity. And this may indeed include a rethinking of the closet as culture, that is, as a question of collective as well as individual experience.[32]

From this perspective, reclaiming shame is not a rejection of all feelings of pride but rather a critique of the rhetoric of progress that mirrors nineteenth-century bourgeois discourses—the same discourses that defined homosexual people as essentially archaic. Think of psychoanalysis's construction of anal eroticism as belonging to the past and of the shame generated by all things anal in modern Western culture. Reclaiming our own archaism is a desire to touch our past, the otherness in us, in order to define our present. This, in turn or perhaps simultaneously, creates intimacy with otherness in general. What produces community in shame is not shame per se—an affect that, like trauma, cannot be articulated in language and, therefore, cannot articulate social relations. What produces community in shame is its memory—always a collective process. Using the term "queer" in its old, negative and singularizing acceptation rather than in its current theoretical sense, Richard Dyer remarks in *The Culture of Queers*, "I remember being a queer and have never been entirely convinced that I ever became gay" (13).[33] And what shame tells us, with its uncanny power to make us relive it at the most unexpected moments, is that our past isolation can never be safely rejected. Once again, to remember shame is to experience it anew, isolation and all. A community in shame is one that can be neither naturalized nor positioned as dominant because it is consciously defined by the active and persistent memory of its own negativity.

As opposed to the family-based models of community so popular in mainstream gay rhetoric these days, queer communities are thus predicated on the impossibility of stability and self-sameness. According to the philosopher Peter Sloterdijk, the myth of the expulsion from Paradise anchors all human self-consciousness in shame:

> From then on, shame, along with feelings of guilt and separation, would become the oldest and most powerful instance of self-referentiality through which the individual "makes an image" of himself. The deepest traces of Being as an extant shortcoming are inscribed in this image.[34]

My point here is that the first conscious image of oneself that young homosexuals often "make" *as homosexuals* is one of failure and separation from the family, a domestic fall from grace in which we realize that we were not exactly made in our parents' image. This "extant shortcoming"—in effect the departure point of the queer diaspora—generates the first instance of gay shame and, from then on, posits identification as difference *from* the family rather than as sameness *with* the family.[35] The memory of our separation from the familial Eden and subsequent isolation remind us that there hasn't always been community and that, therefore, there may not always be community. An identity thus defined by its own negation through an identification mediated by difference cannot produce communities simply on the basis of a shared positive trait. It doesn't *ground* communities so much as disseminate them on a free-floating diasporic model of out-of-placeness and out-of-timeness, in which the self can only be comprehended through its contact with others and experience its selfness always as otherness. Indeed a queer community is a community of spatial discrepancy and asynchronicity, where past and present are concurrent and in which we enjoy the pleasures of the collective and relive our original isolation at the same time.

I may have felt completely out of place when Michel Hermon sang "Black Market," and I may have felt out of time too (I mean, come on, who worships Marlene Dietrich these days?), but in the end it made a pretty good story, didn't it? Its confessional mode, however, does not inscribe it so neatly in the logic of Foucault's *aveu*, according to which the confession of deviance produces the pathological species of the homosexual. In fact, when you tell a story like this one, chances are someone in your audience will retort, "Oh, darling, you think *that's* bad? Well, listen to *this*." Then a third person may join in with an even more humiliating story. And so on and so forth until the story, which must retain its genuine confessional dimension in order to achieve the twofold status of parody, momentarily deactivates the disciplinary power of confession and turns isolation into something like a membership card. Sharing such stories makes a rather interesting community, slightly on the freakish side perhaps, but one where I feel right at home.

[4]

Disaster, Failure, and Alienation

The sentences are instantly recognizable and their effect all the more disastrous in that they often come in familiar forms and settings from people you know and like. The voice of a relative at the other end of a long-distance phone call, the lover across a restaurant table, the friendly doctor you've been seeing for years are now telling you that "There's been an accident" or "We need to talk about something" or "I've got some bad news," and literally in no time, before a second sentence is even uttered, a deathly frigid emptiness descends upon your body and your mind, leaving you with a void where your life used to be, your own past now alien to you and the future all but inconceivable. Somehow you know that the moment articulates a before and an after, but the whole thing is so brutal that the relation between the two looks unclear. Pieces of time no longer seem connected by causality or narrative coherence, or basic chronology, for that matter. Without warning, the friend has become a monster, the room as strange and hostile as a faraway planet, and the familiar suddenly appears distant and other. Nothing has changed, of course, for the otherness you feel is purely your own. You now feel alien, not just in relation to the world around you but, more violently, to yourself. Sometimes experienced as a split and sometimes as a shattering, the sudden obsolescence of your old self feels as though something has been taken away from you, but also as though something has been added, some foreign entity that is now a defining part of you—an ache, perhaps, both a pain and a yearning; or depression, the visitor that just won't leave; or a virus, a foreign body so intimate it makes your own body foreign. What first came to you as emptiness or lack soon turns into a burden: the subtraction was also an addition. What has been stolen from you now has the weight of unwieldy luggage you have to carry along from this moment on—even though you haven't the faintest idea where on earth you could possibly be going now.

AIDS, "AUSCHWITZ," AND THE DISASTER OF COMMUNITY

Not unlike feelings of shame and self-hatred, a personal disaster is initially experienced as the hyper-individualizing sensation of being singled out of the realm of the social even if, as in a nightmare, others do not always seem to notice and your surroundings appear eerily unaffected by any of it. Mado, Charlotte Delbo's friend and fellow deportee, remarks on her return from the camps: "I died in Auschwitz and no one sees it" (267 [*MJ* 66]; translation modified). After his HIV diagnosis, Hervé Guibert wonders, "Does it show in my eyes?" as he moves about the city:

> My blood, unmasked, everywhere and forever . . . , naked around the clock, when I'm walking in the street, taking public transportation, the constant target of an arrow aimed at me wherever I go. (*To the Friend Who Did Not Save My Life*, 6)

> [Mon sang démasqué, partout et en tout lieu, et à jamais . . . mon sang nu à toute heure, dans les transports publics, dans la rue quand je marche, toujours guetté par une flèche qui me vise à chaque instant. (14)]

Personal disasters, however, are no more personal than shame or self-hatred. Caught up in norms and judgments, all are, in fact, always collective in nature. If I didn't specify what statements could follow "There's been an accident" or "I've got some bad news," it's because I didn't need to. People need not share specific experiences to feel the same sinking sensation (just as shame may have different causes in different people yet *feels* the same to all, outlining collectivities of affect rather than of experience). The reason is that these sentences, and others of the same kind, are instantly recognizable for what they are: collectively shared markers of life-altering news. Alienating as they may be, they are first of all familiar statements—repetitions. One is *aware* that there has been a disaster only to the extent that one correctly identifies its common markers, be they linguistic signs or actual events that instantly fall into something like a discursive mold. The awareness of the disaster, in other words, is bound to the idea of community, and alienation is at the core of both.

The actual disaster, a kind of trauma, is itself unarticulated by definition. A classic, fictional example would be the case of Stendhal's Fabrizio, the protagonist of *La chartreuse de Parme*, who, in the midst of the chaos of Waterloo, is unable to perceive that a debacle of tremendous magnitude is happening around him, his whole world unraveling. More recently, one can think once more of Charlotte Delbo, when she notes, "It was almost impossible, later, to explain with words what was happening in that period of time when there were no words" (237 [*MJ* 13]). And in Jean-Claude Grumberg's play *L'atelier [The Workroom]*, set right after the Holocaust in a garment workshop, presumably in the Marais, survivors share their recollections and sorrows while life seems to go on uneventfully.[1] Simone, one of the workers in *L'atelier*, manages at long last to obtain from the French authorities the much-needed death certificate of her husband who was killed in Majdanek. But the document makes no mention of the death camp, stating instead that the man had died in the transit facility of Drancy outside Paris. Hélène, the boss, explodes in anger:

> In that case, no one went there, no one got into their boxcars, no one was burned; if they simply died in Drancy or Compiègne, or Pithiviers,[2] who'll remember them? Who'll remember them?
>
> . . .
>
> Why don't they just put down the truth? Why not put "thrown live into the flames"? Why not?
>
> . . .
>
> And how will her children know? They'll see "deceased in Drancy" and that's it? (203–204)

> [Alors personne n'est parti là-bas, personne n'est jamais monté dans leurs wagons, personne n'a été brûlé; s'ils sont tout simplement morts à Drancy, ou à Compiègne, ou à Pithiviers, qui se souviendra d'eux? Qui se souviendra d'eux?
>
> . . .
>
> Pourquoi ne pas mettre simplement la vérité? Pourquoi ne pas mettre: jeté vif dans les flammes? Pourquoi?
>
> . . .
>
> Et ses enfants comment ils sauront? Ils verront mort à Drancy et c'est tout? (52)]

To which Hélène's husband, Léon, replies, "Those who should know will never know; as for us, we know too much already, much too much" (204 [53]; translation modified). The remark emphasizes that the disaster remains unknowable as such and is framed only by lack or excess of knowledge. Such excess of knowledge is, in effect, what grounds the community expressed in Léon's "we"—an idea that echoes the closing poem of Delbo's volume tellingly titled *Une connaissance inutile [Useless Knowledge]*:

> I have returned
> from a world beyond knowledge
> and must now unlearn.
>
> (230)
>
> [Je reviens
> d'au-delà de la connaissance
> il faut maintenant désapprendre.]
>
> (*CI* 191)

Which came first, the disaster or the community, is a chicken-and-egg sort of question, for if a community emerges from the disaster it recognizes as such after the fact, a pre-existing sense of community is also necessary to understand that a disaster has taken place. In effect, community and disaster *realize* each other simultaneously. Take the AIDS crisis, for example, a historical event that has radically redefined what is understood today as a "gay community." There were, of course, forms of community before AIDS, but the epidemic has profoundly altered what it means to be gay, just as the Holocaust has transformed what it means to be Jewish and the slave trade what it means to be black. In France, the advent of the epidemic, or more accurately the belated *awareness* of its catastrophic dimensions, has effectively ushered in the community in its modern meanings and manifestations. The rise of the Marais, the throngs at gay pride marches, the PACS, the debates on homophobia, the official recognition of Nazi deportations of homosexuals, and so on, have been direct consequences of the awareness of AIDS as a *collective* catastrophe rather than as a mass of individual predicaments only connected by a virus. But ACT UP's central role as the initiator of a new kind of gay communitarian consciousness in France (one that admittedly drew on a network of bars, clubs, and other organizations) suggests that the consciousness it founded was already operative. *Thinking* of themselves as a community, French gays were already engaged in a form of community that could then develop an actual infrastructure, demand rights, and produce its own collective historiography as a means of legitimization after the fact. Simply put, a disaster cannot be understood as foundational until something has been founded. It is thus *collective* awareness that allowed AIDS to be defined as a founding disaster. As a result, disaster may precede community chronologically but it is also contained and remains extant within it. Like shame and self-hatred, it isn't external to or distinct from what it founds, as an early stage *out* of which it would be possible to grow. Disaster signals rather a concurrence of past and present, making community a matter of belated, *post factum* awareness, or what I would call in French, *conscience décalée.*

I'll return to this question later in terms less historically specific, but the topic of the deportations of homosexual men to concentration camps is worth lingering on a little. Neglected for decades by academics and politicians alike, this chapter in the history of Nazi persecutions began to be written with some degree of consistency and significance when visible gay communities had emerged in the West and in particular once the communitarian awareness of the AIDS crisis had finally taken hold in the late 1980s and early 1990s.[3] For one thing, there needed to be a community in place or at the very least in a process of self-formation for such historical research to take place. One of the reasons for that is simply economic. Research and publishing go hand in hand, the former depending on the existence of a potential market, that is, of a group of people who have at least once thing in common, which is an interest in buying the books. That "thing in common" is therefore a shared absence of knowledge, a blank space outlined by desire. In other words, a community of listeners is necessary for stories to be told, at the same time that collective storytelling, as utterance, delineates communities. The publication of scholarly and testimonial writings on the Holocaust, for example, plummeted in the late 1940s when readers, including Jews, showed little interest for them. It wasn't until Jewish communities reclaimed some form of collective standing in the 1960s that, in France and elsewhere, Holocaust scholarship began in earnest and the voices of witnesses started to be heard anew, including, sometimes, those of people who, like Charlotte Delbo or Jorge Semprum, were not, in fact, Jewish. In the case of homosexual men deported to the camps, the return was a far lonelier one since male homosexuality was almost universally stigmatized and, in the case of Germany, actually unlawful until 1969. As Pierre Seel, a gay man from Alsace who was arrested and deported by the Nazis, wrote in his 1994 memoir, "Liberation was only for others" (88 [110]).[4] The cultural recognition finally enjoyed by Jews and long denied to queers serves two related purposes: it inscribes a minority's specific history within national or world history and, by doing so, places the community itself within the nation and the world.

The role that AIDS played in the growing interest in gay deportations is more complex. The characterization of these deportations as a "gay Holocaust" has drawn intense criticism, especially in France, on the grounds that homosexual men, unlike "racials," were not marked for systematic annihilation and that linking homosexuals and Jews in this way trivializes the Holocaust.[5] I admit that I, too, often find this comparison problematic and, because I understand people's discomfort with it, I need to clarify a few points before going any further.

To claim that homosexual men were subjected to a policy of extermination is historically untrue. In fact, some of the men deported to concentration camps for homosexuality, and who managed to survive the particularly harsh treatment they received there, were set free, oftentimes after having been castrated. Yet, the criticism is sometimes specious for two reasons. To begin with, the term "Holocaust," or "Shoah" in France, is often indiscriminately applied in the culture at large to all the categories of deportees and to the entire Nazi concentration camp system without anyone being shocked, *shocked!* about it. In France, it was the term *déportation* that used to serve this all-encompassing purpose, but take a look now at the "Shoah" section of many bookstores and see what you find there. In addition, the criticism rests on the common but false premise that the two terms of a comparison must be connected by identity rather than difference. In fact, all tropes are premised on difference since one can only substitute one thing for *another*. For troping to happen, all that is required is that there be *one* point of contact (paradigmatic for a metaphor, syntagmatic for a metonymy, etc.) between two different words. Tropes, in other words, are relational devices. To claim that the Holocaust may not be used for troping is to imply that it is entirely self-identical and nonrelational, and this, in essence, is a fascist fantasy (as well as a convenient way to turn a blind eye to other crimes unfolding around us and to ignore our responsibilities). I would go as far, then, as stating that the Holocaust *must* be used for troping.

But more important, these condemnations, sometimes blatantly homophobic and sometimes not, miss the point altogether. To call the Nazi persecutions of homosexual men a gay Holocaust is, to a large extent, an indirect comment not on Nazi persecutions but on AIDS, as ACT UP clearly explained.[6] Given the emergency, the question to ask is not whether the comparison is morally acceptable in itself. Words do not have an inherent moral value; they don't even have an inherent meaning, only a differential one. What matters is whether and how the comparison works. (It is, after all, the ways the HIV/AIDS pandemic has been dealt with that have too often been morally unacceptable, not how those affected by it have been using language in order to survive.) Whether a trope works or not can only be determined in relation to its purpose, that is, to its extralinguistic outside and not to its inner workings or "mechanic" (the connection of its parts). For example, Paul Eluard's famous verse, "La Terre est bleue comme une orange" [The Earth is blue like an orange], works as surrealist poetry but it may be of little help at your local grocery store. The metonymy that, in the early years of the epidemic, sought to endow HIV-positive people with the qualities of the virus itself succeeded in withholding the solidarity of the so-called general public. The metaphor comparing the deportations of homosexual men to a Holocaust served to organize the HIV/AIDS community to fight against its possible destruction.

In his 1987 AIDS memoir, *Corps à corps [Mortal Embrace],* Alain Emmanuel Dreuilhe makes this point thanks to his ample use of Holocaust tropes to describe the daily experience of the disease in the early years of the epidemic. He likens AIDS to Hitler, Ronald Reagan to Pétain, his own writing to Anne Frank's diary, and AIDS sufferers to concentration camp inmates, as in this typical passage:

> Many had been struck down after a few weeks; some, like myself, have been lucky enough (if one can call lucky those prisoners in a concentration camp who weren't gassed right away) to see the passage of several seasons and to have survived some of the opportunistic diseases that prey on us. . . . The fallen all weigh the same, all wear the same AIDS mask and the same striped pajamas. (4)

> [Les uns étaient abattus en quelques semaines d'agonie, d'autres, comme moi, ont eu la chance—peut-on vraiment dire que les détenus des camps de concentration aient eu la chance de ne pas mourir tout de suite?—de voir passer plusieurs saisons et de survivre à certaines des maladies opportunistes qui s'acharnent sur nous. . . . Tous ceux qui tombent ont le même poids et portent le même masque sidatique, le même pyjama rayé. (12–13)]

Dreuilhe's book, an angry militant cry for community awareness and the first major text of its kind written for a French audience, may be read as one long allegory that brings together references to the two world wars, the American civil war, Vietnam, Algeria, and many other armed conflicts.[7] But it is his Holocaust imagery that truly allows him to illuminate the link between disaster and community.

Referencing the Holocaust in the context of the AIDS crisis could only be effective at the time of *Corps à corps*'s publication insofar as the specificity of the extermination of the Jews had finally entered French cultural discourses, a process that culminated with the 1985 release of *Shoah.* It comes as no surprise, then, that Dreuilhe should make direct mentions of Claude Lanzmann's landmark film. By doing so, he didn't simply compare AIDS and the Holocaust, but also automatically placed his call for an organized gay community in France alongside the collective recognition that French Jews had recently gained. The question of passive, genocidal complicity is absolutely central here:

In *Shoah*, Claude Lanzmann's film about the Holocaust, we see Polish peasants who still complain, even today, that the Jews in their village, gassed to death forty years before, had exploited them and had never worked with their hands. . . . Some heterosexuals resent the fact that homosexuals don't have to take on the same responsibilities as they do. . . . The hoariest cliché, even within liberal circles, had pre-AIDS gays thinking of nothing but dancing and making love, squandering their money on silly trifles. (35)

[Dans *Shoah*, ce film sur l'Holocauste, des paysans polonais reprochent, encore de nos jours, aux Juifs de leur village, gazés il y a quarante ans, de ne jamais avoir travaillé de leurs mains et de les avoir exploités. . . . Certains hétérosexuels en veulent aux homosexuels de ne pas avoir eu à assumer les mêmes responsabilités qu'eux. . . . D'après le cliché le plus répandu, même dans les milieux libéraux, les gays d'avant le SIDA ne pensaient qu'à faire l'amour et à danser, dépensant leur argent en futilités. (49–50)]

More explicitly even:

That's what the Jewish slave laborers in the camps thought too: the Gentile world had long since lost interest in their fate. Rounded up and transported, they had become invisible. Though I'm not one of those people who think that AIDS was created on purpose by someone somewhere, the fact remains that this epidemic was tolerated during at least the first two years by an entire society that believed itself safe from attack. (51)

[C'est ce que pensaient aussi les travailleurs juifs des camps: le monde des Gentils s'était depuis longtemps désintéressé de leur sort. Relégués, puis déportés, ils étaient devenus invisibles. Je ne suis pas de ceux qui pensent que le SIDA a été voulu par des hommes. Toujours est-il que cette épidémie a été tolérée pendant au moins ses deux premières années par toute une société qui se croyait à l'abri. (71–72)]

In these passages, the comparison between homophobia and anti-Semitism allows Dreuilhe to foreground some of the historical conditions that have made AIDS and the Holocaust possible. What his book exposes—and that's what makes his analogy disturbing to many—is that there is, at the core of liberal democratic societies, an unacknowledged fantasy of purity that brings them into uncomfortable closeness with fascism. Indeed, the accusation of fascism leveled in France at minority groups making community-based political claims is, in the end, nothing but an attempt to deflect attention—in a word, denial.

Dreuilhe's proposition, then, is that AIDS is to gay men what the Holocaust was to Jews. But more importantly, by summoning *Shoah*—an event of the 1980s—as well as the Shoah—an "event" of the 1940s—he is implying that the disaster of AIDS must be for queers in the future what the

Holocaust had become to the Jews, that is, a defining moment in the public affirmation of a heretofore privatized community. The trope—really an
injunction to emulate—may have scandalized many, but what it brings into
uneasy proximity is less historical disasters with arguably little in common
than two instances of something that ultimately remains unrepresentable as
such. The point of contact that authorizes a trope largely derided as excessive is, in the end, a lack or failure of representation—the necessary condition of tropes.[8]

What Dreuilhe's text and other AIDS memoirs have in common with
Holocaust and concentration camps testimonials is also the idea that community *in general* is premised on and inseparable from the demise of a self
conceived as singularity. And in the case of early AIDS testimonials, the
symbolic end of the self is accompanied by the actual death of their authors.[9] For Martine Delvaux, Dreuilhe's "I" thus takes form within the
space of a collective "we."[10] The transformation of the autonomous subject
(I) into one that acknowledges the community that enables it (we) is the
very condition of survival—although probably not his or her own:

> To survive, one must die to oneself and be reborn in a new incarnation of
> one's own making: aggressive, resolute, austere, and disciplined. Discipline is
> *our* only hope of survival. (92; my emphasis; translation modified)
>
> [Pour survivre, il faut mourir à soi-même et se façonner une autre mentalité,
> agressive et résolue, austère et disciplinée. C'èst *notre* seule chance de survivre,
> cette discipline. (118; my emphasis)]

As for Delbo, she writes of herself and her comrades waiting outside in the
freezing cold: "We have lost consciousness and feeling. We had died to ourselves" (35) ["Nous avions perdu conscience et sensibilité. Nous étions
mortes à nous-mêmes" (*ANR* 58)].[11] In both texts, Dreuilhe's and Delbo's,
the use of *soi-même* and *nous-mêmes* in relation to death implies that *sameness*
(*même*) can no longer be understood as a possible basis for the self (*soi*). What
allows witnesses to testify in the first person singular is the erasure of their
autonomous singularity and their redefinition as plural, that is, their self-
alienation. As Thomas Trezise concludes from his reading of Delbo, "What
I wish to suggest, then, is that 'particularity' be here understood to refer, not
to the status of separate and identical particulars, but rather to a *relationality*
that precedes and informs the identity of particulars as such, and only in doing so generates the universal as a condition of community."[12] If relational-
ity/alienation is the universal condition of the self, then the disastrous demise
of the self and its replacement with difference and community are "events"
occurring in succession only when it comes to one's *awareness* of them.

Disaster, I thus want to propose, is the origin of all communities and it, too, has a non-linear relation to time. Given that a community's existence depends on that of its boundaries, it necessarily requires the separation of an inside and an outside and is, therefore, always predicated on the invention, expulsion and loss of an other. The sense of loss, however, suggests that the disaster may never be left safely behind, nor the self separated from its own constitutive (but denied) alterity. In Maurice Blanchot's words, "the disaster always takes place after having taken place" (28 [50]). This is what I call the *disastrous realization*: the realization of community through disaster and the realization that there has been (present perfect, not preterit) a disaster. As a result, the impossibility of isolating the disaster from the present moment makes community inseparable from its own failure. If the purpose of an origin is to be simultaneously embraced and rejected, thus setting into motion a teleological narrative of growth and progress propelled by memory, the ongoing nature of the disaster—an origin that perpetually undoes what it founds—represents a failure to do either; the injunction to embrace annulling the injunction to reject, and vice versa. What follows the disaster is perpetual *ressassement*, a pointless repetition of the past. As Delbo's friend Mado says of her return from Auschwitz: "I'm not alive. I'm imprisoned in memories and repetitions" (261) ["Je ne suis pas vivante. Je suis enfermée dans des souvenirs et des redites" (*MJ* 54)], a fate she shares in one form or another with all her fellow returnees. The work of community, then, is essentially the same as Penelope's, unweaving at night what she had weaved during the day, forever postponing the future by refusing to move on and away from the loss of her companion, and, like the child in Freud's famous *fort-da* example, reliving that loss in the perpetual present of her work of undoing.

———

THAT, in essence, is what I meant in the opening of this book when I stated that my relationship with my father was a disaster and that, if it weren't for disaster, he and I wouldn't have had a relationship at all. It all boiled down to my own shortcomings, of course, or my lacks: my lack of heterosexuality and my lack of Jewishness that never really ceased to be disappointments to my father and sources of mutual alienation. Short of conversion (or cultural drag, depending on what you think a Jew is), I had very little say over the latter, however, since my mother is not Jewish. In that sense, it signals my father's failure as well as mine. (The compromise solution—I was circumcised by a nun in a Catholic clinic—seems to have satisfied no-one, although somebody may want to ask the nun.) But my homosexuality, an object of shame for both of us, was most certainly lived by my father as a failure on his part—the failure of *his* heterosexuality. Heterosexuality is a form of self-policing orthodoxy, that is, something one *must* live up to and, therefore, is always afraid of not being able to do.[13] My father thought he had failed as a father because he had raised a child who failed to become a father. This common failure manifested itself in a shared feeling that can only be described as gay shame. My father and I were both ashamed of *my* homosexuality. To frame this in terms of the question of asynchronicity as I developed it in the previous chapter, I could say that *my* lack of children was *his* loss. This is what is known in French as a *manque à gagner*, a failure that entails loss. Loss is a feeling normally experienced in the present when looking to the past, but in this case what connects past and present is the absence of a future—a peculiar experience of time I defined as queer.

If my father and I had had no relationship at all, none of this would have mattered much. But we *did* have a relationship, and it only began in a mutually satisfying fashion once I had come out to him. My proud gay brothers and sisters would doubtless see this as a result of my self-authenticity and the founding triumph of my relationship with my father. As you've already guessed, I don't see things quite that way. The blend of shame, grief, and loss that my father experienced was passed on to me, just as my queerness was passed on to him. The disastrous realization that affected us stemmed from the recognition that a gay son and a clumsy (rather than outright homophobic) father were in touch with one another and hopelessly loved each other, a very destabilizing feeling that went both ways. When my father told me, "I cannot be proud of your homosexuality," I thought, "I can't either. Welcome to the club!" Because the homo/hetero split is the source of homophobia, our respective sexualities were supposed to disconnect us from one another. In reality, our alienation, from ourselves as well as from each other, turned out to be the founding disaster of our relationship.

IN OTHER WORDS: NEIGHBORLY APPROXIMATIONS AND COMMUNITIES OF FAILURE

Most children of immigrants go more or less through the same experience: a mix of embarrassment and amusement at their relatives' mangling and mispronunciation of their new language. Whether we're embarrassed or amused by this depends, of course, on who's around to hear it. A relative's mistakes are only funny as private jokes, within the family, or a community of other immigrant families; they bother us when they fall on outsiders' ears, and even more so when the awkward-sounding relative is a parent. In private we're *in* on the joke; in public it makes us feel like outsiders. This is another example of the sort of social policing that the two spheres are designed to enforce.

My sister and I still laugh fondly at our father's attempts to sound, and be, French by mastering the most French and most awful form of humor there is—puns—only to fall just a little short because of his Hungarian accent. (It wasn't the puns that were funny, believe me. While there's no mention of them in Leviticus, there ought to be for they truly were an abomination.) And to this day, we still enjoy offering each other *un p'tit visky* for *apéro*. Like most social rituals, the French *apéro*—drinks and finger food before a meal—comes with its own set of colloquialisms. But even though, or *because*, our father was only slightly off, pronouncing a [v] for a [w], the minute mistake brought out his foreignness in even starker relief. Had his accent been impossibly thick and had he not attempted to sound so French, we would have had nothing to laugh about. What was funny was his approximations, the fact that he came so close to sounding perfect but could never quite make it, could never quite fit in.

In public, though, the linguistic shortcomings of one's parents may reflect poorly on their children's own ability to distance themselves from alien origins and find a "normal" place in the dominant culture. At the very least, reminders of a parent's stubborn foreignness further complicate the double injunction to embrace and reject one's origins. Frankly, I wasn't aware that my father had a foreign accent until my franco-French friends informed me that he did. I never stopped hearing it after that. Did that play a subtle (denied?) part in my decision to leave France and in turn become an accented foreigner myself? It's a safe bet that it did and that, if anything, it brought me closer to my father as I was putting a longer distance between us.

In his memoirs, *10 ans en 1938* [10 Years Old in 1938] and *Mon père l'étranger* [My Father the Foreigner], Maurice Rajsfus, the French-born son of Jewish immigrants from Poland, recalls the mix of hilarity and embarrassment with which he and his siblings greeted their elders' yiddishisms: "In private, the effect was often highly comical, but it could become embarrassing in public, for lack of a sense of humor, the Frenchy French being unable to bear seeing their language disfigured" (*10 ans* 35)]. In addition to syntactical errors, some mistakes involve mispronouncing certain sounds, such as the tricky *liaisons* or the dreaded French [y], or simply replacing a French word with a Yiddish one, or a combination of several such lapses. "*Du wilst* apple or *du wilst* banana?" ["*Dou wilst* à pom ou *dou wilsts* à banane?" (*10 ans/* 36)], asks an uncle when young Maurice visits him for an afternoon snack.

Rajsfus's father's attempts at speaking French as best he can reflect his frustrated desire to integrate. On his arrival in Paris, Nahoum (that's his name) decides not to settle in the Marais, for example, opting instead for the

Sedaine-Popincourt district, still a Jewish area, but not as traditionalist and religious as the Marais, and definitely not as Polish. Just as my father did, he reluctantly enters a so-called Jewish trade and, like my father, becomes a *marchand forain* selling garments at outdoors markets. That the word *forain* originally meant "foreign" only heightens the sad irony of his situation, making the very path to integration a reminder of foreignness. Soon, Nahoum begins to attend repertory plays at the Comédie française, the most French of all Parisian national theaters. Things don't always go smoothly, though, as he once tries to purchase a ticket for *Relâche*, misunderstanding the word for "recess" (*Mon père* 81). If trying to buy a ticket to a non-existent play was clearly a problem, some mistakes may have other, unintended consequences. Confusing the operetta *Véronique* with Racine's far more prestigious *Bérénice*, Nahoum accidentally discovers another form of French entertainment, only more "appropriate" perhaps to his lower station in life.

More seriously, when Nahoum, one day, asks passers-by for directions to the place de la Nation where a friend of his lives, he pronounces a [t] sound where there should have been [s]. As a result, he is met with baffled stares and cannot find the way to his friend's place (*Mon père* 78). It is symbolically significant, of course, that it is "nation" the well-meaning immigrant mispronounces and fails to find through no fault of his own. His earnest attempt to pronounce the word properly, in order (literally) to find a place in the city, singles him out as a foreigner and an outsider to the "nation" he's trying to reach. The anecdote takes on a tragic meaning, however, since readers know from the outset that the book tells the story of Nahoum's failure to obtain French citizenship, his arrest by the French police, and his death in a Nazi death camp.[14] Nahoum's place in the nation is what his son seeks to restore, but as an absence or ghostly presence, thus bringing into relief France's failure to live up to its much-vaunted powers of integration.

But the mispronunciation of street names and metro stations also serves the interests of immigrant communities. Rajsfus lovingly recalls how Jewish immigrants collectively renamed and appropriated the Parisian landscape in ways pronounceable and understandable by all members of the Yiddish-speaking community.

> The streets of Paris and the metro stations are subjected to a methodical havoc, an apparent hatchet job but really a practical adjustment to pronounce words that would otherwise be quite a mouthful. The boulevard Sébastopol thus becomes *Shabbés Tépou*. The metro station Barbès-Rochechouart is transformed into *Barbès-Rochechoune*. Yet another metro station, Havre-Caumartin, meets a more noble fate by becoming *Haver-Caumartin*.

[Les rues de Paris ou les stations de métro font l'objet d'un saccage en règle, véritable assassinat apparent mais adaptation pratique pour prononcer des mots qui obstruent le palais. Ainsi le boulevard Sébastopol devient *Shabbés Tèpou*. La station de métro Barbès-Rochechouart se transforme en *Barbès-Rochechoune*. Une autre station de métro, Havre-Caumartin, subit un sort plus noble en devenant *Haver-Caumartin*. (*10 ans* 36–37)]

(A few words of explanation: *Shabbés Tèpou* translates as "the little Saturday pot"; *Rochechoune* is a version of "Rosh Hashanah"; and *Haver* means "comrade."[15]) Collectively accepted "mistakes" and acknowledgments of shared failure, the Yiddish or Hebrew rechristening (so to speak) of French names represents the community's tactic for finding its place in public space—again literally—by remapping the city for their own purposes. In a way, the immigrants familiarize themselves with an alien environment by making it foreign like them. By doing so, they not only forge a unique diasporic parlance for themselves, but also bring immigrant and host cultures closer to one another without reducing the defining singularity of each in relation to the other. Simply put, linguistic approximation emphasizes the neighborly nature of diaspora.

In her own memoir, *Ce que j'ai cru comprendre* [What I Believe I Understood], Annie Kriegel evokes a similar phenomenon, albeit in cultural rather than linguistic terms since her family descends from French, and francophone, Alsatian Jews displaced by the German annexation of 1870 and settled in the Marais. Staunchly secular and steeped in French universalist values, Kriegel's parents nonetheless found ways to claim and downplay their Jewishness at the same time. Years later their daughter recalls their lives with delicate irony—the ideal trope for ambiguous feelings:

> There was, at our home, no religious practice at all, not even residual. *With one single exception, however:* the boys were circumcised at birth. *But* the religious dimension of the act was disguised and rationalized: circumcision was accounted a hygienic precaution. (My emphasis)
>
> [Il n'y avait chez nous aucune pratique religieuse, si résiduelle soit-elle. *A l'exception cependant* d'une seule: les garçons furent circoncis à la naissance. La dimension religieuse de la chose était *toutefois* déguisée et rationalisée: la circoncision passait pour une précaution d'hygiène. (48; my emphasis)]

Note how reason, in the name of which Jews were emancipated, is presented here as a disguise. And also:

> My mother didn't respect dietary prohibitions, *although* she kept cooking with oil, a last remnant of the ancient injunction: "Thou shalt not cook the lamb in

its mother's milk." Similarly, meat was reserved for lunches, when there was no
cheese, while dairy products made up the basis of our dinners. (My emphasis)

[Ma mère ne respectait pas les interdits alimentaires, *encore qu*'elle continuât à
faire la cuisine à l'huile, ultime trace de l'antique injonction: "Tu ne cuiras pas
l'agneau dans le lait de sa mère." Elle réservait de même la viande pour le repas
de midi où ne figurait aucun fromage tandis que les laitages constituaient le
fond du repas du soir. (48–49; my emphasis)]

And later:

We celebrated neither the Shabbat nor the holidays. Not even the Day of
Atonement (Yom Kippur). *Although* my father (consciously?) chose not to be
on the road on Saturdays. The English workweek, however, hadn't yet been in-
stituted and his customers would have been happy to see him on those days. As
for my mother . . . she never failed, in a neutral but insistent tone, to bring our
attention to the Jewish New Year: "Children, *if* we were practicing, today
would be Rosh Hashanah." (My emphasis)

[Nous ne sanctifions [*sic*] ni le *Shabbat* ni les jours de fête. Pas même le Grand
Pardon (Yom Kippour). *Encore que* mon père (consciemment?) eût choisi de
n'être pas sur les routes le samedi. Pourtant, la semaine anglaise n'était pas encore instituée et ses clients auraient volontiers reçu sa visite ce jour-là. De son
côté ma mère . . . ne manquait pas, d'un ton neutre mais insistant, de remar-
quer à notre intention le 1er de l'an juif: "Mes enfants, *si* nous étions prati-
quants, aujourd'hui ce serait *Roch Hachana*." (49; my emphasis except for
Hebrew words)]

Kriegel's father was a traveling salesman, not quite a *marchand forain* but not
grounded in a store either. And as is the custom in Alsace, the children received gifts on Saint Nicholas Day—a convenient way for the family to
avoid both Christmas and Hanukkah while celebrating the holidays all the
same. And if they went for a stroll in the woods on Sundays, they would go
early and head home just before Christian families started arriving after
mass. As for the main synagogue by the place des Vosges, they would only
go there to drop off old clothes for the poor—a civic duty, not a religious
one. Similarly, the Kriegels' devotion to studies and respect for the laws
blended Jewish and republican principles, with books standing for the Book
(51) and laws for the Law (58).

As Kriegel's many "exceptions" and "ifs" and "althoughs" indicate, what
she recognizes as a "subterfuge" was a way for the family to have their strudel
and eat it too, a defining practice of diasporic cultures. She notes that

this slight discrepancy was decisively instrumental in making us feel different
without having to explicitly define and localize the substance of that difference.

[ce décalage subtil contribua de manière décisive à nous donner le sentiment que nous étions différents sans que la substance de cette différence fût explicitement définie et localisée. (49)]

Yet their

> sense of belonging to the Jewish world was first inscribed, as it should be, in space, within the boundaries of a territory. . . . Is it necessary to go so far as to say that it was . . . an extended and flexible version of an original ghetto?" The answer of course: "Yes and no."
>
> [Notre appartenance au monde juif s'inscrivait d'abord, comme il se doit, dans l'espace, par la délimitation d'un territoire. . . . Faut-il pousser la chose jusqu'à dire qu'il était . . . la version élargie et assouplie d'un ghetto originel? Oui et non. (67)]

The family's attachment to the Marais, lovingly described in Kriegel's memoir, is very telling in that it represents a neighborly mode of communitarian localization that need not rely on stable, definable identities and origins. It is the sort of territorialization that deterritorializes. The neighborhood thus provides an apt figure along which to form communities of nearness, bringing together Kriegel's slight cultural discrepancies and Rajsfus's linguistic shortcomings. Both are modes of concurrence of past and present and ways of engaging (in) the dominant culture without having to relinquish difference or singularity.

That Rajsfus chose to entitle his chapter on approximations "Yiddishisms of Yesteryear" was probably intended to remind his readers that Yiddish culture in Paris has been wiped out by the storm that took his father. But I believe it points to something more. To be sure, a foreigner's mistakes are traces of his or her past—a kind of survival—but by definition they can only take place in the present and away from the "home" country.[16] In other words, yiddishisms, like survival, are always of the past and of the present at the same time. In fact, the same could be said of Yiddish itself. Germanic in its spoken form and Hebraic in writing, it, too, encompasses origin and destination, revealing past and present to be concurrent rather than successive. In the end, Yiddish (the already impure source) and yiddishisms (the relational or neighborly trace) may be difficult to disentangle. Failures of language thus bring out the more fundamental failure to sever the link with one's origin just as it testifies to one's distance from it.

Furthermore, as Rajsfus reminds us, immigrants with different native tongues manage to understand each other as well. His mother, one day, explains to an impatient and xenophobic French woman whose stand is next to her own at the market what a heavily accented customer is trying to ask. Rajsfus reads the episode as follows:

> Furtive solidarity of immigrants who always understand each other, even
> though they may not mangle in the same way the language of those who can-
> not tolerate the fact that foreigners have a difficult time speaking in a polished
> language that *the French themselves often do not know*. (My emphasis)
>
> [Solidarité furtive des immigrés qui se comprennent toujours, même s'ils ne dé-
> forment pas de la même façon la langue de ceux qui ne peuvent tolérer que les
> étrangers éprouvent quelque difficulté à s'exprimer dans ce français châtié *qu'ils
> ignorent souvent eux-mêmes*. (*Mon père* 113–14; my emphasis)]

What brings people together, if only for a furtive moment without a future,
is less a common language, whose mastery ultimately eludes everyone in
any case, than the very fact that they *all* get it wrong—their common fail-
ure/alienation, in other words. And as Rajsfus's comment emphasizes, this
applies to the hosts as well. The difference between the natives and their diasporic counterparts is that the former must be in denial of their own defi-
ciencies and limitations (their finitude, as Jean-Luc Nancy would put it) if
they are to exclude the latter on the basis of language use. That very denial,
Rajsfus suggests, is a root cause of xenophobia and, in the case of Nahoum
and other "foreign" Jews, underscores the common genocidal nature of desires for linguistic and racial purity.

What I find especially important in this episode is that a foreigner's errors
also expose the failure of the dominant culture and its own impure, relational, neighborly nature. Those colloquialisms my father enjoyed so much,
don't the French have to learn them too, making mistakes along the way?
Aren't lame puns called *approximatifs* in French? But aren't successful ones
also linguistic misappropriations in their own right? Our own language may
feel natural to us, giving us the sense that we naturally belong to the community it outlines and that those whose slips are different from ours are alien
to it. But no language is natural, obviously, and if even native speakers make
mistakes, language can only be alien and alienating by definition. In that
sense, approximations should be understood, as it were, in the full etymological sense of the term—from the latin *ad proximare*, to come near. Linguistic and cultural approximations outline communities of people who use
them for internal purposes; they bring immigrants closer to the culture
whose language they approximate but fail to reproduce faithfully; and they
bring people into contact with those who approximate in different ways, including the hosts themselves who, logically, also come nearer to those who
fail. My father's linguistic approximations encapsulated his position in relation to French culture but also French culture's relation to him. If the feeling of naturalness is what characterizes the situation of native speakers, it

merely masks the fact that they, too, are neighbors to themselves. Ultimately, a foreigner's failed attempts to reproduce the host's language—his or her capacity only to come near it—reveal that dominant cultures are really approximations of themselves and fall short of their own imagined purity. Accepting and sharing failures may be a sensible way to deal with a predicament one may have no control over, but it also defines communities in terms of difference and self-alienation, that is, as relation rather than sameness. Neighborliness, *in other words*, is a universal.

BACK TO AUSCHWITZ: CHARLOTTE DELBO
AND THE FAILURE OF THE FAMILY

In her trilogy *Auschwitz et après*, Charlotte Delbo often describes the bonds between her fellow inmates in Auschwitz-Birkenau and Ravensbrück with familial metaphors or with indirect references to family relationships. Looking to maintain a functioning collective entity—a community—designed to increase the chances of survival and return of its members, the women act as sisters, mothers, and daughters for one another, providing care, sustenance, and physical and psychological warmth. "Take care of yourself," Lulu tells Charlotte (72 *[ANR* 119]). "What's the matter with you? Are you ill? . . . That's nothing. You'll get over it" (104 *[ANR* 166–67]). "Be good," Carmen tells her (143 *[CI* 45]). "Eat. You've got to eat," says another, "Try" (73 *[ANR,* 120]). Charlotte gets scolded and encouraged by Viva and "it's my mother's voice I hear. The voice grows hard: 'Keep your chin up! On your feet!' And I feel that I cling to Viva as a child to its mother" (65 *[ANR* 106]). Lulu comforts her. "It is as though I had wept against my mother's breast" (105 *[ANR* 168]). And they all look after grand'mère Yvonne (38 *[ANR* 63]) who isn't anyone's grandmother and is therefore everyone's. Ultimately, the community of women becomes metaphorically related by blood during one of these endless morning roll calls on a frigid morning: "Backs to chests, we stand pressed against each other, yet, as we establish a single circulatory system, we remain frozen through and through" (63 *[ANR* 103]). But the roles are rarely fixed, as each woman may find herself playing the protective role, less out of personal motherly disposition than as a response adapted to specific situations and to the needs of others.

The familial metaphors (and I'm using the term metaphor loosely to mean a variety of textual tropes as well as actual instances of role-playing and simulacrum) seek to fulfill more than the urgent needs of individual inmates in given life-or-death situations. The purpose of the camps—one of

their purposes, at least—was to reduce human beings to their most basic animal dimensions—what Giorgio Agamben has called "bare life."[17] Reclaiming
and sustaining a framework, any framework, of social relations within the
dehumanizing world of the camps was intended to reclaim and sustain humanity, a humanity now defined as relational as opposed to a system that
pushed individuals to care only for their own immediate survival. In that
sense, the elemental fight for life in the camps was supposed to be a logical
extension of the Nazis' notions of essentialized identities and *Lebensraum*
policy: both systems—Nazism and the camps—are about animalistic survival. As we shall see, familial metaphors also allowed the inmates to maintain a connection with the past, that is to say, with time itself in a context
where time seemed to have stopped, where past lives had vanished forever
and the future had become, for all practical purposes, an impossibility.

As we know from testimonial narratives of the camps written by men (the
writings of Jorge Semprun and especially Robert Antelme come to mind, as
far as French-language testimonials are concerned), communist networking,
national origin or basic camaraderie often provided them with the necessary
models of group solidarity. But to rely on a model of social relations familiar
to all in one form or another—the family—promotes a more universal type
of community, one that tends to be less susceptible to the discontinuities of
nationality, politics, class, religion, age and, in some instances, gender. And it
should come as no surprise that the family metaphor was favored by women
rather than men.[18] While the latter sometimes use the trope of brotherhood,
and Delbo most commonly refers to her fellow inmates as *camarades*, a dual-
gender noun, male inmates tended to rely on relational frameworks associated with the (masculine) public sphere. The family, to the contrary, pertains
to the private sphere and, as such, provided women with a readily available
model—even those women whose political and Resistance activities may
have disrupted the traditional gender roles so prevalent at the time and landed
them in Birkenau and Ravensbrück in the first place.

Indeed, the women in Delbo's story often attempt to recapture elements
of femininity, and they do so in ways that appear, at first glance, perfectly
traditional. They give moral comfort to the men, for example, and they care
about their looks when it is at all possible, sometimes concocting their own
make up. In one passage, a group of women, out of the camp on a work detail, takes shelter from the rain in an abandoned house. Soon, they start
wondering aloud how they would furnish and decorate the empty rooms:

> "If it were up to me, I'd put a sofa here, near the fireplace."—"Country-style
> draperies would look nice. You know, a nice chintz." The house bedecks itself
> with all its comfortable, familiar pieces of furniture, polished by time. (77)

["Moi, je mettrais un divan ici près de la cheminée."—"Des rideaux rustiques feraient bien. Vous savez, ces toiles de Jouy." La maison se pare de tous ses meubles, patinés, confortables, familiers. (*ANR*, 127)]

And Delbo concludes, "The house has grown warm, lived in [habitée]. We feel good. We look at the rain, hoping it will last till evening" (78 [127]). The French "habitée," however, also means "haunted" or "possessed," and not just "lived in," which makes the simulacrum even more uncanny and suggests that, should these women ever return, it would be as ghosts.

I will allude to this episode again later. For now I will offer it next to a brief poem that appears near the beginning of the same volume, the first of the trilogy:

> My mother
> She was hands, a face
> They made our mothers strip in front of us
> Here mothers are no longer mothers to their children.
> (12)

> [Ma mère
> c'était des mains un visage
> Ils ont mis nos mères nues devant nous
> Ici les mères ne sont plus mères à leurs enfants.
> (*ANR* 23)]

And a few pages earlier, Delbo tells of Jewish families undressing and entering the gas chambers made to look like shower rooms. Mothers take off their children's clothes, then their own,

> and when the men enter the shower room through another door, stark naked, the women hide their children against their bodies. Perhaps at that moment all of them understand. (8)

> [et quand les hommes par une autre porte entrent dans la salle de douche nus aussi elles cachent leurs enfants contre elles. Et peut-être alors tous comprennent-ils. (*ANR* 16–17)]

More than the dehumanizing effect of the lack of privacy, these passages show how the family, along with the private sphere to which it is associated, is rendered inoperative by forced collective nakedness. Family members may actually be together, but their nakedness strips them, also, of their bond—"Here mothers are no longer mothers to their children." In the case of the Jewish families, Delbo imagines that it is the moment they understand that they are about to die. To reclaim the private sphere, as the women do by acting out stereotypical gender roles immediately accessible and shared by all, is thus a tactical way to stay alive by maintaining a social bond and their very humanity.

In the opening section of the second volume, Delbo recounts her stay at the Romainville prison before being deported to Auschwitz. She describes how the men there felt deprived of their manhood because they were no longer in control and could not protect the women.

> They experience the sting of the decline of strength and manly duty since they could do nothing for the women. If we suffered seeing them unhappy, hungry, deprived, they did even more so, realizing their inability to protect and defend us, to assume their destiny on their own. (117)

> [Ils éprouvaient, plus aigu que tout autre, le sentiment d'être diminués dans leur force et dans leur devoir d'hommes, parce qu'ils ne pouvaient rien pour les femmes. Si nous souffrions de les voir malheureux, affamés, dénués, ils souf-fraient davantage encore de ne plus être en mesure de nous protéger, de nous défendre, de ne plus assumer seuls le destin. (*CI* 10)]

Notice the common etymology of *dénué* and *dénudé* and the powerlessness they both signify in this context, linking once more nakedness and failure.

Soon, the women's resourcefulness *as women* has unexpected conse-quences on the traditional distribution of gender roles:

> On the other hand, the men *tried* to seem casual, as though life still followed a normal course. They *attempted* to be helpful, *wondering* what they might do. Alas! The wretchedness of the men's situation precluded any *expectations* on the women's part. Although their distress was just as great, the women still had some resources, those always possessed by women. They could do the wash, mend the only shirt, now in tatters, the men wore the day of their arrest, cut up blan-kets to make slippers. They deprived themselves of a portion of bread to give it to the men. A man must eat more. (118; translation modified; my emphasis)

> [Les hommes, de leur côté, *s'efforçaient* au naturel quotidien. Ils *s'ingéniaient* à nous être utiles, *cherchaient* quels services ils pourraient nous rendre. Hélas! Dans la détresse matérielle où ils étaient, il n'y avait rien que pussent leur *demander* les femmes. Celles-ci, dans une détresse tout aussi grande, avaient encore des ressources, les ressources qu'ont toujours les femmes. Elles pouvaient laver le linge, raccommoder l'unique chemise maintenant en loques qu'ils portaient le jour de leur arrestation, couper dans les couvertures pour leur confectionner des chaussons. Elles se privaient d'une partie de leur pain pour la leur donner. Un homme doit manger davantage. (*CI* 11; my emphasis)]

While the men are reduced to the pretense of being men, acting out their role "for nothing" ("s'efforcaient," "s'ingéniaient," "cherchaient"), the women have, in effect, become the real providers, no longer asking but giving. Their typical "feminine" skills—the very same ones, I can't help but notice, that my father possessed as a tailor and, for a while, contributed to his relative well-being as a war prisoner—are now the source of their strength, while the men's power has all but evaporated. And the dissolution of power relations is ultimately what will happen, after the war, to the family as institution.

The final volume of Delbo's trilogy deals with the return from the camps. Most of the women whose stories are told here either rejoin their families or start new ones. Whatever the case may be, something always seems amiss. The women seldom manage to find their place in the family. Their marriages fail; they become alienated from their parents; they cannot relate to their own children according to traditional expectations. They fail as wives, as daughters, as mothers. For these women, in other words, the family proper didn't survive its tactical metaphorization in Auschwitz. What had once served so efficiently as a life line was no longer operative for the survivors.

Gilberte, in a transit facility in Paris, is terrified at the idea of returning home to Bordeaux to confront her father because her younger sister Andrée didn't make it: "And my father will think: 'And Andrée? What have you done with Andrée?'" (246 [*MJ* 29]; translation modified). The sentence is a transparent allusion to the story of Cain and Abel (perhaps mediated by Victor Hugo's rendition of Cain's hopeless wandering in his famous poem "La conscience,", given that canonical French literature provides Delbo's writing with a more common set of references than the Bible).[19] "And my father will think" echoes the common biblical phrase "And God said," while "What have you done with Andrée?" recalls "What have you done with your brother?" What makes this particularly uncomfortable for the reader is the implication that Gilberte fears being perceived as her sister's murderer by a vengeful, God-like father. Or worse, that she actually perceives herself that way. But what the passage also alludes to is that Gilberte's future, just like Cain's in Hugo's poem, may be one of perpetual departures and endless, aimless wandering. Indeed so it turned out, or rather that was how it felt to her. As she tells Charlotte,

> I had to live elsewhere, leave the house where Dédée was born, where I had brought her up. Everything was wrenching. Settle down somewhere. . . . I'm not settled. (253; translation modified)

> [J'ai dû m'installer dans une autre maison. Quitter la maison où Dédée était née, où je l'avais élevée, tout était déchirement. M'installer ailleurs. . . . Je ne suis pas installée. (40)]

With the death of her sister, whom Gilberte had raised like a mother, filiation ceases to work. (She never had a child.) In the context of the return from the camps, the family no longer functions either as a recoverable origin or as projection into the future. Life and survival are not exactly the same thing. When asked by a fellow returnee, "Where are you from?" she spontaneously tells him, "Auschwitz" (245 [28]); to which he replies, "I've returned from Mauthausen, but that's not what I was asking you." For the rest of her story she never names the man, only referring to him as "the comrade from Mauthausen." The phrase encapsulates both the camps as the disastrous origin that can neither be embraced nor rejected and the only valid form of sociality now available to the returnees—friendship. As Andrée's death is equated with the deaths of others, the family as origin has now been displaced by the camps and the group of friends that formed there:

> I could have shed endless tears after Dédée's death. After the death of Viva, of Grandma Yvonne, of all our companions from Bordeaux, those who had been imprisoned with Dédée and me *since the beginning*. (247; my emphasis)

> [Que de larmes j'aurais pu verser à la mort de Dédée. A la mort de Viva, à la mort de grand'mère Yvonne, à la mort de toutes nos Bordelaises, celles qui avaient étaient emprisonnées avec Dédée et moi *depuis le début*. (31; my emphasis)]

The actual sister has become one among a group of friends.
    Mado, another friend, remarks,

> Our past was our lifeline and reassurance. But since I came back, everything I was before, all my memories from that earlier time, have dissolved, come undone. It is as though my past had been used up over there. Nothing remains of what was before. (258)

> [Notre passé nous a été sauvegarde et rassurance. Et depuis que je suis rentrée, tout ce que j'étais avant, tous mes souvenirs d'avant, tout s'est dissout, défait. On dirait que je l'ai usé là-bas. D'avant, il ne me reste rien. (*MJ*, 50)]

And she immediately adds,

> My real sister is you. My true family is you, those who were there with me. Today, my memories, my past are over there. When I project my thought backward they never overstep these bounds. They butt against this milestone. (258–59; translation modified)

> [Ma vraie soeur, c'est toi. Ma vraie famille, c'est vous, ceux qui étaient là-bas avec moi. Aujourd'hui, mes souvenirs, mon passé, c'est là-bas. Mes retours en arrière ne franchissent jamais cette borne. Ils y butent.]

She then describes how, at the birth of her son, she found herself transported back to the camp and how the ghosts of her comrades left childless suddenly appeared to her. More shockingly perhaps, she likens her baby to a newborn child they once saw in Auschwitz, frozen to death between the legs of its dead mother:

> The silky water of my joy changed to sticky mud, sooty snow, fetid marshes. I saw again this woman—you remember this peasant woman, lying in the snow, dead, with her dead newborn baby frozen between her thighs. My son was also that newborn child. I look at my son and I recognize Jackie's eyes, Yvonne's pout, Mounette's inflection. My son is their son, he belongs to all of them. (261–62; translation modified)

> [L'eau soyeuse de ma joie s'est changée en boue gluante, en neige souillée, en marécage fétide. Je revoyais cette femme—tu te souviens, cette paysanne, couchée dans la neige, morte, avec son nouveau-né mort, gelé entre ses cuisses. Mon fils était aussi ce nouveau-né là. Je regarde mon fils et je lui reconnais les yeux de Jackie, le bleu-vert des yeux de Jackie, une moue d'Yvonne, une inflexion de Mounette. Mon fils est leur fils à toutes. (55–56)]

In the camps, family as metaphor resulted in and from the creation of a group of friends. When Mado says that her relations to others are now reduced to pretending (263) ["faire semblant" (58)], she acknowledges the reversal that has taken place: the actual family is a pretense and the pretend family has become the true one—"My true family is you."

The story of Marie-Louise provides an interesting addendum to that of Mado. Marie-Louise rejoined her husband Pierre when she returned and, after a tough period of readjustment, managed to reconstruct her life. In his eagerness to be supportive of his wife, Pierre developed such an interest in her experience that he effectively made himself something like an honorary member of the group. He greets Charlotte, whom he has only heard of, with a cheerful "I've known you a long time" (281 [88]), and the reader cannot help but cringe a little. What right does he have to act as though he had been to Auschwitz? And how can Marie-Louise put up with it? Delbo, as narrator, keeps her distance. Up until then and, in fact, in the entire third volume, she writes either as herself or assuming the voice of her comrades in the first person and without quotation marks, thus emphasizing the relation of intimacy between self and other, the individual and the collective. When she recounts the story of Marie-Louise, however, the section is written in the third person and Marie-Louise's words appear in quotation marks. Her normalcy, thus bracketed, is made to appear odd. Or is it that whereas the women's simulacrum of the family in Auschwitz served as a defense against radical alienation, Pierre's own simulacrum now alienates Charlotte? The couple's home may be warm and welcoming, but she clearly feels out of place there. When she takes her leave and Pierre tells her, "Charlotte, you know that this is your home" (288 [99]), the remark takes on darkly ironic overtones. Delbo adds, "I left them ["Je les ai laissés] standing on the threshold of their pretty house"; and the verb *laisser*, usually a simple synonym for *partir*, to leave, in similar contexts (as in "Je vous laisse"), conveys here a far more drastic departure.

Yet the oddness of Marie-Louise and Pierre's normal home may also be a powerful marker of the survivors' inability to inhabit their future other than in the mode of haunting suggested by the double meaning of the French "habiter." In that sense, the descriptions of domestic life in this section could also be read as an eerie echo of the mock decoration of the empty house at the end of the first volume. Either way, home, Delbo tells us, does not work. But why? Why has a social model that had proved so useful— literally vital—in Auschwitz suddenly become inoperative afterward? Why was it embraced in the camps for its familiarity and availability only to become radically alien and out of reach after the liberation?

A passage from another book, by another survivor named Odette Elina, a French Jewish woman, begins to shed light on this question. The scene is made especially horrific by its surreal quality. One day, Elina recounts, one hundred women are ordered to push one hundred empty baby carriages from Birkenau, where the exterminations took place, to Auschwitz:

> There were all kinds. Big ones, low ones, old ones, modern ones, pretty ones, poor ones. But all were still warm with the babies they had sheltered and that had just been burned.
> The pillows had kept the shape of the little heads. Here and there hung a bonnet, a blanket, a bib.
> For this sinister journey, one hundred women had been used.
> One hundred women who were themselves mothers or could have been.
> One hundred women whose motherhood could have been the purpose of their lives.
> One hundred women shivered in horror at the touch of the softest of things.
> One hundred women plumbed the depths of distress and hopelessness.
>
> [Il y en avait de toutes sortes. Des grandes, des basses, des vieilles, des modernes, des belles, des pauvres. Mais toutes étaient encore chaudes du bébé qu'elles avaient abrité et qui venait d'être brûlé.
> Les oreillers avaient gardé la forme des petits crânes. Ça et là pendait un bonnet, une couverture, un bavoir.
> Pour faire ce sinistre trajet, on avait pris cent femmes.
> Cent femmes qui étaient mères ou qui auraient pu l'être.
> Cent femmes dont la maternité eût pu être la raison de vivre.
> Cent femmes ont tremblé d'horreur au contact d'une chose qui est douce entre toutes.
> Cent femmes ont touché le fond de la détresse et du désespoir. (21–22)]

At one level, this grotesque mass pantomime of motherhood looks like an odious pastiche of the Nazis' "perfect" community—just as the piles of corpses and stolen objects discovered in the camps echoed, as their murderous flipside, the mass rallies at Nuremberg and revealed their inhuman underpinnings. Indeed, in the aftermath of Auschwitz and the entire system of Nazi concentration camps, certain images have become inescapably tainted. Chimney stacks, trains, and most of all piles of personal belongings often provoke discomfort and even revulsion. Claude Lanzmann, in *Shoah*, was able to channel such reactions with unsettling results, emphasizing the Holocaust's stubborn presence across the contemporary European landscape without resorting to archival footage. In the culture at large, these effects have, of course, been largely attenuated by now, and I know that when images of abundance make me queasy I'm beginning to show my age. Or maybe it is an uncanny manifestation of the overlapping of my family's history with History—the point of contact where personal and historical memories meet, often with devastating consequences. Still, the image of the pile of human hair in Alain Resnais's *Nuit et brouillard* [*Night and Fog*] always has a tremendous impact on my undergraduate students. They just cannot get it out of their minds, and I'm glad.

But at another level, because this passage of Elina's book is about babies, it cannot but foreground the question of the future. The scene begins and ends with the women, whose sheer number (probably not exact and for that reason indicative of a deeper symbolic meaning, hence its repetition) points toward systematization—the systematization that was the Holocaust itself and the systemic consequences of its aftermath. The focus then moves to the baby carriages and, after that, to the absent babies. First we are told that they have just been burned. Then they are alluded to as traces inside the carriages—"The pillows had kept the shape of the little heads." Finally, we return to the women. The structure of the complete passage thus appears to be circular: the women, the carriages, the babies, the carriages, the women. But folded onto itself in the middle and hinging on the babies' death, this scene, a simulacrum of maternity, reveals a lack where there used to be a promise. When they recur, the carriages now bear traces of the absent, while the women have effectively become childless—regardless of whether or not some of them may have in fact survived and had children. If they did, one can speculate that they must have felt something akin to what Mado describes. The future is a baby frozen to death. And without babies, there are no mothers. Abolish the future and you erase origins. The death of the family in Auschwitz, I want to suggest, ushers in a different notion of time and, with it, a different notion of community.

In Western culture, the family is an institution. (Of course, it has been institutionalized in one form or another by most cultures, but Western culture is my focus here.) Like all institutions it has a dual purpose. It seeks to organize and regulate modes of collective life. That is to say, it shows us how to be together through imitation. But, being a model, its primary goal (and this is how institutions differ from other kinds of social relationality) is self-perpetuation. The family as institution, particularly in our post-Enlightenment modernity, naturalizes itself by internalizing compulsory perpetuation within each individual family it encompasses. It thus becomes the institution on which all institutions rest. The family, in a sense, works as a synecdoche, standing for and containing society as a whole. This explains why the family has served as the most fundamental structuring trope for thinking the question of community—whether we imagine community as contract or as sameness.[20]

The idea of perpetuation inscribes time within community. It implies a past (an origin, an ancestry, a history) and a future. Both past and future must be linked by a coherent narrative of development designed to unify the community in the present.[21] Modernity's relationship with its past, I have argued before, is thus one of simultaneous embrace and rejection. We embrace the past because it is the condition of our existence and because our recreation of it as origin brings us coherence in hindsight; we reject it because we find ourselves trapped by our obligation to progress, to improve, to better ourselves. This is the internal logic of modernity as unfinished project. Consider, for example, how France in the early years of the Third Republic sought to stabilize itself after a century of political turmoil by rejecting the familial, non-contractual definition of pre-Revolutionary society and, at the same time, produced an overarching national narrative that went back to ancient Gaul and embraced everything in between, *including* the discarded Ancien Régime. Think of the once famous children's book *L'Histoire de France racontée à deux enfants* [French History as Told to Two Children], in which the story-teller, or history-teller, is a 2,000-year-old Gaul, who represents something like the father of French nationhood. Perpetuation, then, implies change and continuity at the same time.

But in the context of the camps time no longer functions as an unbroken line bringing together past, present, and future. Delbo's comrades often talk about the future, usually imagining their return in great detail, but only as a trick to maintain their will to live because "Those who had stopped believing they would return were dead" (102 [*ANR* 162]; translation modified). However, should anyone ask, "How do you envision getting out?" the disruption of linear time becomes apparent: "[W]e let the question sink in silence." The moment of articulation between the present and the future cannot be imagined, at least not credibly enough to allow the visions of the future to play the trick: "The more detailed her description, the less we were able to believe it" (102 [162]). Where there used to be a link there is now a hole where questions fall silent. Thus disconnected from the present, visions of the future are the stuff of madness. "[O]ur impossible plans were as logical as the words of madmen" (translation modified). Put differently, there may be an after to Auschwitz, as the title of the trilogy implies, but in this case an after is not the same thing as a future insofar as it doesn't have a narrative (causal, logical) relationship to what comes before. This is what Ross Chambers, in *Untimely Interventions*, calls "*aftermath*, the state of perpetually surviving a trauma that is never over" (43; original emphasis).

In a section entitled "Springtime," the season of rebirth and renewal so often celebrated as a return, Delbo depicts the women as if they were rehearsing their deaths:

> all these women . . . were rehearsing the scene of their death on the next day—or close to it for they were to die the next day or close to it. (110)
>
> [toutes ces femmes . . . répétaient la scène qu'elles mourraient le lendemain—ou un jour tout proche car elles mourraient le lendemain ou un jour tout proche. (*ANR*, 176)]

Because of the bitter contrast between its title and the disruption of the cycle of life that it tells, this section reads like an echo of Elina's story of the empty baby carriages, with its equally disturbing heading, "One Sunday in May." And nowhere is the abolition of the future so directly expressed as in the title of the first volume, *Aucun de nous ne reviendra* [*None of Us Will Return*]—even if that very phrase was written by someone who *did* return to write it. Within the perpetual present of the camps, time begins and ends each day—an experience of time that characterizes community as I understand it.

Early in that book, a poem figures in a series of brief periods the succession of disconnected present moments:

> We are waiting.
> For days, the next day.
> Since the day before, the following day.
> Since the middle of the night, today.
> . . . .
> We're waiting for nothing.
> We're waiting for what happens. Night because it follows day.
>   Day because it follows night.
>   (22; translation modified)
>
> [On attend.
> Depuis des jours, le jour suivant.
> Depuis la veille, le lendemain.

> Depuis le milieu de la nuit, aujourd'hui.
>
> . . . .
>
> On n'attend rien.
> On attend ce qui arrive. La nuit parce qu'elle succède au
>   jour. Le jour parce qu'il succède à la nuit.
>
> (ANR 37)]

The next day may come after this day but it will not be its future.

   In Delbo's text, however, the abolition of the future, that is, the failure of each individual to envision it, finds itself at the core of the community. I call this a failure because the women's belief in the possibility of their return served as a powerful psychological tool for survival. Simply put, to believe in the future was equated with life and the failure to do so with death:

> To talk meant that we could make plans about going home, because to trust we would return was a way of forcing luck's hand. Those who had stopped believing they would return were dead. One had to believe, against all odds, incredible as it might seem. One had to lend to our return certainty, reality and color by preparing for it, conjuring up each and every detail. (102; translation modified)

> [Parler, c'était faire des projets pour le retour parce que croire au retour était une manière de forcer la chance. Celles qui avaient cessé de croire au retour étaient mortes. Il fallait y croire, y croire malgré tout, contre tout, donner certitude à ce retour, réalité et couleur, en le préparant, en le matérialisant dans tous les détails. (ANR 162)]

The fact that the return can only take shape ("reality and color") through group discussions emphasizes that the future is inseparable from the performance, or self-actualization, of the community. Once alone, Charlotte begins to wonder whether she'll even survive the day: "Here I am, at the bottom of the ditch, alone, and so discouraged that I wonder whether I will ever reach the end of the day" (103 [164]). Predictably, such failure to believe is shared by each individual and, in fact, constitutes the condition for the existence of the group as a group. As Delbo writes,

> Left alone at the bottom of the ditch, I am filled with despair. The others' presence, their words, made it possible to believe we might return. Now that they have left I am desperate. I cannot believe I will ever return when I am alone. With them near me, since they seem so certain of it, I believe in it too. No sooner do they leave me than I am frightened. No one believes she will return when she is alone. (103; translation modified)

> [Je reste seule au fond de ce fossé et je suis prise de désespoir. La présence des autres, leurs paroles faisaient possible le retour. Elles s'en vont et j'ai peur. Je ne

crois pas au retour quand je suis seule. Avec elles, puisqu'elles semblent y croire
si fort, j'y crois aussi. Dès qu'elles me quittent, j'ai peur. Aucune ne croit plus
au retour quand elle est seule.]

The choice of the verb *faire*, rather than the more common *rendre*, in "leurs
paroles *faisaient* possible le retour," emphasizes the performative nature of
the words. And to the extent that the last sentence of the passage retro-
spectively defines Charlotte's "Je" as exemplary, the possessive adjective in
the third person plural, "leurs," indicates that belief in survival (that is, survival itself) is always located outside the individual and is an effect of community. As we saw in Dreuilhe's AIDS memoir, autonomous individuality is
no longer a viable option.

Consider also the sentence "With them near me, since they seem so certain of it, I believe in it too." Markers of community begin and end the
sentence—"With" and "too"—and the community they point to is made
possible by a collective belief—"I believe in it too." In the middle of the sentence, however, Delbo inserts a clause that negates not just the others' belief
in the return, but Charlotte's own belief in her companions' belief, "since
they *seem* so certain of it." Indeed, "No one believes she will return when
she is alone." Collective belief, therefore, is made up of the sum of individual lacks of belief or failures to believe. In other words, the "collective" and
the "shared" are two different things, unless what is shared is defined only as
a negative—a failure, a lack, a desire.

In a poem with the ambivalent title of "Auschwitz," Delbo recounts how
a column of women is walking through the town adjacent to the epony-
mous camp. The townspeople, turning away from the prisoners in a gesture
of guilt and denial, effectively become faceless or, rather, *confirm* that they
have no faces:

> None of the inhabitants of this city
> had a face
> and in order not to admit it
> all turned away as we passed.
>
> (87; translation modified)

> [Aucun des habitants de cette ville
> n'avait de visage
> et pour n'en pas faire l'aveu
> tous se détournaient à notre passage.
>
> (140)]

Then, passing by empty shop windows, Charlotte raises her arm, hoping to
identify her own reflection and recognize herself. All the women, however,

had had the same idea and each person, expecting to see herself, only saw the group. Given that Delbo had repeatedly described the dead and the near dead as mannequins in the preceding pages of her volume, it comes as no surprise that one's image in a shop window wouldn't bring any sense of individuality and would, in fact, confirm the erasure of autonomous identity. What is different here, of course, is that the facelessness of the inmates extends to the people outside the camp.

A cursory reading may yield a basic truth—the fact that one cannot try to dehumanize others without dehumanizing oneself. But the end of the poem, especially when read in relation to its title, hints at a far bleaker prospect, with a reference to "the town / we had walked through like a wave of morning sickness" (88 [141]). By erasing the distinction between Auschwitz the camp that we now know to be closed and Auschwitz the town that still very much exists (under its Polish name, Oświęcim), the poem foregrounds the question of the aftermath and, in essence, makes us wonder what sort of birth was announced by this morning sickness. Perhaps that of a dead baby whose absence is figured by the facelessness of inmates and passive bystanders alike and whose ghost will forever haunt (*habiter*) the European landscape, that is, perhaps, the birth of community. The future, it seems, has been taken away from all.

As for the past, in the absence of a future it cannot function as origin anymore—"Nothing remains of what was before," "Here mothers are no longer mothers to their children." Like the future, the past is no longer articulated to the present chronologically. And like the future, it serves only as a trick to stay alive. In the camps, when Charlotte and her companions embraced the family as a model and a stand-in for the past in general, they had to embrace it in its most institutional form and with all attending traditional gender roles. For one thing, clichés and stereotypes were the only way something culturally defined as private could, in fact, provide the sort of stable knowledge shared by a group. More important, however, it was only by recapturing the past *as obsolete*, that the women could use it to detach themselves from the frozen present that was Auschwitz. They were quite aware, then, that this was only a trick, a trope; that none of this—family, gender, heterosexual reproduction—was actually valid as institution anymore; and that the old knowledge had now been superseded by a different kind of knowledge.

The passage entitled "Thirst" in the first volume may not be directly about the family, but it provides a telling example of the way Delbo links the dual question of knowledge and unfamiliarity to that of community—in this case, the community she forms with her readers. The passage, which tells the harrowing story of Charlotte being almost driven to insanity by thirst, starts with the following sentence: "Thirst is an explorer's tale, you know, in the books we read as children" (70) ["La soif, c'est le récit des explorateurs, vous savez, dans les livres de notre enfance" (114)]. However, by the second paragraph, beginning with "But" ["Mais"], it has become clear that the sort of thirst she is talking about has very little to do with the familiar images of her and her readers' childhood stories. Here Delbo uses one of her poetic trademarks—a direct address to the readers through the pronoun "vous" combined with the verb *savoir*. Unlike an earlier poem, in which the incantation "O you who know / did you know that" (11) ["O vous qui savez / saviez-vous que" (*ANR*, 21–22)] is repeated with unsettling effects, the "you know" in "Thirst" is meant to be an informal and friendly way to establish contact, and the sentence ends with the reassuringly inclusive "notre enfance" [our childhood, the literal translation of the original French]. At first, Delbo seems to bring her readers into a cozy community based on a shared knowledge and a shared past—the familiar and the familial. Soon, however, she pulls the rug from under us, and we are left to confront something we did not and cannot possibly know. What remains is the awareness of our failure. Yet the sense of community hasn't vanished; it wasn't *that* kind of trick. Like all testimonial writers, after all, Delbo published her books in the hope that they would be read, and that they would be read, largely, by people who had not themselves witnessed the sort of events she describes. Moreover, readers who have read so far have learned to recognize, and accept, that their expectations will fail.[22] So what happened to our childhood then? Like Delbo's it has become not merely irretrievable but a home whose existence has become very much in doubt—a tale we, too, had mistaken for an origin. It is in that sense that what one reads in Delbo's work is the universal condition of community.

The fact that this new knowledge, or awareness, could not, per se, ground any revolutionary transformation of postwar societies is apparent in the title of the trilogy's second volume, *Useless Knowledge* [*Une connaissance inutile*]. This explains why the survivors mostly tell stories of going through the motions of the family, gender, and all the trappings of what we call the private sphere, a cultural site they now know to be as vacant as the house they mentally redecorated on that rainy day. The past had to be embraced in Auschwitz, but as an empty form to be actualized in relation to a specific context and not as an origin, pregnant with the possibility of the future. In the end, the feeling of alienation from the familiar/familial experienced by the returnees reveals that "home" was an effect of history and culture and was never there to be recaptured in the first place. Delbo's injunction to remember "our childhood" invites us, her readers, to partake in a community premised on and defined by the acknowledgement of our own failure and alienation. As Mado tells Charlotte,

[5]

The Queerness of Group Friendship

A few months before my father died and just weeks after I saw him alive for the last time, an old friend of mine paid him a visit. Sophie and I were in high school together. She was smart, funny, seductive, and just plain stunning. (She still is, if you care to know.) My father was crazy about her back then and he never even tried to conceal the fact that he thought she would make a perfect daughter-in-law. Sophie has been living in the States for quite a while now, so when she mentioned she was going back to Caen for the summer, I urged her to go see my father, knowing that their affection was mutual and how happy her visit would make him—and her. So she did, and sure enough my father soon called me, going on and on about the big event and what a wonderful surprise it had been and how gorgeous she looked. After so many years they had fallen once more under each other's irrepressible charm. Sophie was one of the first persons I called with the news that my father had passed away.

During their conversation, he mentioned a few things she felt she had to report to me afterward. One was his puzzlement at my sudden interest in him and his life. For a book, no less! After years of seeming indifference, what was that all about? Not that he objected, mind you, but still, wasn't that odd? Another remark left Sophie a tad bewildered and perhaps even concerned about my father's mental health. Out of the blue, he told her that the happiest period of his life had been his years as a prisoner of war in Germany. Yes, this may sound like a strange statement, especially coming from a Jewish man whose existence in those years was more precarious than that of his fellow POWs. But I can't say it came as a surprise to me. His recollections of captivity had always been tinged with nostalgia; not for the hard labor, of course, or the tough living conditions and lack of proper food

("I ate raw potatoes"—an image that has stayed with me), but for the friends, the buddies, the *copains* whose eventual dispersion after the liberation filled him with grief and a genuine sense of loss.

He never had, for his entire life, the slightest taste for power or status or ambition. In fact, having some sort of power in certain situations embarrassed him. Come to think of it, that may have been the cause of his uneasiness with fatherhood and would also explain the number of unclaimed IOUs I found among his papers. The two are related. This book: my attempt and inevitable failure to discharge the debt. No payback time for us. The accounts were not meant to be settled, and that's what made us friends in the end.

In the camps, there was only the rank and file for him, nothing more and nothing less. After the war, the community was what he missed and never ceased to miss. The *amicale* of former prisoners he briefly joined turned out to be a pale, frustrating ersatz of the friendships he had known during the war and which he briefly recaptured in Israel in 1948. It was the old story of the soldier adrift and lonely at war's end. Not even the family could offer him much solace. You may think, as Sophie did, that as a son I'd be upset by this, but I'm not. I'm not at all. For, you see, I don't think of this as repudiation but as bond. I recognized in my father my own love of friendship.

PUTTING ON A SHOW

When my sister and I emptied our father's apartment after his death we found an old photo album with flower prints on the cover and bearing the title "Souvenir de captivité." It was empty. He had, however, showed me a few photos from a stalag after I'd expressed interest in seeing them, but they had been stuffed haphazardly in old envelopes, and it is safe to assume that it had been a while since he'd looked at them. My father was not one to keep his precious mementos too neatly ordered. Useless crap, sure, but what truly mattered, no. (My mother: "He could have obtained his divorce much sooner if only he hadn't misplaced the papers.")

The photos showed some of his buddies, most of whom he could no longer identify. Sometimes he was in the pictures and sometimes not. One represented a funeral of which he had no recollection. The one he seemed most proud of depicted him and another fellow wearing brand new uniforms which he had tailored himself. "Faits maison!" he exclaimed. "Home-made!" And there was the attestation certifying that he had successfully passed the "Certificat d'études primaires élémentaires," a degree conferred upon him by the "Université du camp" on 11 May 1943, and to be officially validated in France after his return. Final grade: 98.5 out of 120. A resounding success and the first and only diploma my father ever obtained. It wasn't much, but it meant a lot. I don't know whether he actually bothered to have it validated in the end. After all, he would have no use for a degree and he never sought to liberate himself through formal education. I suspect, in fact, that the diploma mattered to him only as a "souvenir de captivité."

He had also kept the programs of a couple of shows the prisoners had put on in the stalag. One of them included a musical comedy entitled *Tertulia sevillana*, a Spanish fantasia whose dramatis personae now reads like a roster of Latin drag queens: La Carmencita, Lolita, Pilaritu, Pepita, and so on. For prisoners of war didn't always wear uniforms, you see, and my father was sometimes called upon to make other, frillier kinds of garments. A second program announces a song-and-dance number called *Mirages hawaïens*, with the princess Hula as its main character. The company is named "Gais Fangen's," a pun on the German word *Gefangen*, prisoners, which made me laugh

Home-made uniforms (my
father on the left)

STALAG XI B   ATTESTATION   Vu pour la légalisation
Université du camp   de la signature de Monsieur

Derouin Marcel

GEORGE GAUTHIER
Homme de Confiance du Stalag XI B
Hauptvertrauensmann

Je, soussigné DEROUIN Marcel, No 54.724, professeur a
l'école primaire supérieure de Chartres (Eure-et-Loir),
certifie que M. Gottlieb Joseph No Mle 114.308 (Stalag XI B)
Kdo 2355
né le 17 août 1919 à Sátora Garyhely (Hongrie)
domicilié à 23. Place Saint Sauveur, à Caen (Calvados)
ou il exerce la profession de
a subi avec succes les épreuves d'examen du Certificat d'études
primaires élémentaires, session du 18 août 1943, dans les conditions prevues par la circulaire fixant les modalités d'applica-
tion de l'arreté de Monsieur le Ministre, Secretaire d'Etat a
l'Education nationale en date du 26 mai 1942.

NOTES OBTENUES PAR LE CANDIDAT:

Kriegsg.-Mannsch.-Stammlager
Stalag XI B
Kommandantur (Betreuung)
Fallingbostel

Dictée.............................. 2 5½ sur 30
Redaction........................... 2 4 sur 30
Calcul.............................. 28½ sur 30
Sciences, histoire et geographie 20½ sur 30
      Total: 98 ½ sur 120

Moyenne exigée: 60

En foi de quoi, la présente attestation lui a été delivrée.
Le diplome definitif, conformement a l'Arreté ministeriel du 26 mai
1942 lui sera delivré par Monsieur l'Inspecteur d'Academie des
Calvados.
      A Fallingbostel, le 11 mai 1943
      (Allemagne)
Directeur de l'Université du camp
Président du Jury

Le Vice-président du Jury

L'Instituteur du Kommando:

27
Geprüft

A diploma in the stalag

[186]

for my own reasons. My father made the costumes, and the back cover of the program bears a mock advertisement that reads:

"French Chic" isn't dead . . .
. . . thanks to "Gottlieb" it lives on!
Gottlieb
The tailor of the company

[Le "Chic Français" n'est pas mort . . .
. . . grace [sic] à "Gottlieb" il vit encor'!
Gottlieb
Tailleur de la Troupe]

I haven't preserved the rhyme in my translation. Notice that only the last name was used. That was often the rule when referring to the *copains*. The cast, for example, reads like an old-fashioned roll call at the *école communale*: Pillon, Cocard, Pichon, Denichère, Lantheaume. It even brings together a Beauboucher and a Boudin (Handsome Butcher and Blood Sausage, respectively). How Third Republic it all sounds! What stands out for me, of course, is my father's name amidst this typically French nomenclature, and not just because it is my father's name. "Gottlieb, the tailor of the company." Is it just me or does that scream "Jew"? Like Poe's purloined letter, in plain sight of all yet noticed by none, there it was: my father's Jewishness. Who said reading wasn't a matter of context?

I am also tempted to decipher the innocuous-sounding slogan ("It lives on!") as a coded affirmation of resilience and survival; an impression reinforced by this other ad: "Furniture created by Gaboriau / . . . is guaranteed to be the most beautiful" [Les meubles signés Gaboriau / . . . sont garantis les plus beaux], followed by an untranslatable play on words: "Mise en scène / Mise en boîte." *Mise en boîte* means "mockery" or "deception," and may be an indication that something more than mere entertainment was going on— as if the Gais Fangen's putting on a show were also putting on their captors.

I later discovered a series of photos of another one of these shows, and I'm including a few here. French maids, geishas, chorus girls, creole beauties . . . All the stock characters of vaudeville seemed to be there. The back of the photograph of the entire company bears the men's signatures, and my father later added the date and place of the event: "July 1941, Stalag VIII C."

The mixture of pride and levity, of drag and community, reminds me of a wonderful, moving scene from Jean Renoir's 1937 film *La grande illusion* [*Grand Illusion*]. Movies never make me cry, not even *Stella Dallas*, but this one never fails to give me goose bumps. Set in World War I, the antiwar, antinationalist movie tells the story of allied prisoners in Germany, of their

A program (cover)

Régisseur Gal   Direction
   Lé n TILLE   J.de LEBRIJE:

        Orchestre Don LE EBVRE "LA SAGANAISE"
        Spectacle présenté par LEROY des Fol's Sag's

Ière Partie	IIème Partie - *Orchestre-*
LE MANOIR DE L'OPALE	**TERTULIA SEVILLANA**

Ière Partie
LE MANOIR DE L'OPALE

Pièce policière en 1 prologue et
3 Actes de LADRIERE & MOREAU tiré
      du Roman de Grégorg

Décors de MARCOU=Mise en scène de
FEURSINGER=Coiffures et costumes
dessinés par MARCOU,exécutés par
DELUC,CASANOVA,PLESSIS,etc... Jeux
de lumière de CARARO & LADRIERE.

        D i s t r i b u t i o n

PRELE, propriétaire du Manoir.....
        DEGUERGUE de.....l'Atelier
Cap.TEVIERES
        AUBELEAU de........l'Odéon
P.SAVOIE,détective.........THENARD
Docteur ROBERT.............MOREAU
JOCKER,Prince Oriental.....CHIGOT
SAMOS,grand joaillier.....LAETHIER
JACQUIN,Détective........... MEA
LEJAUNE,ancien Sergent.....ANDRAC
JANVIER,Détective..........KOHLER
WILL,Secrétaire de Samos.....NEROU
FELLAH,domestique de Jocker..BERA
COURTOIS,ami de Jacquin.....MONET
VAN VERRUCKT..............VARESE
LI SOO,cuisinier Chinois..CHARQUET
2 serviteurs.............(FERRAND
                        (HUIGHES

        -.-.-.-.-.-.-.-.-

        INTERMEDE
Orchestre:"VERS LE SOIR".Molinatti

Création de:
        LA MARCHE DES FOL'S SAG'S
    Paroles de Jean de Lébrijes
        Musique de René Beaux
par.................... Léon TILLE
    des Moissonneurs de Lille

A I D A................... VERDI

ENTR'ACTE
★

IIème Partie - *Orchestre-*
TERTULIA SEVILLANA

Comédie Musicale en I Acte de J.de
LEBRIJES

Décors de MARCOU.= Mise en scène
de FEURSINGER=Coiffures et costumes dessinés par MARCOU, exécutés
par DELUC et son équipe. Jeux de
lumière de CARARO.

Atmosphère Musicale de R.BEAUX,Th.
GOUIN, GADOUX & RUIZ.

Les danses ont été réglées par M.
RICHE,Maître de Ballet, de l'Opé-
ra Comique.

        D i s t r i b u t i o n
        -.-.-.-.-.-.-.

LA CARMENCITA-Prima Dona.....J.JOLY
EL SALTADOR,Premier danseur. RICHE
              de l'Opéra Comique
RAFAELITO,Matador.........ROUSSEAUX
PEPE, le tavernier..........CHIGOT
JOSELITO,Chanteur...........URFI
EL PESANDILLO,Picador.......PONTS
LOLITA,danseuse............PIERRE
PILARITU,danseuse........LAFFORGUE
ELITA,danseuse...........LAETHIER
PEPITA,danseuse...........BERA
EL RUBIO,danseur..........TOUCAS
MANOLO,danseur.........RUGGIERY
JUANITO,danseur..........ROTH
EL CHIQUILLO,danseur.....THENARD
PEDRO,toréador..........MONET
EL BETUNERO..............HUYGHE
                        (GADOUX
LOS FLAMENCOS,musiciens..(RUIZ
                        (BONICHON

        -.-.-.-.-.-.-.

        RETRAITE

        MARCHE DES FOL'S SAG'S

        ....Orchestre

        Tirage SMEILDERS

The same program (inside)

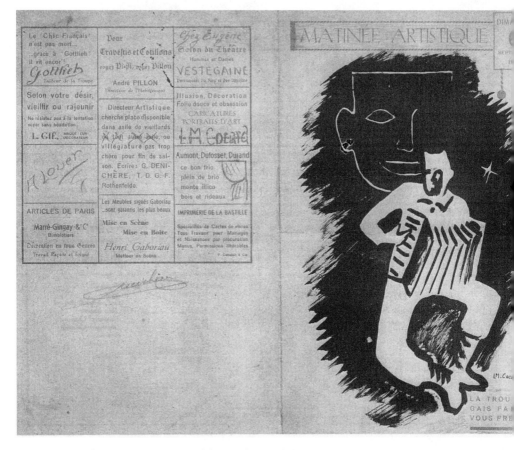

Another program (cover, my father's 'ad' upper left)

camaraderie and of the tensions that sometimes divide them. At one point, the inmates put on a show. British soldiers are on stage, in full drag and dancing a French can-can to the tune of "Tipperary" (maybe they were Irish), when the main character, played by interwar proletarian hero and tragic everyman Jean Gabin, rushes on stage: "Stop the show, fellas!" ["Arrêtez, les copains!"] he shouts, as he announces that French troops have recaptured Douaumont, one of these spots in eastern France that kept changing hands during the bloody, protracted trench warfare that, until much worse happened, came to epitomize the barbarity of modern conflict. Immediately, one of the performers turns to the band: " 'La Marseillaise,' please." He removes his wig and starts singing the French national anthem, English accent and all, followed by the entire multinational audience standing at attention in defiance of the German soldiers present.

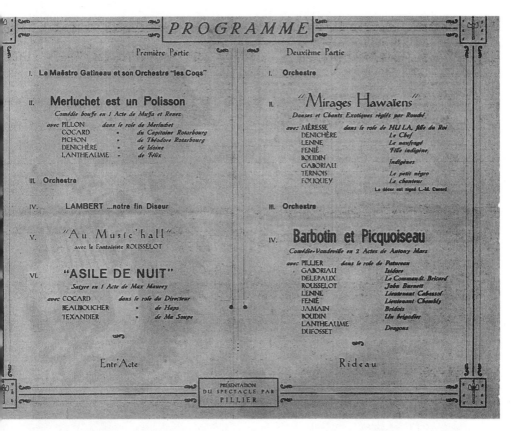

The same program (inside)

What makes the scene so compelling isn't its patriotism. Like the rest of the movie, it isn't patriotic at all, the "Marseillaise" notwithstanding. The scene isn't an unwittingly campy propaganda piece, like the "Marseillaise" sung with great panache in *Casablanca*, whose story takes place during World War II. For one thing, in *La grande illusion* the Germans are never portrayed as evil. While the movie was made in 1937, its German characters are not metaphorical stand-ins for the Nazis, and one of the central friendships in the plot involves a French officer and his German captor, both aristocrats. Furthermore, viewers then and now know how meaningless the victory at Douaumont really is, how futile the celebration, and that in 1916, when the scene takes place, there are still two long years of slaughter ahead. The compelling power of the scene lay not in its expression of triumph but rather, I believe, in its staging of shared failure as defining the community of *copains*.

A show in the stalag

A show in the stalag

A show in the stalag

A show in the stalag (the entire company)

A show in the stalag (the company's signatures)

By definition, all prisoners of war have failed; that's what made my father's remark so unsettling to my friend Sophie. To her dismay, what he was
waxing nostalgic about wasn't his glory days (say, his service in the Israeli
army during its successful war for independence, for example) but the very
opposite. And in the context of the times, when the bellicose and the masculine often tended to be one and the same, to fail as a soldier meant to fail
as a man. I think that's what was performed by the drag shows the inmates
put on, the success of the show resulting from the successful send-up of the
soldier's failure.[1] The men in the audience were watching the comic spectacle of their own failed masculinity and enjoying it—"it" referring both to
the spectacle and to the failure. More importantly, they enjoyed it *as a group*.
(Think of the signatures of the company as a company.) The *mise en scène*
that is a *mise en boîte* may not just be mocking the captors under whose noses
the prisoners affirmed their power of survival, but also the very idea that a
community must necessarily be based on the sharing of something positive.
Look again at the first program and at the lace-adorned black mask partially
covering the watchtower, as a flaunted emblem of a masquerade's power to
liberate as it deceives. In the movie, when the soldier removes his wig and
belts out the "Marseillaise," one shouldn't read the gesture as a sign that he
and the others have recaptured their masculinity, just as the French have recaptured Douaumont. Again, the victory was futile and more than likely to
be short-lived anyway. That the soldier is still wearing his dress suggests,

rather, that success and masculinity can never be fully recovered and shall remain, from now on, concurrently and inescapably defined by their own negation. Success and failure have ceased to function as a meaningful distinction. They have been hopelessly queered.

It goes without saying that, while in captivity, my father wished with all his heart for an ultimate victory over the Nazis. That's why he enrolled in the Foreign Legion in the first place. But after victory was finally achieved, his failure could never be undone, and what he missed was the community of men with whom he shared it—the happiest days of his life. What followed was triumph, plain, drab, boring triumph—and the gradual realization that his family had been exterminated. His war years had been the last time he didn't have to live with this impossible knowledge.

I often wondered why, a few short years after the conclusion of World War II, my father would choose to join another conflict. I knew he wasn't a violent man and that he had no particular taste for bloodshed. Oh, he was a man's man all right. Many photos of him show that he loved to pose next to symbols of masculinity, such as a car, a motorcycle, a plane, even a tank on a picture taken during a brief stint in the Israeli army reserve in the mid 1990s, unaware of course that the fetishistic nature of these dangerous supplements expose the lack they attempt to deny. So many of my father's pictures, I came to realize, were not about himself but about his desire to belong, to fit in. The fact that this desire was so often frustrated is what makes these photos so moving to me. There he is, looking perfectly French in France and perfectly Israeli in Israel. (Look again at the portraits I selected for the preface.) He poses in uniform next to other soldiers or prisoners, also in uniform. He stands proudly by a motorcycle and a plane. When on earth did my father ever ride a motorcycle or fly a plane? Never, as far as I know. To see him wear the accoutrements of his ever-changing identities is to witness how elusive the objects of his desires always were—and how unstable such objects always are in the first place.

Only recently did I understand that his decision to go to Palestine and fight for the creation of the State of Israel was motivated in equal measure by a sense of duty toward his fellow Jews and by a desire to recapture (so to speak) the feeling of community military service had brought him. What both reasons had in common was a desire to melt into the group, to muster a sense of life's purpose in and through the collective. Selflessness—to serve, to share, and to give—was, all through his life, my father's way to take on the burden of community and to lift the burden that is the self . Existence as unclaimed IOU: I can live with that.

A RETURN TO THEORY AND A THEORY OF RETURN

In my preface I described in greater detail how disappointed my father had been that the group friendship he enjoyed so much during his war years all but dissolved after liberation. The few buddies with whom he managed to stay in touch for a while seemed to have become different people. Perhaps they thought the same thing of my father. I don't know, he didn't say. But something that had seemed so strong, so vital even, had ceased to function as the friends returned to normal peacetime activities, such as family and work—the defining values of postwar normality. Surely you remember *It's Always Fair Weather*, the 1955 MGM musical directed by Gene Kelly and Stanley Donen. (Of course, you do. That's the one where the three war buddies dance on a New York street with trashcan lids on their feet.) At war's end, the guys swear that they'll be friends forever. When they meet again ten years later they realize they can't stand each other, until they rekindle their friendship by banding together once more against America's (and Hollywood's) latest evil enemy: television. The movie may be very entertaining on one level, but its undercurrent is dark and depressing, which, of

Left: The buddies in the stalag (my father standing on the right)
Right: The buddies in the Israeli army (my father in the center)

course, makes me want to raise a host of questions. What is it about group friendship that seems to deprive it of a future? What, then, is its larger relation to time and to social normality? What is its purpose? How does it work? And what happens when group friendship, rather than the family, becomes the structuring metaphor for community?

The French *copain*, so prevalent among soldiers, is an interesting word. Translatable as "buddy" or "pal," its etymology indicates that it has to do with sharing bread, as in the English "companion." In French, *copain* isn't quite the same thing as *ami*, a relationship etymologically related to love. That's the whole difference: whereas *amis* must love each other, *copains* need only love bread, or whatever it is that they share in lieu of bread. Or better yet, they must love the act of sharing—especially when the bread has run out and the bond itself is all that remains. *Amitié*, friendship, is usually understood as self-willed and a function of individuality. Its template remains Montaigne's famous essay "De l'amitié" ["On Friendship"] and its oft-quoted line describing his deep attachment to his friend La Boëtie: "Because it was he, because it was I" ["Parce que c'était lui, parce que c'était moi"]. The essay, a work of mourning after the death of the friend, complicates the self at the same time that Montaigne pretty much invents it. Yet it does posit the self as whole first before making it the repository of loss and absence. This internal relationality—I as non-I—may be a complex form of binary, it is nonetheless a binary. The relationship between *copains* owes much to Montaigne's simultaneous making and unmaking of the modern self, to be sure, but it is a function of its necessarily collective context and as such external to the individual. This, in a nutshell, is what I call group friendship, meaning friendship within or as a group and friendship *for* the group.

There are the *copains d'école* [school friends] and the *copains de régiment* [army buddies]—although the latter may eventually vanish now that mandatory conscription has been abolished in France. And there are, of course, the buddies during war or imprisonment. All these bonds are created by the external and temporary circumstances that brought these people together, not by decisions made by individual members of the groups and not by a preexisting common trait, be it an essence or any other form of identity defined by sameness. In *La grande illusion,* for example, the friendship between the two genteel officers, one French and one German, who belong to the same social class and have common acquaintances, comes to an end when the French officer sacrifices himself to allow two of his fellow countrymen to escape. (The escape was made possible when the prisoners staged a cacophonous concert after curfew in order to create confusion—a parody of the earlier drag show and another form of *mise en boîte.*) The two escapees, the Gabin character named Maréchal and a wealthy Jewish bourgeois named Rosenthal (the two men couldn't be more different but, tellingly, their names rhyme in French), are eventually given shelter by a German peasant woman who has lost her husband at the battle of Verdun and found herself alone to tend the farm and care for her little girl. People, land, and livestock need all the help they can get, and the four soon form an unlikely but short-lived friendship. The message is not one of sentimental reconciliation between social classes, religions, and nationalities, as if something good could come out of war. In fact, in the late 1930s, when the movie was made, another conflict was looming on the horizon. In the story, Maréchal promises to return and marry the German widow; the context of the film indicates otherwise. What we are left with is a sense that community is allowed by circumstances, made up of lacks and absences, and contained in the present moment.

In other words, it isn't the friendship that creates the group but the group that creates the friendship. The first logical consequence is that as the circumstances change so does the group. Furthermore, if the enabling circumstances were to disappear altogether, the group wouldn't survive. In other words, group friendship isn't predicated on and justified by the past (that is, the presence of autonomous selves that would pre-exist the group), and it doesn't hold the promise of a future. It exists solely in and for the present. In that sense, a community modeled on the dynamics of group friendship would resemble neither its contractual nor its essentialized counterparts. To recall the late-nineteenth-century framework I used earlier in this book: neither Renan nor Barrès; neither the heirs of Rousseau and the Enlightenment nor their protofascist critics. Family as the structuring metaphor for community serves two related purposes in modern Western cultures. Applied to minority communities, the metaphor seeks to privatize the tribal, the archaic *ethnos*, the old nation within the new nation, and to remove such communities from the realm of the political—the *res publica*. Applied to the state, it transcends and naturalizes the social, universalizes it, and equates the future with reproduction. Group friendship, to the contrary, does not have a future. Its moments may come in succession but they are not connected by causation or narrative thrust. This is why life in concentration camps was, in certain circumstances, conducive to such modes of groupings. Not only did inmates form single-sex communities and therefore fell outside the dynamic of reproduction, but the communities they formed were constantly made to reshape themselves from scratch. In the camps, chronological time had been abolished. Community could help to keep individuals from dying right away, but being alive at the end of the day or after a work shift meant nothing more than just that. It did not increase your chances of surviving the next day or the next shift. In other words, what followed could not build or capitalize on what preceded.

In the context of the AIDS crisis, especially in the years when no effective treatments were available and death was a near certain outcome, group friendship played a similar role. In *Corps à corps*, for example, Dreuilhe advocates it as the only way to fight for and as a community:

> We ought to return somehow, beyond the current confusion and the dark ages through which we are trying to clear our way, beyond the desert our people must now cross, back to the cool, ancient oasis that is homosexual camaraderie. (127; translation modified)

> [il faudrait pourtant que nous retrouvions, au-delà de la confusion actuelle, de l'ère obscure dans laquelle nous devons nous frayer un passage, du désert que notre peuple doit franchir, la fraîche et antique oasis de la camaraderie homosexuelle. (163)]

The return to the mythical homeland, both Hebrew and Greek in Dreuilhe's Proust-influenced vision of it, is not, however, an attempt to recapture chronological time but rather the recognition that, for homosexuals, there has never been anything but the present since a community of friends, unlike a family, is neither an outcome nor a promise of birth. About homosexuality, Dreuilhe writes:

> Now more than ever we must refuse to disown our homeland, adopted though it may be; we must refuse to betray our friends. . . . I don't see why we couldn't . . . cherish the country of our choice without having to apologize to strangers for our devotion to such a rocky and infertile place" (125; translation modified).

> ["C'est maintenant plus que jamais que nous devons refuser de renier notre patrie, même d'adoption, de renier nos amis. . . . Je ne vois pas pourquoi nous ne pourrions exalter . . . notre terre d'élection sans chercher à nous excuser auprès des étrangers de notre attachement à une patrie aussi infertile et rocailleuse. (161)]

The fundamental timelessness of group friendship—its flattened asynchronicity and haphazard relationality—is what makes it so problematic and difficult to accept as a metaphor for community. This is especially true in France's universalist culture, where the group is often associated with the tribal. That modern French culture should condemn all political expressions from minority communities *as communities* betrays the fact that, in France, such communities are thought of as family-like. The family may be a basic social unit, but only on the condition that it be privatized. When Jean-Pierre Chevènement, then Minister of the Interior and a staunch defender of the values of the Republic, once chastised lawless kids from the projects, most of them associated in the public mind with immigrant communities and whose "successors" were to riot so spectacularly in the fall of 2005, he called them *sauvageons*, little savages. Enlightened as Chevènement thought he was, his choice of word was *not* a reference to Rousseau's "noble savage." As for the debates surrounding the use of headscarves by Muslim girls in public schools, their bewildering passion arose from the cultural link between public assertions of religion (and especially of Islam, a religion associated with France's colonial past) and social archaism. Politicians and social commentators routinely describe urban projects home to large foreign and/or nonwhite populations as "lawless spaces" ["espaces de non-droit"] and as ruled by the "law of the jungle." Given the French equation of laws with Reason, these terms unmistakably signify premodern modes of grouping.

As John R. Bowen explains in his book *Why the French Don't Like Headscarves*, proponents of a law banning all "ostensible" signs of religion in public schools (with the exception of universities), organized their arguments by bringing together three perceived threats to French society: *communautarisme* (a word Bowen renders as "communalism" and I as "communitarianism"); Islamism, that is the political expression of Islam; and sexism. What unites these three ideas, I shall add, is that they are presented as antithetical to social progress and throwbacks to pre-Enlightenment values and, therefore, to the very idea of Frenchness.

Communautarisme is said to constitute a return to a non-contractual concept of the nation and to premodern notions of personhood. Islamism is said to return to the ancient alliance of church and state and sexism to the power of the family over social institutions. In the latter part of the argument, Muslim girls are presumed to be wearing headscarves under pressure from their fathers and, especially, from their brothers—the very same young Arab men stereotypically represented in the culture at large as rioting thugs, bigoted rappers, and gang members, and in ways that echo certain representations of young black males in the United States. The entire debate around the social status of communities in France has been caught up in these issues. So I ask the question again: what happens when group friendship, rather than the family, becomes the structuring metaphor for community?

With all the talk of late, in Europe and the United States, about gay marriage, gay parenting, gay families, it looks as if the process of familialization of homosexuality is in full swing, and perhaps irreversible. Yes, even in the United States. This bothers me a little. For one thing, what about those of us, gay or straight or anything, for whom the family is not a possibility or even a coveted ideal? What are our options? To let ourselves be further marginalized by the liberal extension of the concept of family? Or, at best, to imagine our modes of social grouping as family-like and our friends as kin? Most disturbing in all of this is the fact that the rhetorical move that consists in using the family, alternative though it may be, as metaphor for community now threatens to undo community altogether by privatizing it. To ask the question differently: can there be community at all within the private sphere or any other symbolic space defined as private? If so, how could such a community be appropriate for queers? That said, the fashionable revival of the 1970s in the early years of the twenty-first century, apart from making boys and girls in the streets rather sexy, may well provide us with the opportunity to envisage once again some alternative models of socialization. Considering such a comeback less as a consumerist fad than a manifestation of survival could allow us to rethink how we wish to associate with one another and connect with the world.

If the seventies were just about shoulder-length hair and afros, hiphugging bell bottoms, and barely toned bodies under open shirts, I'd be happy enough with their return. But of course they weren't just about that, and their revival owes much of its power of seduction to its irony, to its distance from the object of its pastiche—to its repetition as farce. We shouldn't forget, however, that when theorized—and what a great decade the seventies were for radical theories!—the aesthetic rejection of traditional masculine standards was often accompanied by a radical, if often ambiguous, questioning of the norms and power dynamics enforced in and through masculinity and the family. For queers, this translated into the production of a new kind of public culture. I ask you, if bell bottoms are back, isn't it time we also returned to the radical, sexy theories that came with them? With this in mind, I propose what follows as a return to theory and the outline of a theory of return.

Guy Hocquenghem wrote *Homosexual Desire* in 1972 in the wake and under the influence of Gilles Deleuze and Félix Guattari's landmark book *Anti-Oedipus*. Drawing on their concept of reterritorialization, Hocquenghem makes the following claims. With Oedipus and its triangular structure of desire internalized (and heterosexuality thus naturalized), the phallus becomes the central organizing principle of society. Those who have it can legitimately partake in the public sphere; those who don't can't. As a condition, the anus has to be sublimated, that is, reduced to its sole and solitary excremental function. In Hocquenghem's words,

> The anus has no social position except sublimation. The functions of this organ are truly private; they are the site of the formation of the person. The anus expresses privatization itself. The analytic case-history . . . presupposes that the anal stage is transcended so that the genital stage may be reached. (82)

And later, "The constitution of the private, individual, 'proper' [pudique] person is 'of the anus'; the constitution of the public person is 'of the phallus' " (83). Modern capitalism, with its strict dichotomization of public and private spheres, rests on this privatizing move and, more crucial to my point, on the process of maturation that provides its narrative framework.

The anal stage, as Freud calls it, is one of undifferentiated, amorphous desire that must be transcended. It is essentially presocial in that it precedes the rise of the phallus and of the symbolic, and as such it may be extremely dangerous if left unchecked. For Hocquenghem, "The anus does not exist in a social relation, since it forms precisely the individual and therefore enables the division between society and the individual to be made. . . . [O]ne does not shit in company" (83). Knowing when and where to shit, and when and where not to, is what constitutes selfhood. The expression "to forget oneself" [s'oublier] indicates how control of one's excremental functions is inseparable from one's sense of identity. "In contemporary society," Hocquenghem writes, "total degradation [déchéance] is to live in one's own waste, which only prison or the concentration camp can force us to do. 'To forget oneself' is to risk joining up, through the flux of excrement, with the non-differentiation of desire" (85). For men, such loss of control and social identity through a private act performed in public is also a loss of masculinity. What defines a man (as opposed to an infant, a woman, or a very old person) is the ability to use his will in order to control or conceal bodily flux—except sometimes when it is associated with the penis, which accounts for the popularity of pissing contests. Failure to exercise such control represents a return to what preceded the establishment of the public-private distinction and the accompanying gender system that grants men power over women.

Because it is associated with a regression to a stage of pre-personhood, the sexualized anus is, literally, a thing of the past, and the sublimation of homosexuality parallels the modern, linear narrative of progress. Looking ahead is what makes a man a man. In the American cultural psyche, for example, young men were encouraged to "go west" in order to become real men, while the east coast remained the domain of Europeanized sissies. That the Village People managed to make "Go West" a rallying cry for gay men in search of sex and community is nothing short of genius. For in psychoanalytic thought, homosexuality as perversion is wholly conceived as a movement backward, a "counter-current." The male homosexual individual is socialized only to the extent that he is defined not by the future generations he may spawn but by his fixation on the past in the persons of his parents. As Hocquenghem writes:

The homosexual can only be a degenerate, for he does not generate. . . . The only acceptable form of homosexual temporality is that which is directed towards the past, to the Greeks or Sodom. . . . Homosexuality is seen as a regressive neurosis, totally drawn towards the past; the homosexual is incapable of facing his future as an adult and father, which is laid down for every male individual. Since homosexual desire is ignorant of the law of succession—the law of stages—and is thus unable to ascend to genitality, it must therefore be regression, a counter-current to the necessary historical evolution. . . . Freud undoubtedly establishes a topographical coexistence of drives rather than successive stages; but temporality asserts itself as the absolute need for parents and children to succeed each other, and for full genitality to follow the anal stage, even if the preceding stages reappear throughout the individual's history as the relics of an ever-threatening past. (94)

This naturally raises the question: What if we just screw sublimation and embrace this backward, downward turn instead? This is precisely what Hocquenghem advises us to do. "It is good to try, in contradistinction to Gide, to follow one's inclination as long it descends" (81; translation modified). The result would be a radical destabilization of the order organized by and around the phallus—the end of the social as we know it and the birth of "the group." If society rests entirely on its repudiation of homosexual desire, to embrace such desire places one outside and against the heteronormative social:

The desires directed towards the anus, which are closely connected with homosexual desire, constitute what we shall call a "group" mode [mode groupal] of relations as opposed to the usual "social" mode. . . . Homosexual desire is a group desire; it groupifies [groupalise] the anus by restoring its functions as a desiring bond, and by collectively reinvesting it against a society which has reduced it to the state of a shameful little secret. . . . *To fail one's sublimation is in fact merely to conceive social relations in a different way.* Possibly, when the anus recovers its desiring function . . . the group can then take its pleasure in an immediate relation where the sacrosanct difference between public and private, between the individual and the social, will be out of place. (96–97; translation modified, my emphasis)

As a result of this immediacy, what characterizes such groups is their absence of goal and any kind of social usefulness defined by the future. Flattened in an eternal present, animated only by their internal unruly relationality, that is, by sharing rather than transmission, they serve no purpose other than themselves and go nowhere in particular. This, I want to suggest, could be the universal model for community, and its manifestation would be group friendship.

The family as model is caught in a double bind. The narrative of progress, the accumulation of greater and greater wealth, provides the motor with which capitalism propels itself and sustains its existence. Should the final stage of progress be reached (and there is no way to know what it could possibly look like) that would be the end of capitalism. Therefore the system must produce constant dissatisfaction by constructing ideals that can never be reached. Heterosexuality, the cultural avatar of capitalism, is one of these ideals. Think of it this way: Can one ever be absolutely certain of someone's purely heterosexual desire? What would be the irrefutable proof? The absence of homosexual acts during one's entire lifetime? No. A successful marriage and family life? No. A person's sincere word? No. The appearance of perfect gender appropriateness? Please! On the other hand, if an effeminate man has sex with other men and says he's gay, he is. But *in theory*, pure heterosexual desire is impossible to prove and is, therefore, inherently fragile.

That leaves us with practice. A person's heterosexuality must constantly be demonstrated, but because it can't, it must be performed through the repeated repudiation of homosexuality. (I am tempted to read "demonstrate" as "to make unmonstrous" by stretching its etymology ever so slightly. The idea that heterosexuality is produced by making the homosexual a monster is Roddey Reid's thesis in *Families in Jeopardy*.) In other words, if heterosexuality was conceived to remain forever unfulfilled in order for the system to keep propelling itself into existence, and if the ideal family is an unattainable goal, why would anyone willingly choose to follow such a frustrating path? Simply because one doesn't want to be a homosexual, that is, radically desocialized. Just as capitalism displaced *compagnonnage* (think of the *copains* again) at the core of the organization of labor (Hocquenghem 80), the family now stands, instead of group friendship, as the structuring metaphor for community. Conceived in this way, community is bound endlessly to repeat the collective repudiation of the monstrous outsider. Homosexual desire, however, is self-fulfilling. It does not follow a linear narrative path and has no other goal than itself. It is not looking toward an elusive future but rather toward the past, which it keeps bringing back into the present. Queers are the Jews of desire: as the latter have in relation to the Christian West, queers irritate the system by reminding it that its self-fulfillment is impossible. They figure, in short, the point of departure that may never be fully left behind.

This is the nature of male group friendship. Like the anal stage, it is not supposed to last. Socially, it occurs in temporary, evolutionary stages of apprenticeship—schools, sports, military service, war, etc.—and exceptional situations in which the individual is threatened with disappearance—

prisons or concentration camps, to mention Hocquenghem's earlier examples. These are the contexts in which men, or boys, are allowed to have groups of friends, or *copains*—when they are in the process of learning to be men but not there yet, or when their existence as men is threatened. The term *copains* suggests such immaturity. While a man is allowed to have buddies and to keep a close (but not *too* close) friend into adulthood, perhaps as relic/repellent of a type of social relation that is no longer allowed, the group of males must not be the primary mode of social identification. The stereotypical comedic situation in which a man's girlfriend and future wife is in conflict with his old buddies is emblematic of this tension. The man must discard his buddies, grow up, and get married. That women do not face exactly the same pressure to repudiate their community of female friends is due to the fact that they have been privatized *as a group* in the first place. No maturity is necessary there, and female group friendship is as (deceptively!) easy to dismiss as a sewing circle, a Tupperware party, or a gossip network. However, with the advent of male maturity and in states of social normalcy, the public sphere is supposed to be the only legitimate site of the male collective. In fact, the public sphere *is* the male collective, the sublimated, socially constructive form of homosexual desire, while the private sphere, as Hocquenghem contends, is the site of the individual. In short, male group friendship, like homosexual desire, is an archaic social stage, and because men are destined to join the public sphere as male collective, to return to immaturity is to emulate female group friendship, forsake masculinity as identity and, as in the prisoners' drag shows, embrace gender indeterminacy. Reclaiming such archaism in the present—in a never-ending present—could entail a radical rethinking of the social far beyond the sexualized gay male focus that is Hocquenghem's and that I use as a starting point. To a large extent, what he calls "homosexual desire" may be a misnomer, since what the phrase describes—the survival into adulthood of the pre-Oedipal stage that preceded the existence of "homosexual" and "heterosexual"—is, in effect, an undoing of the foundational categories of sex and gender identities and perforce of identity *in general*. Without selves capable of laying claim to distinct identities, "all" we are left with is the perpetual interplay of difference that I call the queerness of community.

Unlike Hocquenghem, however, I'm not all that interested in the Revolution. It suffices to me that I look backward and live *with* the past rather than *in* the past. This is why I enjoy the *return* of the 1970s today far more than I did the actual 1970s. (I was a teenager then. Need I say more?) As I've said before, queer life often involves practices of return. Camp, as a mode of group rereading, is such a turn to the past through acts of faggotry, such as mourning the passing of Hedy Lamarr (don't laugh, I'm still not over it) or

There exist, in the so-called normal world, certain privileged meeting places: libraries, stadiums, theaters, museums, university lecture halls, even waiting rooms in train stations. In the Lager, THE "heavenly" spot was none other than the collective shithouse of a group forced into a collective nonlife. A place where information was exchanged and where the men's morale was read like barometric pressure. . . . At night, it was the place to get together with the other men from the block, and it was possible to chat there.

[Il existe dans le monde dit normal, des lieux de rencontre privilégiés, les bibliothèques, les stades, les théâtres, les musées, les amphis des facs, voire les salles d'attente des gares. Au Lager, CE coin "paradisiaque" n'était autre que les chiottes collectives d'un groupe contraint à une non-vie collective. Lieu d'échange d'informations, de relevé barométrique du moral des hommes. . . . Le soir, on y retrouvait les autres habitants du block et on pouvait discuter. (103)]

The conjunction of nonlife, anality, and group relations finds its most glorious expression in a scene that Hocquenghem would surely have appreciated. One day, shortly after his arrival, Joseph has to use the latrines and there, to his surprise, he runs into Maurice, a childhood friend of his from Belleville. The two buddies catch up while taking a shit side by side. Maurice is a more seasoned inmate and he begins to inform the newcomer of what is really going on. At one point, with no toilet paper in sight, Maurice hands his friend a large 5,000-franc note to wipe his ass with. Money, capitalism's phallus and the central organizer of heteronormative sociality, finds itself defiled and replaced by friendship and the anus:

The banknote bears the mark of the "Bank of France" and the customary inscriptions printed on the largest bill in use in our country at the time. . . . And Maurice and I start imagining the Bank of France transformed into a gigantic toilet paper factory. . . . A brief moment of relaxation, and that is how I had the unique experience of wiping my ass with the national currency.

[La coupure porte le sigle "Banque de France" et les inscriptions usuelles de la monnaie nationale imprimées sur la plus grosse unité monétaire en usage à l'époque dans notre pays. . . . Et je me mets à imaginer avec Maurice la Banque de France metamorphosée en gigantesque usine de papier-toilette. . . . Bref instant de détente et c'est ainsi que, expérience inédite, je me suis torché avec la monnaie nationale. (108–9)]

Antelme, while not given to Bialot's crude and irreverent brand of Parisian working-class humor, also emphasizes the communal role played by the latrines. He recalls how, one morning,

some guys have already headed for the latrine, so as not to be in the field, so as to be fenced in on all four sides along with the happy anxiousness that goes with hiding out. They can't ask anything of us at night; there's no way they can make us work out of doors, since they wouldn't be able to watch us. (40; translation modified)

[des copains sont partis aux chiottes, pour n'être pas dans le pré, pour être entre les quatre planches qui les entourent avec la bonne angoisse de la planque. La nuit, on ne peut rien nous demander; rien ne peut faire que nous travaillions dehors dans la nuit parce qu'on ne pourrait pas nous surveiller. (47)]

Another day, at a factory,

I went to the new latrine that had been set up recently at one end of the factory. There was always a crowd there, guys ducking out of work. When we'd been sufficiently stupefied by the noise of the compressor and the hammers, we'd go to the latrines and *do nothing*. There were several stalls, a toilet in each one; when a kapo came in, we'd sit on the toilet and *pretend*. (143; my emphases)

[je suis allé aux nouvelles chiottes qui avaient été aménagées depuis peu à une extrémité de l'usine. Là, il y avait toujours du monde, les types s'y planquaient. Quand on était suffisamment abruti par le bruit du compresseur et des marteaux, on allait aux chiottes et *on ne faisait rien*. Il y avait plusieurs boxes avec une cuvette dans chacun. Quand un kapo venait, on s'asseyait sur une cuvette, et *on faisait semblant*. (149; my emphases)]

The SS and kapos tolerate the fact that prisoners take piss and shit breaks because they see the satisfaction of these needs as signs of further servitude and humiliation (34 [40]). But this too must be done according to the rules. When the prisoners, sickened one night by the dog biscuits they had eaten, cannot make it to the latrines and start shitting uncontrollably inside the church where they are spending the night, the kapos become enraged: "The kapos arrive. They know we've shit in the church. *Alle Scheisse!* They're furious, and happy to be, for they'll be able to settle [régler] some accounts" (227 [237]). This flagrant breakdown of order, collectively defiant as it may be, is also involuntary, and it ultimately gives the kapos and the SS the opportunity to reinforce their domination. (*Régler* also means "to regulate.") But tricking them by *pretending* is a hidden declaration of independence. Together in the latrines, their pants down around their ankles, the prisoners put on a show of degradation. *Doing nothing* is unacceptable to the SS. Indeed, they would abolish night itself if they could. "Our work doesn't have any beginnings. All it has is interruptions; the one at night, though official, is scandalous" (41 [47]). Knowingly sharing "nothing," a nothing that is simultaneously displayed and hidden, is what makes the prisoners a community.

Nothingness is what also characterizes the conversations, or rather the words, shared by the men in the latrines. Nothing truly meaningful is ever said there, except the unsurprising news that so-and-so has died, for example. What matters is not the content of the exchange, but the fact that contact is established:

> It was in the latrine that the guys would first say hello to each other in the morning and question one another.
> "What's new?"
> "Nothing's new." (67)

> [C'était aux chiottes que les copains se disaient bonjour pour la première fois le matin, et se questionnaient.
> —Quoi de nouveau?
> —Rien de nouveau.] (73)

Or this other exchange between a night watchman and a prisoner on his way to the latrines:

> "Okay?
> The other would nod his head and reply:
> "Okay."
> At the door he would put on his shoes, then go out and piss. The watchman would go back to his pacing. (10; translation modified)

> [—Ça va?
> L'autre hochait la tête et répondait:
> —Ça va.
> Arrivé à la porte il enfilait ses chaussures, puis sortait pisser. Le veilleur du block reprenait sa marche. (16)]

In a different context, this sort of exchange finds an echo in Guillaume Dustan's AIDS novel *Je sors ce soir*. The narrator, wandering into a Pigalle dance club after a long absence from Paris, runs into old friends and acquaintances who, like himself, have been HIV-positive for a while. The year is 1996 and important breakthroughs in treatments are beginning to change the course of the epidemic in Western countries. Given the loud music and the festive purpose of a night out, most conversations are brief and avoid the topic that is on everyone's mind. The encounters, however, are opportunities to check on how the others are doing, how well or visibly ill they are, and to convey the same kind of information about oneself (and *to* oneself as well to the extent that, as in a concentration camp, when one is caught in the middle of a disaster, one always sees oneself in the others)—to gauge, in other words, the state of health of the community. Part tact and part denial, words in such circumstances seldom are about what they denote. Such is the case in this typical encounter:

> That's when Jean-Luc and Stéphane walk by, an eternal couple I haven't seen in ages, and we all say to each other,—Hi!,—How's it going?, genuinely happy to see that we're not dead or visibly ill. I wonder if I should ask them for details, but what about? Their jobs? Too vulgar. Noteworthy tricks they've had lately? Indiscreet. Their recipe for not splitting up? Now that would be interesting but it doesn't occur to me at the time. Anyway, what really matters *has* been said. There is a silence. And then they say,—We're gonna walk around, later!, and they leave.

> [C'est là que passent Jean-Luc et Stéphane, un couple éternel que je n'ai pas vu depuis des siècles, et on se dit tous,—Salut!,—Ça va?, sincèrement contents de voir qu'on n'est pas morts ni visiblement malades. Je me demande si je vais leur demander des détails, mais sur quoi? Leur boulot? Vulgaire. Les coups les plus marquants qu'ils ont faits ces derniers temps? Indiscret. Leur recette pour ne pas se séparer? Ça, ça serait intéressant mais je n'y pense pas sur le moment. De toute façon l'essentiel a été dit. Il y a un silence. Et puis ils disent,—On va faire un tour, à plus!, et ils partent. (28)]

It may also be worth noting, with Antelme in mind, that a great deal of Guillaume's evening is spent in the men's room because he is high on ecstasy and it makes him shit.

In *L'espèce humaine*, this phatic use of language, in which both referent and signified are unimportant (of the anus rather than of the phallus, Hocquenghem would say), eventually extends beyond the latrines into the work details and becomes another mode of community formation. In the following passage, the group is defined as heterogeneous *and* as made up of interchangeable members—that is, both as continuity and discontinuity:

> The civilian foreman . . . couldn't prevent words from passing from one man to another. Only a few words; it wasn't conversations these men would hold, since work in the mine wasn't done by homogeneous groups, and one guy couldn't stand beside the same buddy for several hours at a stretch. Sentences were broken up by the rhythm of the picking and shoveling and the coming and going of the wheelbarrow. . . .

> This would be going on in the tunnel, and was being said by one beast of burden to another. And from that a language was taking shape that wasn't just one of insults and belches. . . . In the depths of the mine, in their bent bodies and disfigured faces, the world was opening up. (193–94; translation modified)

> [Le contremaître . . . ne pouvait pas empêcher les mots de passer d'un homme à l'autre. Peu de mots, d'ailleurs; ce n'était pas une conversation que ces

hommes tenaient, parce que le travail de la mine ne se faisait pas par groupes homogènes, et chacun ne pouvait donc pas rester auprès du même copain plusieurs heures de suite. Les phrases étaient hachées par le rythme du travail à la pioche, le va-et-vient de la brouette. . . .

Ça se passait dans le tunnel, et ça se disait de bête de somme à bête de somme. Ainsi un langage *se tramait*, qui n'était plus celui de l'injure ou de l'éructation du ventre. . . . Au coeur de la mine, dans le corps courbé, dans la tête défigurée, le monde s'ouvrait. (201; my emphasis)]

The group is not "homogeneous." Because its composition changes with the constant turnaround of the *copains* and its "broken" language never articulates a coherent whole, such a group is stuck in the present moment. The words circulating from inmate to inmate may be those of encouragement uttered by their friend Gaston, with his inspiring resilience, but what matters most is the very dynamic of circulation. The verb *se tramer*, unlike "to take shape" used in the translation, suggests some sort of (forgive the pun) underground conspiracy, of which there is none, but *trame*, the noun, means both the plot of a story and the intermeshing threads of a fabric. In this context, because the words work phatically the story is the fabric itself. Here, the primary function of *langage* (as opposed to *langue*) is not to represent reality or to convey information, but rather, like gossip or small talk, to establish community for its own sake.

The same goes for the French language as a whole. Despised by the SS as the national language of people they rank just above the Jews, it functions among prisoners as an oppositional practice—and it does so *in itself*. Connotatively speaking, the meanings conveyed by the French language are obsolete in the context of Buchenwald because the social and cultural realities that this language simultaneously refers to and produces have been forever destroyed. (Even after the liberation things may look the same, but the survivors know better, for they knowingly embody the empty core of a culture that functions pro forma.) The world of French as they knew it being gone forever, every word now feels archaic. This makes the use of French precious in all senses of the term. Because language is shared not *in spite* of its obsolescence but *because* of it and preserved in its most pristine form to the point of making it blatantly unreal, its surviving use *as old form* implies the survival of the prisoners themselves. In a different context, this collective use of old forms for present oppositional purposes might be called campy. The same language, thus used, is the vector of new social relations. Antelme writes:

[L]anguage . . . [is] the same back there as it is here; we use the same words, pronounce the same names. So we begin to worship that language, since it has become the ultimate thing that we possess in common. Sometimes when I am in the neighborhood of a German I speak French with special attentiveness, *in a way I don't ordinarily speak it back home*; I construct sentences better and pronounce all the liaisons. . . . Next to German, our tongue rings, I see it shape itself *as I speak it and make it*. . . . Inside the barbed wire, in the land of the SS, you speak the way you do back home and the SS, who don't understand a word of it, put up with it. Our language doesn't make the SS laugh; it merely confirms our condition. (45–46; translation modified; my emphases)

[[L]e langage . . . est le même là-bas qu'ici; nous nous servons des mêmes mots, nous prononçons les mêmes noms. Alors on se met à l'adorer car il est devenu l'ultime chose commune dont nous disposions. Quand je suis près d'un Allemand, il m'arrive de parler le français avec plus d'attention, *comme je ne le parle pas habituellement là-bas*; je construis mieux la phrase, j'use de toutes les liaisons. . . . Auprès de l'allemand, la langue sonne, je la vois se dessiner *au fur et à mesure que je la fais*. . . . A l'intérieur du barbelé, chez le SS, on parle comme là-bas et le SS qui ne comprend rien le supporte. Notre langue ne le fait pas rire. Elle ne fait que confirmer notre condition. (51; my emphases)]

Ten pages earlier, Antelme had remarked,

The SS . . . must think that, for prisoners, pissing is nothing other than an obligation whose fulfillment should . . . render them more dependent on their task; the SS do not know that, by pissing, you get away. So sometimes we stand in front of a wall, open our flies, and pretend. (34)

[Le SS . . . doit croire que pisser est exclusivement pour le détenu une servitude dont l'accomplissement doit . . . le rendre plus dépendant de sa tâche; le SS ne sait pas qu'en pissant on s'évade. Aussi, parfois, on se met contre un mur, on ouvre la braguette et on fait semblant. (40)]

And later:

Since I wasn't your extraordinary prisoner, a machine-tool operator or a mechanic, I was the waste prisoner who with his feet forges ahead, with his hands picks up waste. A perfect coinciding of the task with the man. The harmony in all this was reassuring to them, I'm certain . . .

What they didn't know was that when you're randomly picking up scraps— bent over, totally ignored—you can also be happy, the way you are when you're pissing. (68; translation modified)

[Puisque je n'étais pas ce détenu extraordinaire, tourneur ou mécanicien, j'étais le détenu déchet qui avec ses pieds avance, avec ses mains ramasse les déchets. Coïncidence parfaite de la tâche et de l'homme; cette harmonie les rassurait, c'était sûr. Ils ne savaient pas qu'en ramassant les déchets au hasard, courbé, parfaitement ignoré, il arrivait qu'on soit heureux, comme en pissant. (73–74)]

Degrading work, bodily functions, and language are similar practices of freedom, especially when performed in this empty way.

Now consider Nazi language, which I define as the literalization of tropes: the total aesthetic gesture that seeks to erase the difference between figure and literality and to obliterate the distance of language from the real—a relationality that is itself the instantiation of the communal core that enables/activates the self and defines the human. By contrast, Nazi language seeks to embody a mode of *Gemeinschaft* based on the communion or fusion of all its members into totalitarian self-sameness.[3] The extermination of Jews was made possible from the moment they were thought of as *literally* vermin—which makes the Holocaust the essence of Nazism and its deniers' claim that Zyklon B was used only for delousing a true statement as well as a lie. The "harmony" (really a metonymy) between waste and the person who collects waste is another telling example. So is the fact that for the guards, the prisoners, especially the French prisoners, are shit. The word *Scheisse* is as ubiquitous in Antelme's text as the actual shitting scenes. In one particular instance, its use reveals how Nazi language works. This is the episode in which a dying prisoner lets out a gush of diarrhea in front of the men assembled for roll call. When the kapo yells "Scheisse!" (29), it must be read all at once as an exclamation ("Shit!"), the naming of what is under his eyes ("This is shit"), and an insult directed at the dying man ("You are shit"). Similarly, when another kapo uses the same word after the prisoners have defecated in the church, it appears that the metonymic relation between "shit" and "he who shits" is abolished.

Nazi language being that of the masters, there is no way for the prisoners not to abide by it, just as there is no way for them to escape defecating in public or to restore the lost meanings of the French language. In the camps, there is no other meaning than Nazi meaning. All that is left to the men is to shit as a group because they are called shit as a group and to be the rubbish they are forced to eat. For Antelme,

> You can acknowledge the self you recall rummaging like a dog among rotten leftovers. But, on the other hand, the memory of the moment when you didn't share with one of the guys what you should have shared with him will finally give rise to doubts even as concerns the former behavior. Conscience errs not when we "sink" to "a lower level," but when we lose sight of the fact that degradation must be of all and for all. (96; translation modified)

> [On peut se reconnaître à se revoir fouinant comme un chien dans les épluchures pourries. Le souvenir du moment où l'on n'a pas partagé avec un copain ce qui devait l'être, au contraire viendrait à faire douter même du premier acte. L'erreur de conscience n'est pas de "déchoir," mais de perdre de vue que la déchéance doit être de tous et pour tous. (101–2)]

Being made to shit in public and to eat trash is *meant* (by the Nazis) to dehumanize the prisoners. Yet the latter rehumanize themselves through the act of sharing, regardless of what is being shared and which is, by the very act of sharing, deprived of its intended meaning.[4] For the men, "A buddy's bread is sacred" ["Le pain d'un copain, c'est sacré"].[5] Etymologically, the *pain* is that which must be shared for there to be *copains*, that is, community. But in the end *co* is more sacred than *pain*. Antelme's phrase, "la merde du copain" (34), frustratingly translated as "the guy's shit" (29)—the *copain* here is the one who shits and dies in front of all the others—is oddly beautiful. On one level, it reads like a contradiction in terms since shitting in public marks you as a radical outsider; on another, it rewrites the lowest, loneliest state of degradation as the source of community: "*A thousand men together* had never seen that before" (my emphasis).

This is not, however, the case of a community being unified negatively in opposition to what it repels, as in the injunction "One does not shit in company," which tells us that the social may be performed by eating bread with others, as the etymology of "company" indicates, but on the condition that the waste thus produced be disposed of privately. "La merde du copain," however, implies that the community of a thousand men is enabled by incorporating, and not rejecting, the inmate who loses control of his bodily orifices (thus ceasing to be a man) and lets out a gush of shit in plain view of all. Embracing the dying prisoner as a friend among friends implies that the group is founded on and by a repudiation of masculinity as identity: "degradation must be of all and for all." The thousand onlookers may be men, but they now embody manhood without a gender system. In *L'espèce humaine*, returning to something like a presocial stage is what grounds community and simultaneously repudiates identity. Given the context of his story, there was no other choice, of course, but because all oppressions are forms of dehumanization, Antelme's relevance extends beyond his particular experience.

Comrades on a Train

In *La douleur* [Pain], Marguerite Duras, once Antelme's lover, tells of his return from Buchenwald. The man she once loved and alongside whom she fought in the French Resistance is all but unrecognizable. Unable to eat solid food because it could kill him, all he does is defecate in a seemingly endless stream of diarrhea. But whereas diarrhea, in the camp, signified community, it singles him out after his return once he finds himself in the company of people who do not and cannot fathom what he has been through. Duras describes Antelme's shit as something radically alien to her that impedes all possibility of community—as does Buchenwald itself:

> When he sat on his bucket, he went all at once, with an enormous, unexpected, and outsized gargling sound. . . . He expelled this dark green, sticky stuff that bubbled, shit the like of which no one had ever seen. . . . For seventeen days, that shit remained the same. It was inhuman. It separated him from us more than his fever and emaciation did, more than his fingers that had lost their nails, more than the traces of the S.S.'s blows. We fed him pap of the golden yellow kind we give infants, and it came out of him dark green like the sludge in a marsh. . . . It had indeed a dark smell whose thickness evoked the thickness of the night he was awakening from and that we would never know.

> [Une fois assis sur son seau, il faisait d'un seul coup, dans un glou-glou énorme, inattendu, démesuré. . . . Il faisait donc cette chose gluante vert sombre qui bouillonnait, merde que personne n'avait encore vue. . . . Pendant dix-sept jours, l'aspect de cette merde resta le même. Elle était inhumaine. Elle le séparait de nous plus que la fièvre, plus que la maigreur, les doigts désonglés, les traces de coups des S.S. On lui donnait de la bouillie jaune d'or, bouillie pour nourrisson et elle ressortait de lui vert sombre comme de la vase de marécage. . . . C'était là en effet une odeur sombre, épaisse comme le reflet de cette nuit épaisse de laquelle il émergeait et que nous ne connaîtrions jamais. (68–69)]

Duras and her friends are helpless: "In the face of the unknown we scrambled for explanations. . . . How could we know? How could we know what unknown, what pain this belly still contained?" (70). Ultimately, Duras's only means of evoking her friendship with Antelme lies in the unbridgeable gap she maintains between her writing and the experience of the camps, as if her tactical erasure as a writer echoed, as a form of inevitable failure, the unspeakable she attempts to convey to her readers in order to involve us, too, in that friendship. She soon acknowledges that the only way to keep death at bay is through a form of tact: to touch by keeping a distance.

> The struggle with death began very early. We had to go easy with it, with delicacy, tact, and dexterity. It surrounded him on all sides. But there was still a way to reach him. It wasn't a large opening through which to communicate with him, but life was still in him.

> [La lutte a commencé très vite avec la mort. Il fallait y aller doux avec elle, avec delicatesse, tact, doigté. Elle le cernait de tous les côtés. Mais tout de même il y avait un moyen de l'atteindre lui, ce n'était pas grand, cette ouverture par où communiquer avec lui mais la vie était quand même en lui. (67)]

The question that seeps through the gaps and silences of Duras's account is one I raised earlier. How is a community to be based on a disaster that

cannot and must not be repeated yet must somehow be recalled as a founding moment? In *Untimely Interventions*, Ross Chambers has shown how testimonial writings of trauma and disaster have to rely on rhetorical tactics of
untimeliness and inappropriateness that make a haunted narrative, in turn,
haunt its readers. Community, then, is essentially a matter of return. So let
me return to Charlotte Delbo and, specifically, to the section of the third
volume of *Auschwitz et après* entitled "The Funeral." In this episode, Delbo
gives us an idea of how the community of friends may be maintained beyond its founding event when that event, Auschwitz in this case, is too trau-
matic to remember.

The trilogy is framed by two train rides, two train rides toward death.
The first one, although it isn't directly described in the trilogy, is of course
the one that led the group of two hundred and thirty French women to
Auschwitz in January 1943 and is implied in the opening of the first volume
when Delbo depicts the "train station" of the camp;[6] the second, whose date
and destination are not specified, is the one that a few of the forty-nine survivors take many years later to attend the funeral of one of their comrades,
Germaine, and that is related in the section I would like to read here. This
second train ride toward death, a *re-union*, is a symbolic repetition of the
first one that abolishes both the past and the future in the sense that the
"original" train ride cannot be celebrated as foundational yet cannot be rejected either. The second train ride—a form of timeless *ressassement* rather
than a marker of chronological linearity—figures a "return" that allows the
community of comrades to maintain itself by locating its origin "in between," "in transit," that is to say, by figuring the return *of* Auschwitz without returning *to* Auschwitz.

There is another mode of transport I would like to talk about first. At one
point in the second volume, *Une connaissance inutile*, Delbo mentions some
of the tricks she resorted to in the camps in order to stay connected to her
past, such as remembering phone numbers, poems, shops along a particular
street, and all the stops on a metro line. Her purpose is to recapture time
where time has ceased to mean anything and thus maintain her very self
through and as connection:

> Since Auschwitz, I always feared losing my memory. To lose one's memory is
> to lose oneself, to no longer be oneself. I had invented all kinds of exercises to
> put my memory to work: memorize all the telephone numbers I used to know,
> all the metro stations along one line, all the boutiques along the rue Caumartin
> between the Athénée theater and the Havre-Caumartin metro station. I had
> succeeded, at the price of infinite efforts, in recalling fifty-seven poems. (188)
>
> [Depuis Auschwitz, j'avais peur de perdre la mémoire. Perdre la mémoire, c'est se
> perdre soi-même, c'est n'être plus soi. Et j'avais inventé toutes sortes d'exercices

pour faire travailler ma mémoire: me rappeler tous les numéros de téléphone que
j'avais sus, toutes les stations d'une ligne de métro, toutes les boutiques de la rue
Caumartin, entre l'Athénée et le métro Havre-Caumartin. J'avais réussi, au prix
d'efforts infinis, à me rappeler cinquante-sept poèmes. (124)]

By reviving the past the future becomes imaginable, and the survival of individuals may be envisioned through the work of memory. And in addition
to time, the recollections have to do with space as well—urban space, such
as the metro and the street, but also cultural sites, such as the poems. Memory may be a way to keep a sense of self, its objects, however, are collective
in nature and define the self as an effect of the group.

More significant perhaps is the comrades' earlier attempt to remember the
text of Molière's play *Le malade imaginaire* in order to put on a show.
Claudette, with some help from the others, is in charge of rewriting the text,
while the other women put together the costumes and the set—a collective
form of *bricolage* that is also textual and textile—a *trame*. Reconstructing the
past in order to ensure individual survival is, it turns out, something better
done as a group. To reconnect in this way what has been radically disrupted
is not an act of denial but a brief moment of respite. As Delbo concludes:

It's magnificent because each one of us performs the play with humility, without thinking of foregrouding her own role.

. . .

It was magnificent because, for the space of two hours, while the smokestacks
never stopped belching their smoke of human flesh, for two whole hours we
believed in it. (171; translation modified)

[C'est magnifique parce que chacune, avec humilité, joue la pièce sans songer à
se mettre en valeur dans son rôle.

. . .

C'était magnifique parce que, pendant deux heures, sans que les cheminées
aient cessé de fumer leur fumée de chair humaine, pendant deux heures, nous
y avons cru. (95–96)]

The staging of the play isn't an attempt to restore continuity between past
and future as if nothing had happened in between. What has happened is
the disastrous realization that community has become the condition of selfhood. In more theoretical terms, because it constitutes a form of fidelity
and acknowledges a debt to the past, memory is akin to loyalty. It obliges us,
expropriates the self (etymologically, it locates its properties outside or removes it from the domain of the proper), and therefore makes community
an inherent, perhaps the *only* inherent property of the self.

But what the comrades also attempt to summon is the national community the canon and the French public school system were designed to produce. The eventual performance of the play in the camp is not faithful to the original words of Molière, of course. The complete text cannot be restored nor the continuity between past and future seamlessly reestablished. While the plot of the play is more or less all there, Claudette, in spite of the others' help, cannot remember exactly where each act ended and the next one began, and exact lines from Molière's play are interspersed with the women's own approximations. In the end, their version of *Le malade imaginaire*, not by Molière but "after Molière, by Claudette" (169 [92]), comprises only four acts instead of the original five. The community thus performed by this imperfect act of collective rereading/rewriting is figured in the "flawed" structure of the play: it works beautifully but it isn't a faithful repetition of the original. It is in these gaps of memory, in the inability to articulate elements as they once were, in the failure to reproduce, that Auschwitz lurks and is allegorically conveyed to us with a sense of its historical, national, and cultural implications. In other words, there is something not quite right with Molière after Auschwitz. Like the metro, Molière is, in Delbo's text, a mode of mass transport, or *transport en commun*, in that it transports the comrades out of Auschwitz together but takes specters along for the ride.

When thinking of the two train rides that frame Delbo's trilogy, an aphorism by Jean Cocteau comes to mind: "Everything we do/make in life, even love, we do on the fast train that leads to death" ["Tout ce qu'on fait dans la vie, même l'amour, on le fait dans le train express qui roule vers la mort"]. This observation is about life as much as it is about death, of course, since each one makes the other possible. In that sense, the train ride to Germaine's funeral is different from the original one, the one to Auschwitz. Germaine's death is arguably a normal death, unlike death in Auschwitz, which is not the opposite of life as a natural course of events. The obsolescence of a dichotomy so fundamental to our understanding of pretty much everything is conveyed by Delbo in what she twice describes as "the feeling of being dead and knowing it" (70 [*ANR 115*]; translation modified)—a figural undoing of that dichotomy, since death is the unknowable by definition. In a way, death in Auschwitz is to death what life in Auschwitz is to life: both are radically altered in themselves and in their relation, and both are unknowable. "[T]he feeling of being dead and knowing it" is a figure that questions "meaning" altogether.

Let us now turn to the text of "The Funeral." Delbo and a group of surviving comrades are meeting at a station to take a train together to attend Germaine's funeral. The first sentence of this section contains most of the ideas I have been discussing. The original French sentence is "Nous devions nous retrouver au train" (*MJ* 185) and is rendered rather faithfully as "We were supposed to meet at the train" (337). As is often the case with Delbo's writing, however, the attempt to translate reveals a multiplicity of possible meanings. To begin with, the first word, "nous," indicates that this section is going to be about the community of comrades. The very short opening paragraph contains the word "nous" six times, as subject, object, and reflexive pronouns. The last sentence, "How many of us d'you think there'll be?" ["Combien croyez-vous que nous serons?"], soon confirms this indication while locating the community's exact contours in the realm of uncertainty and interrogation. The second word, the verb "devions," *devoir* in the imperfect tense, lends itself to a plurality of interpretations. Given the context that follows the opening sentence, the obvious translation would indeed be: "were supposed to." But what happens if we read "nous devions" as "we had to" or "we were bound to"? Then the other possible meanings and connotations of *devoir* come to mind: duty, debt, inescapability. Again, the community of comrades finds itself defined in terms of loyalty, ethics, and obligations.

As for "nous retrouver," it can mean "to meet up with each other," but also "to find ourselves again" if we read the second "nous" in the sentence as both reflexive and reciprocal and if we deploy both senses of "retrouver." The latter meaning suggests that community is the condition of selfhood and the idea that to be with each other and to find oneself is the same thing. The prefix "re" signals that the community is enacted through a process of repetition or return, which is, of course, what is taking place in the passage.

Finally, "au train" (and not *à la gare*, at the station) echoes the original train journey and locates the community and its origin not in a definable, knowable space—which Auschwitz, as trauma, can never really be for survivors—but in a more elusive and forever changing *transit*. The figure of the train, as we know, has become a common trope to signify the camps, and its connotations are unavoidable in this passage. But I am also thinking of Jorge Semprun's first testimonial account of his deportation and internment at Buchenwald, *Le grand voyage [The Long Journey]*. The journey by train forms the narrative backbone of the entire book, interrupted by a series of flashbacks and flashforwards. For the duration of the journey, the narrator engages in conversations with a man he calls "the guy from Semur," a fictional character designed to figure textually the impending fragmentation of the narrator's self. At the end of the book, when the train pulls into Buchenwald, the narration shifts from the first person to the third, the narrator's ability to say "I" having disappeared. In Delbo, as in Semprun, membership in a community of comrades is not determined by a principle of identity, as traditional one-on-one friendship according to Montaigne would be, but rather by one of alienation or self-alteration—literally, becoming other.

In a passage from *Convoy to Auschwitz*, the women who have just arrived in the camp try to make sense of their new surroundings little by little:

> Near the entrance, a sign made from a board nailed to a spindly post . . . said "*Vernichttunglager*" [*sic*]. "You know German—what does it mean?"—"*Nichts* means 'nothing, nothingness. Toward nothing, nothingness.' In other words, 'Annihilation Camp.' "—"Oh, that's cheerful." (5; translation modified)

> [Près de l'entrée, un écriteau fait d'une planchette clouée à un méchant piquet . . . disait "Vernichttunglager" [*sic*].—Toi qui sais l'allemand, qu'est-ce que ça veut dire?—"Nichts, c'est: rien, néant. Vers le rien, vers le néant. Cela veut dire: camp d'anéantissement."—"Eh bien, c'est gai." (12)]

One could then read the opening sentence of "The Funeral," "Nous devions nous retrouver au train," as an echo of that initial scene: "We, survivors, owed it to each other to think of ourselves as a collective journey toward nothing, nothing but one another." The question, "Combien croyez-vous que nous serons?" (how many do you think we'll be, in word-for-word translation) would then mean: "How many fragments of one another do you think each one of us is made of?"

Soon after this introduction, the four comrades who have already arrived at the train notice a woman standing alone and looking around. One of them says, "It might be one of us, but I don't recognize her" (337 [186]. In fact, none of the friends recognize her for certain: "Jeanne? How she must have changed . . ." (translation modified); until the woman introduces herself, "You don't recognize me? Jeanne." And Delbo writes, "She no longer seemed changed. As soon as we recognized her, it was she" [Dès qu'on l'avait reconnue, c'était elle]." Jeanne's identity, then, is conferred upon her solely by her recognition by the other members of the community. Before she was recognized, Jeanne was not Jeanne. And Delbo adds, "We may be the only ones to see the truth of our comrades" (338 [187]; translation modified). Such truth, therefore, is relational. It stems from a debt that cannot and must not be discharged for there to be friendship.

On the train, the women start to reminisce and, as they did with the Molière play, to reconstruct a common past with fragments of incomplete personal memories—only this time, the past is Auschwitz, that is, a past that should be recalled but not reopened. As with the play, though, the collective not only conditions personal memories but is memory's very purpose. As one of the friends remarks, "Only when I'm with all of you do I remember, or perhaps I ought to say recognize what you remember" (344 [198]; translation modified). Indeed, what good are memories if those who share them are no longer with you? What is the point of remembering alone? Is it even possible? But if what matters is less the thing remembered than the act of remembering, a form of faithfulness and obligation to the others, then the others don't need to have actually shared your past. This may be the only way for us, readers, to *be* with survivors, to relate to them in friendship and, in turn, to acknowledge *ressassement* as our own inescapable condition.

Epilogue
My Father and I

On 25 February 2004, sometime in the evening, my father collapsed in his apartment from a massive blood clot to the brain. After a brief coma, he died in the hospital the next day at the age of eighty-four.

————————

I spent most of 2002 in Paris doing research for this book. During that time, my father made several brief trips there, as he often did even when I was not around, to visit my sister and her kids. He and I soon settled into our own little routines. I would go pick him up at Saint-Lazare, the train station that connects Paris to western France and vice versa, and from there we would go for a beer and a walk and chat. After that, I would put him on a commuter train to my sister's place in the suburbs. On the day of his return to Caen we would meet at noon in the Marais, always at the corner of the rue des Rosiers and rue des Ecouffes, the heart of the Pletzl, as he still called the neighborhood, and have some falafels. He was often in charge of doing a little shopping for his friends in the community whenever he went to Paris—smoked sprats at Goldenberg's, Yiddish Broït at Finkelsztajn's, pickles at Panzer's, and so on. All the time we would talk and talk, and I would take him back to Saint-Lazare, his travel bag full and smelly, until the next visit.

One day I took pictures. I photographed him standing in front of 29 rue du Roi de Sicile where his business used to be, and 7 rue des Blancs-Manteaux, where he once lived. I photographed him in the restaurant where we had lunch that day, and in front of Florence Finkelsztajn's bakery, and by the Saint-Paul metro station, and at a few other very Jewish and somewhat folkloric landmarks. Except for the first two sets of pictures, of which I shall talk later, this was all a bit futile but fun. He had taken so many

By Florence Finkelsztajn's Yiddish bakery

pictures of us kids years ago that there was also something enjoyable for
both of us in this role reversal. But most of all he liked the attention. At last,
it seemed, I was interested in him. I always had been, of course, but never
showed it much, so he didn't know for sure. Finally, I took pictures of him
at the train station, standing at the car's door as if saying goodbye. He asked
to borrow my camera as he wanted to take one of me waving back at him
from the platform. This wordless exchange had been a nice little "moment," as people say, one of these rare times when we awkwardly recognized our mutual affection without expressing it directly. That always
worked better for us somehow than our attempts at intimate conversations.
(*Pudeur* is what the French call this quiet feeling of restraint or modesty,
while Americans must, by now, have added it to the growing list of named
affective disorders.) When I returned to my apartment that evening, I began
to look at the photos on my laptop. I was rather pleased with the first two
sets. Not that they were masterpieces or anything, but they were interesting
and thought-provoking. I could definitely write something about them. But
when the last ones popped up on the screen, I was horrified.

What was I thinking? How could I have not realized what I was doing?
All I could see now was that I had taken pictures of a Holocaust survivor

boarding a train and saying goodbye, and that it was an awful thing to do, even involuntarily. I was overcome with that familiar feeling of shame, burning cheeks and all. My original intent was to have a cool shot of a typical nineteenth-century train station with the kind of industrial steel structure so popular in those days that Eiffel built a tower that way. For the same aesthetic reasons, I also enjoyed the Gymnase Japy, across the street from my apartment in the eleventh arrondissement, in the neighborhood once known as Little Istanbul. With its heavy steel beams, knots and bolts, the former covered market is truly a little gem of the Haussmann era. As with Saint-Lazare, there is something deliciously Parisian about it and the sense of old-fashioned modernity it exhales. Until, as in the train station, another side of history impinges on your memory. Several plaques at the entrance of the gym explain how thousands of Jews, including children from nearby schools, were rounded up there in 1942 before being deported to Auschwitz where they were all killed. Symbols of the glorious "capital of the nineteenth century," to use Walter Benjamin's famous phrase, are thus often tainted by what happened in the twentieth.

For some reason I can't quite explain, the ghostly presence of Holocaust victims was all the more striking in that the awareness of it took me by surprise. Had I known beforehand that the Gymnase Japy was historically connected to the Holocaust I probably wouldn't have had the same uncanny impression that the deaths of thousands of Jews had infected the Parisian landscape in such a lasting way. It probably has to do with the paradoxical effect of officialized memory, or memorialization—when regularly timed rituals end up generating forgetfulness as they purport to do just the opposite. On the other hand, being unexpectedly reminded of that same past, as I was when I discovered the plaque by the gymnasium's doors, has an unsettling power and a near sensorial reality—Proust's involuntary memory, in a sense, but applied to the collective past of the nation rather than to personal experience, and a lot less blissful. Indeed the feeling that unmistakably signals the brutal return of history is often shame. To commemorate our past misdeeds is to attempt to free ourselves of our shame, but shame's inevitable return reveals that to remember the past in order not to repeat it is not to remember it at all. It is about rejecting the past. It is, in a word, denial. Shame, in one of its many, complex aspects, is experienced as a sudden collapse of the safe distance between ourselves and the past, between what is current and what is no more, in short between life and death. The feeling of mortification—in the full etymological sense—that I had when I opened the picture of my father looking as if saying goodbye to me from the train was, literally, a feeling of being in touch with death. Saint-Lazare was not used as a departure point for the death camps during the German occupa-

The gymnase Japy, a historical marker on the corner

tion of France, but my father's figure in the picture was enough to make the old train station look as if it were filled with ghosts, as if this Jew stood for other Jews, this train for other trains, and the survivor for the dead. But why? Although nowhere explicitly (or even implicitly) signified by decipherable signs, such as the commemorative plaques outside the Gymnase Japy, the Holocaust was nonetheless readable in these pictures, as a trace perhaps or what Peirce would call an indexical sign. Yet my father's presence at the station does not suffice to explain the irruption of Holocaust ghosts, nor does my own presence as someone who, as a scholar and as a son, is particularly receptive to such matters. Both circumstances are important, probably necessary even, but they are not enough. My father and I often went to Saint-Lazare for the exact same purpose, repeating more or less the same scene and gestures, probably even the same words—"Take care of yourself,

The entrance of the gym, a memorial plaque on the far left

watch your health, see you next time." I was always worried about his health because he was old; he worried about mine because, although he never said so outright, he was constantly afraid I would get AIDS. What was different this time was, of course, the fact that I took pictures. Or rather not the fact that I took these pictures, because the thought of the Holocaust never entered my mind at the moment I was taking them, but the fact that I looked at them *as pictures*, that is, as signs. And the awareness of signs triggered the urge to read.

So what was there to read in these pictures? They showed my father and me bidding farewell to one another, there, that day, just as we had done several times before. But as soon as these farewells became tokens of farewells, they immediately acquired the potential to stand for other moments of separation. At one level, this exemplarity or representativeness was already evident at the time, since the subject of the pictures was in fact a staging of the "real" exchange of waves and smiles that was to take place a few minutes later and constitute the actual farewell—the copy preceding the original, as it were. Our separation is spatially figured by the two different pictures. He's on the train, I'm on the platform; I watch him leave, he watches me stay. But, when looking at the photographs, it became apparent to me that another, equally real separation was being staged at that moment, a separation that was also to take place in the future, albeit a more distant one—the final goodbye. The relatively unconscious desire to perform, or rehearse, the final goodbye in advance stems from the recognition that it may never actually take place. My father was eighty-two years-old when the pictures were taken, and we lived so far away from each other. Chances were I would not be there with him when he went. Indeed I was not. We had several such final goodbyes, that is, none at all since we couldn't know ahead of time whether this farewell would be the last. But we knew it could be.

The momentousness of the seemingly innocuous event that took place that day must have registered on his mind just as it did on mine. Taking photos always raises the question of time. We know that what happened a second ago is already in the past, but to record it always endows the most banal occurrence with fatefulness in that it kills the present and turns it into a memory. The next time my father came to Paris and we, once again, parted at Saint-Lazare, he told me, with visible emotion and in clear violation of our code of *pudeur*, "Every time we say goodbye at the train station I can't help but think it may be the last time I will ever see you." When the photos appeared on my computer screen just moments after we took them, I saw my father dead. Now that he is dead, I look at them and I see him alive.

That my father's death to come was instantly connected in my mind with the Holocaust wasn't exactly a surprise. All Holocaust survivors have cheated death, and when they actually die, no matter how many years later and how natural the cause of death, it feels as if the Nazis had finally caught up with them. Survivors should never die lest they be deprived of their status of survivors. I mean, can there be such a thing as a dead survivor? Could this explain why so many survivors, most famously Primo Levi, commit suicide, sometimes decades afterward: as an attempt to retain control over their own death and to rob the Nazis of their final victory? In my father's case, the awareness that he may never have the chance to say his final goodbye to his son was doubtless connected to an episode he had recounted to me a few weeks earlier when I interviewed him. My hidden agenda that day was to have him recognize that he had left Hungary not only to flee anti-Semitic persecution but also, just as I had when I came to America, to get away from his family. I was secretly hoping we would share that feeling of guilt so typical of people who are in fact glad to be far away from home and family but slightly embarrassed to admit it. Instead of going where I wanted him to go, however, he began to tell me very movingly about the day he left his hometown in Hungary, walking across a bridge over to Czechoslovakia from where he was going to take a train to Paris. His mother had accompanied him up to the Hungarian end of the bridge. When he was halfway across, he turned back and looked at her. At that point in the story, my father stopped talking. His eyes seemed to stare at that image of the past, a memory of sixty-six years. He was seventeen years old then and he didn't know that he would never see his mother again, let alone in what circumstances she was to die. This was the last image he had of her. His parents had planned a visit to Paris but it never happened. Even if it had that wouldn't have allowed for a final goodbye anyway—obviously they wouldn't have returned home if they had known what was waiting for them there. And since his relatives have had no final resting place, no ritualized mourning was ever possible either. (When I visited an exhibition entitled "The Destruction of the Jews of Hungary" at Paris's Jean Moulin museum in June of 2004, I was unable to locate the names of my relatives on the long list of victims.) Again, as my father stared silently for a few seconds, the safe distance between the present and the past, between life and death, had suddenly and uncannily collapsed. Again I felt like shit. His gaze was lost in pain and sadness. I averted mine in a last-ditch attempt at tactfulness. I was feeling singled out and erased at the same time. Shame had overwhelmed me once more; the quickened heartbeat and the knots in my stomach telltale signs that something was happening. Never before or since have I sensed with such acuity the reality of my relatives' death and its haunting, unspeakable power. That day something of it, and of them, touched me and was passed on to me.

Looking at my pictures, I understood how one goodbye could stand for other goodbyes, one train for other trains, and how the personal was almost immediately inscribed in history. This may be a little late in this book to justify my allegorical use of the personal but, as my relationship with my father during his final years exemplifies, better late than never. My father's future death, announced by the photos taken at Saint-Lazare, reminded me of the death he escaped decades earlier but that, as a European Jew, was supposed to have been his fate, erasing the very possibility of my own life in the same gesture. Like most children of survivors, I exist thanks to a lucky historical fuck-up. My life may be my own, but I share with many others like me the reasons why it was at all possible. There lies the inherent duality of the *exemplum*: thinking of myself rhetorically, I am both singled out and representative—of something that necessarily erases our singularity as it showcases it. The *exemplum* is therefore, and at once, affirmation and negation of singularity.[1] Or, put differently, the *exemplum* is a singularity *in common*.

With this in mind, I present my father's life in my work not as a biography whose intention would be to offer a coherent and complete narrative portrait of the man, but rather as a collection of what Roland Barthes has called biographemes,[2] singular fragments, but ones I can playfully, or painfully as the case may be, recombine and connect with others.

Thinking of Barthes, I am tempted to say about the specific goodbye supposedly represented in the Saint-Lazare pictures, that is, their avowed subject: "That hasn't been." In *Camera Lucida*, Barthes explains how "Photography's Referent is not the same as the referent of other systems of representation, and he calls

> "photographic referent" not the *optionally* real thing to which an image or a sign refers but the *necessarily* real thing which has been placed before the lens, without which there would be no photograph. . . . The name of photography's *noeme* will therefore be "That-has-been." (76–77; original emphasis)

Naturally, my father and I were present in front of the camera when the pictures were taken, and I am not so much refuting Barthes as bending him a little. (I'm sure he wouldn't mind.) What I mean here is that what I, as a participant in these pictures, see in them is not what they appear to represent. The present moment whose reality they were supposed to testify to seemed, as I looked at them, erased or absorbed by the past they evoked— the Holocaust and the death of my father, which was supposed to happen but didn't—and the future they foreshadowed—the death of my father that was surely to happen. The present moment, or photographic referent, that is to say life, appears to be the least significant thing about the photos; it certainly weighs very little compared to the deaths that elliptically frame them. In other words, it has become impossible to consider my father's life in isolation from the way millions of others died, and that the way they died has stubbornly resisted representation so as to let itself be felt, in pure negative fashion, as ellipsis or trace or gap.

For Barthes, death is an inextricable element of photography. Looking, after his mother had died, at a picture of her as a child, he writes, "I shudder . . . *of a catastrophe which has already occurred.* Whether or not the subject is already dead, every photograph is this catastrophe" (96; original emphasis). And reflecting on a picture of himself, he observes that being photographed, for a portrait, "represents that very subtle moment when, to tell the truth, I am neither subject nor object but a subject who feels he is becoming an object: I then experience a micro-version of death . . . : I am truly becoming a specter" (14). Death is also what, according to Barthes, links photography to the theater:

> [If] Photography seems to me closer to the Theater, it is by way of a singular intermediary . . . : Death. We know the original relation of the theater and the cult of the Dead. . . . Now it is the same relation which I find in the Photograph; however "lifelike" we strive to make it (and this frenzy to be lifelike can only be our mythic denial of an apprehension of death), Photography is a kind of primitive theater, a kind of *Tableau Vivant*, a figuration of the motionless and made-up face beneath which we see the dead. (31–32)

The little staging my father and I engaged in that day at Saint-Lazare did, in fact, more than transform us into specters; it accidentally awakened many other specters—the ghosts of the Holocaust. (Of course, I also couldn't help but notice that the experience happened under the symbolic patronage of Lazarus, a Jew who was raised from the dead, although we may want to leave Jesus out of it.) If looking at the future the Saint-Lazare photos announce is like the micro-experience of death Barthes describes, the unexpected reemergence of the past is more like a historical and political macro-experience of it. But when the conductor between a singular moment one was a part of and a past one hasn't directly known happens to be one's own father, a figure Emmanuel Levinas described as simultaneously same and other,[3] it becomes rather difficult to separate familiarity from difference and, if it comes to that, the personal from the historical.

(In presenting parts of this epilogue as professional talks and as friends read early versions of it, I was often asked why I chose not to show the pictures taken at Saint-Lazare. There are three main reasons for this choice. The first is ethical. By taking the picture of my father on the train, I felt that I had somehow harmed him, albeit involuntarily and unbeknownst to him. The second reason is more intellectual. The uncanny effect I've described was made possible by a set of conditions: what the picture represents, how it was taken, and how it first appeared to me on my computer screen. Because this convergence cannot be reproduced, the effect cannot either. Finally, there's a third, perhaps campier reason. By not showing the picture, I am referencing the text I am using as a theoretical framework, citing lack with lack and absence with absence, since Barthes didn't show the picture of his mother that had moved him so much. As for the photo of myself, it is simply too unflattering to display.)

I experienced an odd feeling of overlapping when my father gave me a few reproductions of photos of his family taken in Hungary before and during World War II. Naturally, I could have written "*my* family," since by virtue of the fact that I am my father's son his family is also mine. But that's what was so odd about discovering these pictures. I had never had any interest in my roots or personal genealogy. At least I thought I hadn't. Call it homosexual rebelliousness or plain old denial, either way my professed indifference seems to have been shaken by the irruption of the family's ghosts and images I didn't even know existed. The photos represent or evoke things that are almost completely foreign to me—Hungary, Jewishness, the Holocaust, a culture that no longer exists, and people I have never met. And yet here are my grandparents and my uncle Zoltan and my cousin David. And I was moved by them.[4] But how could I have an uncle named Zoltan? Or, stranger even at my age, a first cousin who died in Auschwitz? Sure, my uncle Albert came from Transylvania and I got a lot of prestige in school out of that, but I actually knew my uncle Albert and he was no vampire. These old photos were different; they brought up the question of family and otherness in a far more serious and unsettling way than spooky images of Bela Lugosi.

The pictures are interesting and moving for a variety of reasons. One shows Zoltan, one of my father's brothers, sometime in the mid 1930s. He is pressing raspberries that were to be used to flavor tea in the winter. He did that professionally, for paying customers, so the photograph is an interesting depiction of an old profession. Except that Zoltan died in a Hungarian-controlled labor camp somewhere in Russia during the war. Another picture, probably taken in the mid 1910s shows my aunt Hélène posing for a professional portrait with her maternal grandparents. Mr. Fuchs, my great-grandfather, looks so perfectly ancestral with his long black double-breasted coat and huge Austro-Hungarian white beard that you'd swear he was actually born a patriarch. (Again I think of Barthes and his own great-grandfather whom he calls "the Stock," "la Souche.") To look at my great-grandfather's portrait is to contemplate the beginning of all things. How could such a man possibly have been a boy?

Another picture represents three of my uncle Abraham's children. They're only toddlers here, smiling and looking both cute and weird. There's Clara, David, and between them another little girl whose name my father couldn't remember. (Who will now?) They were my cousins. They died in Auschwitz, probably when they were in their teens. Because they are children in this particular picture, this is the one that almost invariably makes people ask, "What happened to them? Did they also . . . ?" This reaction irritates me, I must say. It reminds me of kids who watch a movie again and again hoping that a beloved character won't make the same fateful mistake this time around. We all know what Nazis and their henchmen did to Jewish children. So why the phony disbelief? Do people who ask such questions hope against hope that the answer will be negative? That the whole thing will turn out to have been a bad dream after all? Or worse, do they expect that the Nazis will come out nicer than we thought? Is this, in other words, another instance of Holocaust denial? "What happened to them?

Did they also . . . ?" Yes, they did, and one of them was named David like me, as my father made sure to emphasize.

There was also a later photograph in that batch, an informal snapshot of my uncle Jacob with his wife and two children, flanked by his parents, my father's parents, my grandparents. The year is 1943 and they are in mortal danger. Do they know it? Does it show on the photograph? In my grand-parents' grave and weary expressions perhaps? All were rounded up and sent to Auschwitz the following year; all but Jacob were killed there. Of all these photos, this may be the one that affects me the most. It is undoubtedly my family: I met Jacob once years later in Jerusalem, so he is my contact, in a sense, my point of entry into this image. But it is also a picture of Jews in Hungary in 1943. Although, or perhaps because, it is so tightly framed and it is impossible to know what was in the immediate surroundings of these six people, the sense of enveloping danger is so compelling in hindsight that it engulfs them and becomes the (absent) focal point of the entire scene when we look at it today. This, in other words, is a picture of *my* family caught in the middle of catastrophic historical events.

The photograph that I kept for last, because it is at the same time the most banal and the most revealing, is one of these typical early-twentieth-

My uncle Zoltan

Hélène and her grandparents

century professional family portraits. It was taken in 1920 and is the only one with my father in it, or rather with a one-year-old baby who would one day be my father. He is perched on some kind of stool, surrounded by his mother Deborah in the center and her mother, a widow by then, both sitting down as women were supposed to on such portraits; standing behind them are his brother Abraham (Avrum), his father Henri (Chaim), and his sister Hélène (Etuska); finally his brothers Jacob (Yankel) and Zoltan (Zalme Leib), sitting next to their mother. Hélène is holding a bouquet of flowers, Jacob and Zoltan a hoop and an open book respectively. All are dressed up in what must have been their best clothes (or did the clothes belong to the studio?), and all are looking straight ahead, some right at the camera—all except Hélène who seems lost in mysterious thoughts and looks all the more beautiful for it. At first glance, this is a picture perfect example of what Pierre Bourdieu describes as the ideological role of photography in the production of the Family as a coherent and cohesive unit of the Bourgeois social system.[5] At second glance, Hélène's diverging gaze begins to

Abraham's children

undermine that wishful unity by suggesting that there is something else out there that she, as a teenage girl, longs for. (What I was hoping to find in my father—my own desire to run away from home, country and family—was it in my aunt Hélène all along?) But more important, it is the knowledge we now have that most of these people will be murdered in Auschwitz's gas chambers that shatters the dream of the ideal family. One is reminded that photography, enlisted in the service of bourgeois legitimization, also served to define deviance and construct and catalogue a wide array of social undesirables, such as the insane and the criminals, the homosexuals and the Jews.

Looking at this photograph of a Jewish family, one feels there is great cruelty in the discrepancy between their attempt at, and belief in, normalization through modern technology and the ultimate futility of such an attempt. To read in it the traces of the Holocaust, another attempt at normalization through modern technology, is to see this family portrait, in hindsight, as depicting both normalcy and catastrophe at the same time and revealing the intimacy that links the two. In that sense, the pictorial traces that allow me to reconnect with my familial history also prevent all possibility of my doing so through, or as, normalization. The myth of familial cohesion being shattered *to begin with*, all sense of connection with this

1943: My grandparents, my uncle
Jacob, his wife and their kids

particular family can only be marked by discontinuity, that is, gaps, lacks, and fractures, and therefore defined by difference rather than sameness. To put it more succinctly, if these photos evoke or index the destruction of *my family*, they also signify the destruction of *the family* to me. But I am alive to write this, so my family also managed to survive, and survival suggests the possibility of an alternative model for the family. By that I do not mean what is usually referred to as "alternative families"; that is, I do not consider relationships defined neither by blood nor legal contract but by choice as normal families. In fact, I mean just the opposite—*not* considering relationships defined by blood or legal contract as normal families. Thus deprived of all normative power, *the family* could make way for *families*—if we want to keep the term—understood as having community without identification. In the specific case I have been discussing, I may not place any value on the fact that I am biologically and legally related to the Gottliebs and the Fuchses of Sátoraljaújhely, but the fact that I was touched by their portraits forced me to recognize that I have established some sort of contact with

The family

them. Yet this is a relationship that neither erases their difference (or mine, for that matter) nor reasserts the family as norm. The sort of friendship my father and I enjoyed in the years before his death, for example, would fall into that category. Which sends me back to the train station.

In a sense, the pictures my father and I took of each other bidding farewell at Saint-Lazare are family pictures. But instead of "sustaining imaginary cohesion" (Hirsch, *Family Frames*, 6–7), as traditional family portraits seek to do, they represent separation—the future separation they rehearsed and the past separations of which we are reminded by the ghosts of history. So if these are family pictures, they acknowledge that separateness is at the core of this family, and perhaps of all families. For one thing, we were not and could not have been on the pictures together, since we didn't ask a third party to take them, thus getting rid of the legitimating or authenticating position automatically occupied by the picture-taker. By alternately occupying and removing ourselves from that position in our little staging or role-playing my father and I implicitly recognized that the function of authenticator is immanent to the process of representation and cannot, therefore, claim the transcendent authority necessary to make law. Yet this very recognition is itself an act of togetherness—separateness is what connects us to one another. Connectedness as separateness may ultimately be the real subject of these photos and of all the other photos, for contact first requires distance. And that's what's so queer about them. Queer and diasporic.

Finally, there are the photos I took of my father at the exact sites in the Marais where he used to work and live. At 29 rue du Roi de Sicile, where his store was located, now stands a quaint little shop selling flowers and accessories in a faux rustic setting. Nothing there that will leave a meaningful trace in history, I'm afraid, unless as a testimony to the middle class's baffling taste for pastel. Given the popularity of all things "French provincial" among wealthy foreign tourists, however, *Comme à la campagne*, as the shop is called in a seeming admission that it is only an approximation, may be a good indicator of what the neighborhood has (also) become. More interesting are the pictures taken of rue des Blancs-Manteaux, number 7, by the door of the apartment building where my father lived in the 1950s. I didn't look inside but, unlike the upper levels of the façade, the entrance clearly hadn't been renovated yet, which, on the picture, makes it stand out as a remnant of the old, poorer, more Jewish Marais in an otherwise gentrified and gayer area hinted at by the swanky design store next door (called *Repérages Maison,* of all things). In fact the entrance of the building is very run down, which may be why these photos are more touching to me. In a way, both the building and my father were survivors, the photos a reunion. But survival isn't always pretty (my father hadn't been gentrified either), and the passage of time shows with equal harshness on both of them. But this emphasizes continuity in space and in time in spite of everything, whereas the same man in front of daisies and lavender only reveals a more brutal chasm. (Did Parisian Yiddish culture go up in smoke so that our apartments may take us back to the eternal French countryside?) Today the entrance of 7 rue des Blancs-Manteaux has been fully restored to its original seventeenth-century glory, all traces of its decrepitude in the hands of generations of poor Jewish immigrants erased. I can't help but think that this final transformation and the death of my father are more than just coincidental. He too is a ghost now, and it is his absence that I now read in the picture.

But the day I took the first pictures, and just as it happened at Saint-Lazare albeit in a more obvious and intentional fashion, the staging of a scene for the purpose of a photograph revealed a point of contact between the present and the past and between space and time. Modestly, or immodestly I should say, my intention was to try to duplicate for my own purposes Claude Lanzmann's approach in *Shoah*—to prod memory and provoke testimonial by placing the witnesses exactly where they were "at the time" or

7 rue des Blancs-Manteaux, before renovation

The same address today

having them go through the same motions years later, thus fulfilling our duty to remember while circumventing the ethical and ideological problems posed by representation. Since my father lived and worked in the Marais only after the Holocaust, I don't know exactly what I was expecting from these photos—other than the unexpected. Which, luckily, happened when a young straight couple with a child and a friend walked out of the building just as my father was posing in front of the entrance. They noticed that we were taking pictures and struck up a conversation. With good grace he explained that he used to live right there fifty years earlier, and they seemed interested, or perhaps just amused. At any rate, this brief incident felt like an encounter between neighbors across time, a fleeting coincidence of spatial proximity and temporal difference. Another family portrait, perhaps.

My role in all this can be seen from different perspectives. On the one hand I was a mediator or an enabler. I decided to provoke certain situations and recollections by my desire to take these pictures. More often than not, however, things got out of control, although loss of control was also what I was looking for in a way. As for the old photos my father showed me, my first reaction was, "I had no idea these existed. Why didn't he show them to me before?" That's simple: because I never asked. Until recently, I had

Neighbors

manifested little interest in my family's history. I knew how they had died and, somehow, that was enough for me. As many Holocaust and concentration camp survivors have noticed, relations with their children are so complex that the latter are often the least receptive audience. In fact, Jorge Semprun writes in *L'écriture ou la vie* [*Literature or Life*], survivors communicate much better with their grandchildren. *They* are the ones who want to know. But when I started interviewing my father for this book, he probably felt that the time had come, as if, with time, I had myself become the grandchild he once complained he would never have from me. My sudden and unexpected availability as a listener set the narrative into motion by providing, as Mieke Bal writes, the second-personhood that creates the cultural context without which there can be no memory.[6]

Yet, I have also been something other than a mere listener. My own memory was set into motion in that process. Pierre Nora once remarked that, "Being Jewish is to remember being Jewish" ["Etre juif c'est se souvenir de l'être"]. This definition could apply to pretty much all minority communities whose present conditions are less than ideal and to whom cultural and historical memory provides a mode of resistance. Still, it does seem especially apt to describe the Jews and their unique history of exile and displacement. Before they even had a history, *Zakhor!* [Remember!], was one of God's early injunctions to the Jewish people—although nobody is quite sure what it is they're supposed to remember. The need to remember Zion when exiled by the rivers of Babylon at least made sense, and memory, in that case, was attached to a somewhat tangible, if mythified, object; the duty to remember the Holocaust is meant to have practical effects in that it is supposed to prevent the reoccurrence of genocide. But *Zakhor!* implies that Judaism and what we now call Jewishness are defined by the very act of remembering, with the object of memory, should there be one, all but a figurative stand-in for memory itself. Even the memory of the Holocaust, for all its intended practical purpose, is also a trope—at least, and perhaps especially, for the Jews who will never forget or deny that it happened. Obviously this doesn't in any way suggest that there was something inherently Jewish about the Holocaust, other than the fact that Jews were its designated victims. But the memory of it, its aftermath, is necessarily affected by the defining role memory has always had for the Jewish people. While all collective memory is determined in part by the status each individual culture assigns to "memory" in general, it is necessarily different when "memory" is *the* defining element of that culture, as it is for the Jews. Nora's Möbius strip of a definition opens up an abyss—"Being Jewish is to remember to remember to remember . . . ," on and on until what we are supposed—indeed obligated—to remember becomes more elusive as we try to seize it.[7]

Needless to say, being Jewish has never been an easy proposition for me. To begin with, I am not even Jewish in the religious sense of the term, and my relationship with Jewish culture was always tenuous at best. Like many kids whose family is culturally different from that of their friends, I first felt embarrassed by the weirdness of my foreign-looking, foreign-sounding relatives, before embracing them when, as an adolescent, I needed to make myself look special. Of course, I already *was* special—I was queer. But that was a little *too* special at the time. So I did what many others did, and still do, in a similar situation: I asserted my Jewishness as a substitute for coming out. And like all overstated assertions, it was denial. Twice. I first denied my homosexuality by endorsing another difference that wasn't really mine to endorse; and later, when I did come out, my Jewishness found itself relegated to the status of a stage, to be discarded once it had served its purpose in my personal development. In essence, I had treated Jewishness as archaic. Of course I didn't know then what I know now—that all identities are fraudulent—so it took me a while to deal with the multiple levels of shame and guilt that I felt: the shame of having weird relatives; the shame of being gay; the guilt of having instrumentalized Jewishness for the purpose of committing fraud; the guilt of having then rejected it.

What does it mean to be with other people? That was the question this book set out to answer. But "to be with" is an uneasy proposition in that it always entails to be with what one would often rather be without—ghosts, family, country, origin, etc.—and because relationality is the very definition of life, it implies being without what one would rather be with—a unified, autonomous self. In the course of writing this book, I have neither reclaimed my "roots" nor embraced my "origins." I decided long ago to put some distance between me and all that—a distance that was always already there, of course—and I've been quite happy that way. I haven't reconnected with my father; I have connected as a friend with a man who was my father and whose presence, therefore, could not so easily be conjured away. This connection—the "and" in "my father and I"—doesn't presuppose the naturalness of identities, of "father" and of "I." Rather it reveals and conveys the instability of each, and it thrives on a mutual dependency that no longer feels oppressive. Alfred Jarry once said that it isn't fun to be free alone. Indeed it isn't possible at all. Leaving home, I sought to free myself from my family, from my country, from my social class, and from the power structure that rests on my being assigned a space. The thing, though, is that to be free *from* is to be free *with*. That's the paradox of freedom, so often cloaked in the familiar logic of denial. And that is the queerness of community.

So now I remember. I have established contact with a past that is both mine and not mine, a community that is both me and not me. When I

Notes

1. The Old Neighborhood

1. There *were* Jews at Ravensbrück. See Rochelle G. Saidel, *The Jewish Women of Ravensbrück Concentration Camp.*

2. See René Rémond, *Le "fichier juif."*

3. See Jean-Marc Léry, "Evolution du quartier du Marais," 40.

4. In the 1560s according to Clément Gurvil, "Le Marais au XVIème siècle," or the seventeenth century according to Léry, "Evolution du quartier du Marais," 70.

5. See Boris Bove, "L'urbanisation et le peuplement du quartier Saint-Gervais au Moyen Age," 60.

6. Ibid., 70–71, and Léry, "Evolution du quartier du Marais."

7. Gurvil, "Le Marais au XVIème siècle," 134.

8. Jean-Pierre Babelon, "Essor et décadence du Marais," 103.

9. See Robert Descimon, "Le Marais du XVIIème siècle," Azéma, *Vivre et survivre dans le Marais,* and Patrick Maunand, ed., *Le Marais des écrivains.*

10. I thank Marie Ymonet for this wonderful quotation. When no English translation appears in the bibliography, the translation is mine.

11. *Tableau de Paris,* quoted by Babelon, *Le Marais,* 121.

12. See Babelon, *Le Marais,* 116.

13. See Louis Bergeron, "Le quartier Saint-Gervais à l'aube du XIXème siècle."

14. Quoted in Maunand, *Le Marais des écrivains,* 124.

15. For this and much of what follows, see Roger Berg, *Histoire des juifs à Paris.*

16. See Esther Benbassa, *Histoire des juifs de France,* 54–60.

17. Berg, *Histoire des juifs à Paris,* 49.

18. Ibid.

19. Ibid., 189.

20. For these figures and a more detailed description of the different waves of immigration, see Michel Roblin, *Les juifs de Paris,* 64–74.

21. See Benbassa, *Histoire des juifs de France,* 162–63.

22. See Paula E. Hyman, *The Jews of Modern France,* 117.

23. Ibid., 119.

24. On this particular wave of immigration, see Vicki Caron, *Uneasy Asylum.*

25. See Marie-Claude Blanc-Chaléard, "Les étrangers," 285 ; Hyman, *The Jews of Modern France*, 121.

26. Berg, *Histoire des juifs à Paris*, 191.

27. For this and much of what follows, see Nancy L. Green, "The Contradictions of Ac-culturation."

28. See Marc Walter's documentary, *Les rosiers du Marais*.

29. See Jean-Claude Kuperminc, "La presse juive en France" and Green, "The Contra-dictions of Acculturation."

30. See Green, *The Pletzl of Paris*, which focuses on the pre–World War I period but whose description still applies to the interwar period. See also Hyman, *The Jews of Modern France*, and her *From Dreyfus to Vichy*.

31. Hyman, *The Jews of Modern France*, 122.

32. Jean-Claude Kuperminc, "Les mouvements de jeunesse juive en France."

33. Hyman, *The Jews of Modern France*, 120.

34. Nicole Priollaud, Victor Zigelman, and Laurent Goldberg, eds., *Images de la mémoire juive de Paris*, 139.

35. See Aline Denain, "Le Pletzl," Bernadette Costa, "*Je me souviens du Marais*," and Jeanne Brody, *Rue des Rosiers*, among others.

36. See Brody, *Rue des Rosiers*, 37–38, Annie Kriegel's autobiography, *Ce que j'ai cru com-prendre*, and Roger Ascot's novel, *Les enfants du square des Vosges*.

37. As told to Jeanne Brody by an old resident of the Marais, 17.

38. See Brody, *Rue des Rosiers*, 115, and Colette Bismuth-Jarrassé and Dominique Jarrassé, "Fragments d'un quartier juif," 228.

39. Quoted by Jean Laloum, "Entre aryanisation et déportations," 367 and 372–73, re-spectively.

40. The theft of Jewish-owned buildings in the *îlot 16* is contentious to this day and con-stitutes a relatively large portion of the recent exhibit and its companion book. See in partic-ular Laloum, as well as Yankel Fijalkow, "De l'îlot no 2 à l'îlot no 16," and Françoise Janin, "Spoliations d'habitants de 'l'îlot 16.' "

41. Anne Grynberg, "Le retour et la reconstruction."

42. Mark Kurlansky, *A Chosen Few*, 39.

43. Grynberg, "Le retour et la reconstruction." 468, and Kurlansky, *A Chosen Few*.

44. The books of Fleischman's trilogy, *Rendez-vous au métro Saint-Paul*, *Nouveaux rendez-vous au métro Saint-Paul*, and *Derniers rendez-vous au métro Saint-Paul*, are collections of short stories in the style of Sholem Aleichem, in which the dead have a propensity to come back and advise the living. I like to think of these volumes as stories of communities as well as communities of stories.

45. See Hyman, *The Jews of Modern France*, 194, and Benbassa, *Histoire des juifs de France*, 279–80. Berg has slightly different figures.

46. See the work of Michel Abitbol, particularly "La cinquième République et l'accueil des Juifs d'Afrique du Nord" and "The Encounter between French Jewry and the Jews of North Africa." See also Hyman, Benbassa , and Berg, as well as Claude Tapia, *Les juifs sépha-rades en France*.

47. I want to thank my friend Cyril Royer for this.

48. Jeanne Brody shows this very well in all her work on the rue des Rosiers, insisting that stories of the medieval presence of the Jews in the Marais work as a founding myth.

49. Brody,*Rue des Rosiers*, 71 and "La rue des Rosiers, un quartier-mémoire," 31.

50. For a parallel between the two events, see John Tagliabue's *New York Times* article, "A French Lesson."

51. These figures are only approximations. On this and what follows, see Tai Hong Yuen, "L'immigration chinoise en France" and Véronique Poisson, "Les grandes étapes de 100 ans d'histoire migratoire entre la Chine et la France."

52. For a detailed account of how Chinese trades and businesses have interacted with Jewish ones, see Nadine Vasseur, *Il était une fois le Sentier*.

53. Kristin Ross, *Fast Cars, Clean Bodies*, 152.

54. Jacqueline Costa-Lascoux and Live Yu-Sion, *Paris-XIIIe, lumières d'Asie*, 98–100.

55. On human trafficking and other forms of slavery in the French Chinese community, see Gao Yun, "Nouvelles formes d'esclavage parmi les Chinois récemment arrivés en France."

56. On the controversy in the Marais and the Sedaine-Popincourt district, see Anne-Louise Couvelaire and Maël Thierry, "Murailles de Chine à Paris" and Justine Pribetich, "La construction identitaire d'un quartier."

57. Sabine Moreno, "Le projet 'Chinois d'Europe et intégration.' "

58. Alain Finkielkraut, who has now become a reactionary crusader for French cultural identity, once made similar observations in *The Imaginary Jew*.

59. On the role of colonial cadres in the new ministry, see Herman Leibovics, *Bringing the Empire Back Home*; for a larger picture of what Leibovics calls "the reinvention of French culture" by Malraux, see his *Mona Lisa's Escort*.

60. Cyril Royer, "Le Marais."

61. I found this information in the provisional version of a study commissioned by the city of Paris. I was not authorized to see this document and I must therefore remain vague. I will say, however, that no mention of these incidents can be found in the final report.

62. See Florence Tamagne, "Montmartre" and *Histoire de l'homosexualité en Europe*, as well as Michael Sibalis, "Paris."

63. Sibalis, 25. J. K. Huysmans once described a "gay" bar on the rue des Vertus. See Lucey, 73–74.

64. For an interesting depiction and first-person testimonies of homosexual life in Paris in the interwar years, see Gilles Barbedette and Michel Carassou, *Paris gay 1925*.

65. For specifics on Vichy and homosexuality, see Sibalis, "Homophobia, Vichy France and the 'Crime of Homosexuality.' "

66. Georges Sidéris, "Saint-Germain-des-Prés" and Sibalis, "Paris."

67. Cyril Royer, "Rue Sainte-Anne" and Sibalis, "Paris." Didier Lestrade's *Kinsey 6* gives an interesting first-person account of Parisian gay life at that time.

68. Olivier Fillieule, "Lesbian and Gay Pride," and Sibalis, " 'La Lesbian and Gay Pride' in Paris."

69. For this and much of what follows, see Sibalis, "Paris" and "Urban Space and Homosexuality," Royer, "Le Marais," Laurent Villate, "La place des gays," and David Caron, "Le quartier du Marais," among others.

70. Caron, "Le quartier du Marais." See also David Caron, *AIDS in French Culture*.

71. Royer, "Le Marais," 105–107.

72. Villate, "La place des gays, 508–509. New bars keep opening and old ones closing, though, so the actual number may vary.

73. Philippe Baverel, "Le drapeau gay flotte rue Sainte-Croix-de-la-Bretonnerie," 11.

74. Again, for a first-hand description of the atmosphere of the times, see Lestrade, *Kinsey 6*.

75. For more on this, see my book *AIDS in French Culture*.

76. Fillieule, "Lesbian and Gay Pride," 288.

77. For an analytic overview of articles on the Marais in the weekly press, see Guillaume Huyez, "Dix ans de ghetto."

78. Again, I thank Cyril Royer for sharing his knowledge with me.

79. On this and how the gay Marais is depicted in tourist guidebooks in ways that tend to exaggerate its festive atmosphere, see Villate, "La place des gays."

80. See Huyez, Dix ans de ghetto," on how ethnic neighborhoods served as a model to frame news magazine stories on the gay Marais.

81. This critical analysis of the Marais is best exemplified by Jean Le Bitoux, "Marcher dans le gay Marais."

82. I want to thank Didier Eribon for telling me this story.

83. More on this question in chapter 3.

84. For comparison, see David Colman, "Rich Gay, Poor Gay," Patricia Leigh Brown, "Gay Enclaves Face Prospect of Being Passé," and Robert Andrew Powell, "Is Key West Going Straight?"

2. A Queer Ghetto

1. Caron, "AIDS/Holocaust."

2. From *Archives parlementaires*, Assemblée nationale, 23 December 1789, 756; quoted in Dominique Schnapper, "Les Juifs et la nation," 299.

3. "Qu'est-ce qu'une nation?" was presented at the Sorbonne on 11 March 1882.

4. See the work of Zeev Sternhell, in particular, *Maurice Barrès et le nationalisme français*. Sternhell's thesis that the origins of fascism can be traced to France and to Barrès's political thought is still controversial, but it is a thesis I subscribe to.

5. For more, see Susan Rubin Suleiman, "The Jew in Jean-Paul Sartre's *Réflexions sur la question juive*." Post-structuralist theorists, needless to say, have shed a far more complex light on the question of identity, which Sartre approached from a phenomenological standpoint.

6. Respectively Tim Madesclaire and Jean-Robert Pitte, quoted by Michael Sibalis, "Ghetto," 195.

7. See Guillaume Huyez, "Dix ans de 'ghetto.' "

8. See Caron, "Ghetto."

9. I am relying on Simon Watney's work in which he shows how AIDS, first associated with gay men in Western countries and ignored for that reason, was then de-gayed ("Everybody can get AIDS") in a way that seemed more inclusive but, in fact, further excluded and endangered gay men when they were still the hardest hit demographic. See Watney's *Practices of Freedom*.

10. It is worth noting the arrival of the word *homophobie* in French public discourses at that time. The term has even popularized the suffix *-phobie* to describe other types of discriminations and group-hatreds. Most interesting of all is the coinage of the word *judéophobie*, used to describe a new type of anti-Semitism supposedly popular among young French Arabs. See Pierre-André Taguieff's *La nouvelle judéophobie* which, I believe, introduced the new word.

11. See *Discipline and Punish*.

12. *Nous, Juifs de France*, 39.

13. On the PACS, see Daniel Borillo and Pierre Lascoumes, *Amours égales?*, Daniel Borillo, Eric Fassin and Marcela Iacub, ed., *Au-delà du PaCS*, and Caroline Fourest, *Les anti-PaCS*.

14. See Jeanne Brody, *Rue des Rosiers*, 112–13.

15. A *mellah* is a Jewish quarter in Morocco.

16. For an extended discussion of this question, see Tony Judt, *Postwar*.

17. Some survivors did testify but, just like non-Jewish returnees from the "regular" concentration camps, their words fell on deaf ears and they soon retreated into silence. It is also worth recalling that the silencing of the Holocaust was also the case in Israel more or less until the 1961 trial of Adolf Eichmann.

18. See Annie Benveniste, "Sarcelles, du grand ensemble à la ville juive" and Laurence Podselver, "De la périphérie au centre."

19. The original French adjective in Dustan's text is "merveilleux," which translates more readily as "wonderful," especially when attached to the noun "world"—as in *The Wonderful World of Walt Disney*. Guillaume Dustan is no Walt Disney, however, so I have opted for Ross

Chambers's translation of the phrase in *Untimely Interventions* (313). "Fabulous" conveys several meanings that apply here: the sort of excess that borders on unreality and mythic or fable-like storytelling; and there is no gayer word than "fabulous." If I may milk the cartoon analogy a bit more, I'll say that some children may find Mickey Mouse wonderful, whereas Bugs Bunny, that cross-dressing live wire of a rabbit, who, judging from his accent must be from Brooklyn, is fabulous.

20. The expression "warts and all" has no literal equivalent in French, but it's still worth noting that Dustan (who knows English) does mention his plantar warts in his later novel *Nicolas Pages* as Guillaume and his lover Nicolas sleep together in a spooning position: "He caresses my feet with his, to show me that my warts don't matter" ["Il me caresse les pieds avec les siens pour me montrer que mes verrues c'est pas grave" (97)]. In the context, warts may be read as standing in for AIDS, Nicolas's gentle gesture signifying love and safety.

21. *La vie des morts est épuisante* [The Life of the Dead Is Exhausting], 107–108.

22. See *Agir pour ne pas mourir*.

23. This could also be an indirect reference to Dominique Fernandez's famous 1978 novel *L'étoile rose* [*The Pink Star*], a rather weepy plea for tolerance that may have made some kind of sense in its context.

24. *Kinsey 6*, 344

25. Eric Loret, quoted in Dustan, *Nicolas Pages*, 394.

26. See Loret, "Dustan qui passe."

27. The pool is in Les Halles and it is very cruisy.

28. Didier Eribon adapted and transformed Sartre's argument in *Réflexions sur la question juive* for his own *Réflexions sur la question gay*, translated as *Insult* in its English-language edition.

29. See "Gossip and the Novel" and *Gossip* respectively. See also Caron, *AIDS in French Culture*, for a discussion of gossip in the specific context of AIDS.

30. More on this idea follows in chapter 3.

31. *Untimely Interventions*, 313.

3. Things Past

1. On this question, albeit with a different take, see in particular Jonathan Freedman, "Coming out of the Jewish Closet With Marcel Proust."

2. See chapter 2. See also Didier Eribon, *Insult*.

3. See Michel Foucault, *History of Sexuality*.

4. Mark W. Turner entitled his book on queer street cruising *Backward Glances*, but he doesn't make the point about the past that I am making here. In *Who Was That Man?* Neil Bartlett does present such cruising as a means of being in contact with the past.

5. As far as I can tell, Lot's wife is never named in the Bible, but she is called Ildeth in a work with which I am more familiar, Robert Aldrich's and Sergio Leone's 1963 film masterpiece *Sodom and Gomorrha*.

6. See *Homosexual Desire*.

7. *Nicolas Pages*, 280. The French expression is "vouloir le beurre et l'argent du beurre," to want the butter and the money to buy the butter.

8. *Les nuits de Paris ou le spectateur nocturne*, quoted in Maunand, 134.

9. *Paris vécu*, quoted in Maunand, 135.

10. In today's marketing context, the favored term would be "early adopters."

11. On homosexuality as degeneracy, see my book *AIDS in French Culture*.

12. Then minister of Justice, socialist Elisabeth Guigou made a few notorious remarks to that effect. See Fourest and Venner, *Les anti-PaCS*, 34, for this and a useful overview of the homophobic discourses that flourished during the PACS debates in 1998 and 1999.

13. Ibid., 84.

14. Ibid., 53.

15. Ibid., 96–97.

16. Caron, "AIDS/Holocaust."

17. *No Future*, 9.

18. On the relation between jokes and minority communities, see Ted Cohen, *Jokes*.

19. For a critique of the way the Down Low controversy has been presented in the mainstream media and elsewhere, see Keith Boykin, *Beyond the Down Low*; for a far more problematic discussion of the phenomenon, see J.L. King, *On the Down Low*.

20. Eileen O'Sullivan and Breana Wheeler respectively, 17 August 2003, 10.

21. Following complaints from patrons of the museum, the hedges have now been trimmed.

22. This is the focus of Samuel R. Delany's *Times Square Red, Times Square Blue*, his essay on the area's now defunct, mostly straight porn theaters as points of contacts between men. In the Parisian context, see Jacques Nolot's feature film *Porn Theater* [*La chatte à deux têtes*].

23. Lothar Machtan, *The Hidden Hitler*.

24. *The History of Sexuality*

25. Again, Nancy, *Being Singular Plural*.

26. Ibid., 39–40. The same idea is scattered throughout his earlier book, *The Inoperative Community*.

27. Caron, *AIDS in French Culture*.

28. In *What Do Gay Men Want?* David Halperin argues that HIV/AIDS prevention that appeals to the neoliberal values of the self and the good citizen may not easily convince people who often identify with and through their exclusion from these very norms. See chapter 4 of his book. While Halperin is specifically referring to gay men, much of his analysis is pertinent to other groups as well. Halperin draws in large part from Kane Race's groundbreaking work.

29. *Blush*, x.

30. Why I feel no closeness whatsoever with Mel Gibson, another Jew-hating (and homophobic) idiot, has to do, I think, with the fact that he isn't connected to me through the sharing and witnessing of the embarrassing episode. He didn't *touch* me. Another factor, in all likelihood, is that Mel Gibson has power, which changes everything.

31. See also Halperin's reading of Miller in "Homosexuality's Closet." There is much in Miller's and Halperin's analyses that intersects with mine, especially when they underscore the limitations of explicit gay identification in relation to desire.

32. A website called Closet Culture, developed on a non-profit basis by graduate students from the University of Michigan School of Information (but no longer in operation "due to security concerns and lack of volunteers"), defined its mission as follows: "Closet Culture (CC) is a unique online community that connects closeted and questioning individuals in an anonymous environment. At CC, you will find *community without being outed*" (http://www .closetculture.net; my emphasis).

33. I thank Nadine Hubbs for this quote.

34. Sloterdijk, 25; quoted by Spector, 24.

35. If I posit queerness and family as incompatible, I do not imply that queer individuals cannot enjoy good relations with their families. What I mean is that if a queer's queerness is not to be erased, the family has to be queered. See Caron, "Intrusions."

4. Disaster, Failure, and Alienation

1. Robert Bober's novel *Quoi de neuf sur la guerre?* [What's New with the War?], whose themes and setting are, in part, similar to those of Grumberg's play, was adapted for the screen under the apt title *Un monde trop paisible* [Too Peaceful a World]—excess being here the denial and flipside of lack.

2. Compiègne and Pithiviers were the other two main French camps where future deportees were held before being sent to the camps.

3. See Heinz Heger, *The Men With the Pink Triangle*, 12, who notes the dates but does not explicitly make the connection with AIDS that I make here.

4. *Moi, Pierre Seel, déporté homosexuel.* Interestingly, the English title of the book is *Liberation Was for Others: Memoirs of a Gay Survivor of the Nazi Holocaust.* The systematic deportations of homosexual men as such took place only in Germany and in the countries and territories it had annexed, not just occupied, which included Alsace and Moselle in eastern France.

5. See Martel for a typical example of this line of argument. If Martel is intellectually dishonest in his denunciation, I recognize that it isn't the case for everybody.

6. See Christophe Broqua, *Agir pour ne pas mourir*, 267–71.

7. On the use of allegory in Dreuilhe's work, see Martine Delvaux, "Des corps et des frontières."

8. For more on the Holocaust metaphor in the context of AIDS, see my "AIDS/Holocaust."

9. On some of the ramifications of this question, see Ross Chambers, *Facing It.*

10. Delvaux, "Des corps et des frontières," 89.

11. In the context of the Nazi camps, one could also mention the end of Elie Wiesel's *La nuit* [*Night*], when the young narrator catches a glimpse of himself in a mirror and sees a corpse looking back at him; or the switch from the first to the third person in Jorge Semprun's *Le grand voyage* [*The Long Journey*], after the death of another character standing in as the narrator's alter ego. There are many such examples.

12. "The Question of Community in Charlotte Delbo's *Auschwitz and After*," 880; original emphasis.

13. As Elspeth Probyn provocatively remarks on another sort of orthodoxy, "The potential for shame is all the greater because feminism has put forward ideals that often inspire the best in people and of which it is also easy to fall short" (*Blush*, 76).

14. Rajsfus's book is a bitter indictment of the French, whom he deems responsible for his father's killing. It is impossible to know what might have been, of course, but given Vichy's policy of stripping recently naturalized Jews of their French citizenship, making them deportable in the process, it is statistically unlikely that Nahoum would have survived anyway.

15. These are my translations of Rajsfus's own translations.

16. In *The Lost*, Daniel Mendelsohn paints a very similar portrait of his grandfather.

17. See *Remnants of Auschwitz.*

18. It would be a mistake, however, to assume that female inmates in concentration camps formed one vast community, impervious to other markers of social divisions. In Ravensbrück, for example, French women were routinely ostracized and mistreated by the more established and powerful Polish women. See Jack G. Morrison, *Ravensbrück*, 94–98. Moreover, many French women in the camps emphasized their Frenchness as a way to maintain a degree of femininity. See Morrison, and also Margaret-Anne Hutton, *Testimony from the Nazi Camps*, especially chapter 3.

19. It is also possible to read here an echo of Verlaine's poem: "What have you done, O you there / Crying relentlessly / Tell me, what have you done, O you there / With your youth?" ["—Qu'as-tu fait, ô toi que voilà / Pleurant sans cesse, / Dis, qu'as tu fait, toi que voilà / De ta jeunesse?"] I thank Ross Chambers for this insight.

20. See the discussion of Renan and Barrès in chapter 2.

21. Here I rely mostly on Etienne Balibar's thesis.

22. For an excellent analysis of reading Delbo, see Sharon Marquart, "Witnessing Communities and an Ethics of Reading."

5. *The Queerness of Group Friendship*

1. The fact that soldiers who were not prisoners also performed such shows in wartime doesn't change anything in my analysis of what took place in the context of captivity.

2. See *Babel-ville* and *Le salon du prêt-à-saigner*.

3. I am using Jean-Luc Nancy's terminology in *The Inoperative Community*.

4. This is what I had in mind when I suggested in chapter 3 that reclaiming one's stigmatization as shit could offer a mode of queer communal relationality.

5. Antelme, "On m'a volé mon pain," in *Textes inédits*, 62.

6. The arrival of the women in Auschwitz is told in Delbo's *Le convoi du 24 janvier* [*Convoy to Auschwitz*], which also appeared in 1965.

Epilogue

1. See Gelley, *Unruly Examples*.

2. *Sade, Fourier, Loyola*.

3. *Totalité et infini*, 254.

4. Marianne Hirsch's concept of postmemory, the mediated memory of children of survivors, plays a part in my reading. For Hirsch, postmemory is characterized by "displacement" and "belatedness," is "cultural and public, and not merely individual and personal," allows "interconnectedness with others," and constitutes "an *ethical* relation to the oppressed" ("Projected Memory," 8–9; original emphasis).

5. *Un art moyen* [*Photography*].

6. "Introduction" to *Acts of Memory*, x.

7. On the relationship between Judaic memory and Jewish history, I send the reader to Yosef Hayim Yerushalmi's classic study *Zakhor*.

Bibliography

Abitbol, Michel. "The Encounter between French Jewry and the Jews of North Africa." In *The Jews in Modern France*, edited by Malino and Wasserstein, 31–53.

———. "La cinquième République et l'accueil des juifs d'Afrique du Nord." In Jean-Jacques, and Wieviorka, eds. *Les juifs de France,* edited by Becker and Wieviorka, *287–327.*

Agamben, Giorgio. *Remnants of Auschwitz: The Witness and the Archive.* Translated by Daniel Heller-Roazen. New York: Zone Books, 1999. [*Quel che resta di Auschwitz.* Turin: Bollati Boringhieri, 1988.]

Antelme, Robert. *The Human Race.* Translated by Jeffrey Haight and Annie Mahler. Evanston: The Marlboro Press/Northwestern, 1998. [*L'espèce humaine.* Paris: Gallimard, 1957.]

———. *Textes inédits, Sur L'espèce humaine, Essais et témoignages.* Paris: Gallimard, 1996.

Ascot, Roger. *Les enfants du square des Vosges.* Paris: Fayard, 1977.

Azéma, Jean-Pierre, ed. *Vivre et survivre dans le Marais: Au coeur de Paris du Moyen Age à nos jours.* Paris: Le Manuscrit, 2005.

Babelon, Jean-Pierre, ed. *Le Marais: Mythe et réalité.* Paris: Picard, 1987.

———. "Essor et décadence du Marais: De la Renaissance à la Révolution." In Babelon, ed., *Le Marais,* 56–146.

Bal, Mieke, Jonathan Crewe, and Leo Spitzer, eds. *Acts of Memory: Cultural Recall in the Present.* Hanover, NH: University Press of New England, 1999.

Bal, Mieke. Introduction to Bal, Crewe, and Spitzer, *Acts of Memory* vii–xvii.

Barbedette, Gilles, and Michel Carassou. *Paris Gay 1925.* Paris: Presses de la Renaissance, 1981.

Barber, Steven M., and David L. Clark, eds. *Regarding Sedgwick.* New York: Routledge, 2002.

Barthes, Roland. *Sade, Fourier, Loyola.* Translated by Richard Miller. New York: Hill and Wang, 1976. [*Sade, Fourier, Loyola.* Paris: Seuil, 1971.]

———. *Camera Lucida: Reflections on Photography.* Translated by Richard Howard. New York: Hill and Wang, 1981. [*La chambre claire: Note sur la photographie.* Paris: Gallimard/Seuil, 1980.]

Bartlett, Neil. *Who Was That Man? A Present for Mr. Oscar Wilde.* London: Serpent's Tail, 1998.

Baverel, Philippe. "Le drapeau gay flotte rue Sainte-Croix-de-la-Bretonnerie." *Le monde,* 22 June 1996, 11.

Becker, Jean-Jacques, and Annette Wieviorka, eds. *Les juifs de France de la révolution française à nos jours.* Paris: Liana Levi, 1998.

Benbassa, Esther. *Histoire des juifs de France de l'antiquité à nos jours.* Paris: Seuil, 1997.

Benveniste, Annie. "Sarcelles, du grand ensemble à la ville juive." In Bordes-Benayoun, ed., *Les juifs et la ville,* 71–78.

Berg, Roger. *Histoire des juifs à Paris: De Chilpéric à Jacques Chirac.* Paris: Cerf, 1997.

Bergeron, Louis. "Le quartier Saint-Gervais à l'aube du XIXème siècle." In Azéma, ed., *Vivre et survivre dans le Marais,* 209–14.

Bialot, Joseph. *Le salon du prêt-à-saigner.* Paris: Gallimard Série noire, 1978.

———. *Babel-Ville.* Paris: Gallimard Série noire, 1979.

———. *C'est en hiver que les jours rallongent.* Paris: Seuil, 2002.

Birnbaum, Pierre, ed. *Histoire politique des juifs de France: Entre universalisme et particularisme.* Paris: Presses de la fondation nationale des sciences politiques, 1990.

Bismuth-Jarrassé, Colette, and Dominique Jarrassé. "Fragments d'un quartier juif." In Babelon, ed., *Le Marais,* 221–31.

Blanc-Chaléard, Marie-Claude. "Les étrangers, des Parisiens à l'épreuve des convulsions nationales (1840–1940)." In Azéma, ed., *Vivre et survivre dans le Marais,* 279–92.

Blanchot, Maurice. *The Writing of Disaster.* Translated by Ann Smock. Lincoln: University of Nebraska Press, 1986. [*L'écriture du désastre.* Paris: Gallimard, 1980.]

Bober, Robert. *Quoi de neuf sur la guerre?* Paris: P.O.L, 1993.

Bordes-Benayoun, Chantal, ed. *Les juifs et la ville.* Toulouse: Presses Universitaires du Mirail, 2000.

Borrillo, Daniel, Eric Fassin and Marcela Iacub, ed. *Au-delà du PaCS: L'expertise familiale à l'épreuve de l'homosexualité.* Paris: Presses Universitaires de France, 1999.

Borrillo, Daniel and Pierre Lacoumes. *Amours égales? Le Pacs, les homosexuels et la gauche.* Paris: La découverte, 2002.

Bourdieu, Pierre. *Photography: A Middle-Brow Art.* Translated by Shaun Whiteside. Stanford: Stanford University Press, 1990. [*Un art moyen: Essai sur les usages sociaux de la photographie.* Paris: Minuit, 1965].

Bove, Boris. "L'urbanisation et le peuplement du quartier Saint-Gervais au Moyen Age." In Azéma, ed., *Vivre et survivre dans le Marais,* 59–80.

Bowen, John R. *Why the French Don't Like Headscarves: Islam, the State, and Public Space.* Princeton: Princeton University Press, 2007.

Boyarin, Daniel. *Unheroic Conduct: The Rise of Heterosexuality and the Invention of the Jewish Man.* Berkeley: University of California Press, 1997.

Boykin, Keith. *Beyond the Down Low: Sex, Lies, and Denial in Black America.* New York: Carroll & Graf, 2005.

Bret, Antoine. *Mémoires sur la vie de Mademoiselle de Lenclos, par M. B*****.* Amsterdam: F. Joly, 1758.

Brody, Jeanne. *Rue des Rosiers: Une manière d'être juif.* Paris: Autrement, 1995.

———. "La rue des Rosiers, un quartier-mémoire." *Archives juives* 31.1 (1998): 26–38.

Broqua, Christophe. *Agir pour ne pas mourir: Act Up, les homosexuels et le sida.* Paris: Presses de la fondation nationale des sciences politiques, 2005.

Brown, Patricia Leigh. "Gay Enclaves Face Prospect of Being Passé." *New York Times,* 30 Oct. 2007, natl. ed., A1+.

Cairns, Lucille, ed. *Gay and Lesbian Cultures in France.* New York: Peter Lang, 2002.

Camus, Albert. *The Plague.* Translated by Robin Buss. London: Penguin, 2001. [*La peste.* In *Théâtre, récits, nouvelles.* Bibliothèque de la Pléiade. Paris: Gallimard, 1967.]

Camus, Renaud. *Tricks: 25 Encounters*. Translated by Richard Howard. New York: St Martin's Press, 1981. [*Tricks: 33 récits*. Paris: Mazarine, 1979.]

Carco, Francis. *Jésus-la-caille*. Paris: Calmann-Lévy, 1947.

Caron, David. "Intrusions: The Family in AIDS Films." *L'esprit créateur* 38.3 (1998): 62–72.

———. *AIDS in French Culture: Social Ills, Literary Cures*. Madison: University of Wisconsin Press, 2001.

———. "Le quartier du Marais." In Eribon, ed., *Dictionnaire des cultures gays et lesbiennes*, 312–13.

———. "Ghetto." In Eribon, ed., *Dictionnaire des cultures gays et lesbiennes*, 218–19.

———. "AIDS/Holocaust: Metaphor and French Universalism." *L'esprit créateur* 45.3 (2006): 63–73.

Caron, Vicki. *Uneasy Asylum: France and the Jewish Refugee Crisis, 1933–42*. Stanford: Stanford University Press, 1999.

Casablanca. Dir. Michael Curtiz. Warner Brothers, 1942.

de Certeau, Michel, Luce Giard, and Pierre Mayol. *Living and Cooking*. Vol. 2 of *The Practice of Everyday Life*. Translated by Timothy J. Tomasik. Minneapolis: University of Minnesota Press, 1998. [*Habiter, cuisiner*. Vol. 2 of *L'invention du quotidien*. Paris: Gallimard, 1994.]

Chambers, Ross. "Gossip and the Novel: Knowing Narrative and Narrative Knowing in Balzac, Mme de Lafayette and Proust." *Australian Journal of French Studies* 23.2 (1986): 212–33.

———. *Facing It: AIDS Diaries and the Death of the Author*. Ann Arbor: University of Michigan Press, 1998.

———. *Untimely Interventions: AIDS Writing, Testimonial, and the Rhetoric of Haunting*. Ann Arbor: University of Michigan Press, 2004.

Christ, Yvan. *Le Marais*. Paris: Veyrier, 1974.

Closet Culture. http://www.closetculture.net.

Cohen, Ted. *Jokes: Philosophical Thoughts on Joking Matters*. Chicago: University of Chicago Press, 1999.

Colman, David. "Rich Gay, Poor Gay." *New York Times*, 4 Sept. 2005, natl. ed., sec. 9:1+.

Costa, Bernadette. *Je me souviens du Marais*. Paris: Parigramme, 1995.

Costa-Lascoux, Jacqueline, and Live Yu-Sion, *Paris-XIIIème, lumières d'Asie*. Paris: Autrement, 1995.

Couvelaire, Anne-Louise and Maël Thierry. "Murailles de Chine à Paris: Dans les 3ème et 11ème arrondissements, l'atmosphère s'envenime." *Le nouvel observateur/Paris-Ile-de-France*, 14 Dec. 2000, vi–vii.

Crimp, Douglas. "Mario Montez, For Shame." In Barber and Clark, ed., *Regarding Sedgwick*, 57–70.Daudet, Alphonse. *L'évangéliste*. Paris: E. Dentu, 1883.

Daudet, Léon. *Paris vécu*. Paris: Gallimard, 1930.

Delany, Samuel R. *Times Square Red, Times Square Blue*. New York: New York University Press, 1999.

Delbo, Charlotte. *Auschwitz and After*. Translated by Rosette C. Lamont. New Haven: Yale University Press, 1995.

———. *Convoy to Auschwitz: Women of the French Resistance*. Translated by Carol Cosman. Boston: Northeastern University Press, 1997. [*Le convoi du 24 janvier*. Paris: Minuit, 1965.]

———. *Aucun de nous ne reviendra*. Paris: Minuit, 1970.

———. *Une connaissance inutile*. Paris: Minuit, 1970.

———. *Mesure de nos jours*. Paris: Minuit, 1971.

Deleuze, Gilles, and Félix Guattari. *Anti-Oedipus: Capitalism and Schizophrenia.* Translated by Robert Hurley, Mark Seem, and Helen R. Lane. Minneapolis: University of Minnesota Press, 193. [*L'anti-Oedipe: Capitalisme et schizophrénie.* Paris: Minuit, 1972.]

Delvaux, Martine. "Des corps et des frontières: Les lieux du sida." *L'esprit créateur* 37.3 (1997): 83–93.

Denain, Aline. "Le Pletzl: Tentative de définition d'un espace yiddishophone parisien." In Azéma, ed., *Vivre et survivre dans le Marais,* 305–21.

Denizet-Lewis, Benoit. "Double Lives on the Down Low." *New York Times,* 3 Aug. 2003, natl. ed., sec. 6:28+.

Descimon, Robert. "Le Marais du XVIIème siècle." In Azéma, ed., *Vivre et survivre dans le Marais,* 137–42.

Dietrich, Marlene, perf. *Morocco.* Dir. Josef von Sternberg. Paramount, 1930.

——. *A Foreign Affair.* Dir. Billy Wilder. Paramount, 1948.

Diner, Hasia R. *Lower East Side Memories: A Jewish Place in America.* Princeton: Princeton University Press, 2000.

Dreuilhe, Alain Emmanuel. *Mortal Embrace: Living with AIDS.* Translated by Linda Coverdale. New York: Hill and Wang, 1988. [*Corps à corps: Journal de sida.* Paris: Gallimard, 1987.]

Drumont, Edouard. *La France juive.* Paris: Marpon & Flammarion, 1886.

Duras, Marguerite. *La douleur.* Paris: P.O.L., 1985.

Dustan, Guillaume. *In My Room.* Translated by Brad Rumph. London: Serpent's Tail, 1998. [*Dans ma chambre.* Paris: P.O.L., 1996.]

——. *Je sors ce soir.* Paris: P.O.L., 1997.

——. *Nicolas Pages.* Paris: Balland, 1999.

Dyer, Richard. *The Culture of Queers.* New York: Routledge, 2002.

Edelman, Lee. *No Future: Queer Theory and the Death Drive.* Durham, NC: Duke University Press, 2004.

Elina, Odette. *Sans fleurs ni couronnes: Auschwitz 1944–1945.* Paris: Mille et une nuits, 2005.

Eribon, Didier. *Insult and the Making of the Gay Self.* Translated by Michael Lucey. Durham, NC: Duke University Press, 2004. [*Réflexions sur la question gay.* Paris: Fayard, 1999.]

——, ed. *Dictionnaire des cultures gays et lesbiennes.* Paris: Larousse, 2003.

Esposito, Roberto. *Communitas: Origine et destin de la communauté.* Translated by Nadine Le Lirzin. Paris: Presses Universitaires de France, 2000. [*Origine e destino della comunitá.* Turin: Einaudi, 1998.]

Fargue, Léon-Paul. *Le piéton de Paris.* Paris: Gallimard, 1939.

Fernandez, Dominique. *L'étoile rose.* Paris: Grasset, 1978.

Fijalkow, Yankel. "De l'îlot no 2 à l'îlot no 16: L'évolution de l'idée d'insalubrité (1900–1920)." In Azéma, ed., *Vivre et survivre dans le Marais,* 391–407.

Fillieule, Olivier. "Lesbian and Gay Pride." In Eribon, ed., *Dictionnaire des cultures gays et lesbiennes,* 287–88.

Finkielkraut, Alain. *The Imaginary Jew.* Translated by Kevin O'Neill and David Suchoff. Lincoln, University of Nebraska Press, 1994. [*Le juif imaginaire.* Paris: Seuil, 1980.]

Fleischman, Cyrille. *Rendez-vous au métro Saint-Paul.* Paris: Le dilettante, 1992.

——. *Nouveaux rendez-vous au métro Saint-Paul.* Paris: Le dilettante, 1994.

——. *Derniers rendez-vous au métro Saint-Paul.* Paris: Le dilettante, 1995.

Foucault, Michel. *Discipline and Punish: The Birth of the Prison.* Translated by Alan Sheridan. New York: Pantheon Books, 1977. [*Surveiller et punir: Naissance de la prison.* Paris: Gallimard, 1975].

——. *The History of Sexuality*. Translated by Robert Hurley. New York: Pantheon Books, 1978. [*Histoire de la sexualité*. Paris Gallimard, 1976.]

Fourest, Caroline, and Fiametta Venner. *Les anti-PaCS ou la dernière croisade homophobe*. Paris: ProChoix, 1999.

Freedman, Jonathan. "Coming Out of the Jewish Closet with Marcel Proust." *GLQ* 7.4 (2001): 521–51.

Gelley, Alexander. *Unruly Examples: On the Rhetoric of Exemplarity*. Stanford: Stanford University Press, 1995.

Genet, Jean. *Our Lady of the Flowers*. Translated by Bernard Fretchman. New York: Grove Press, 1963. [*Notre-Dame des fleurs*. Lyon: L'arbalète, 1948.]

Gilman, Sander. *The Jew's Body*. New York: Routledge, 1991.

——. *Freud, Race, and Gender*. Princeton: Princeton University Press, 1993.

——. *Jewish Frontiers: Essays on Bodies, Histories, and Identities*. New York: Palgrave Macmillan, 2003.

Green, Nancy L. "The Contradictions of Acculturation: Immigrant Oratories and Yiddish Union Sections in Paris before World War I." In Malino and Wasserstein, ed., *The Jews in Modern France*, 54–77.

——. *The Pletzl of Paris: Jewish Immigrant Workers in the Belle Epoque*. New York: Holmes & Meier, 1986.

Grumberg, Jean-Claude. *The Workroom*. Translated by Catherine Temerson. New York: Ubu Repertory Theater Publications, 1993. [*L'atelier*. Paris: Actes Sud- Papiers, 1985.]

Grynberg, Anne. "Le retour et la reconstruction." In Azéma, ed., *Vivre et survivre dans le Marais*, 465–76.

Guibert, Hervé. *To the Friend Who Did Not Save My Life*. Translated by Linda Coverdale. New York: High Risk Books, 1994. [*A l'ami qui ne m'a pas sauvé la vie*. Paris: Gallimard: 1990.]

Guland, Olivier, and Michel Zerbib. *Nous, juifs de France*. Paris: Bayard, 2000.

Gurvil, Clément. "Le Marais au XVIème siècle: Le grand bouleversement." In Azéma, ed., *Vivre et survivre dans le Marais*, 127–36.

Halperin, David M. "Homosexuality's Closet." *Michigan Quarterly Review* 41.1 (2002): 21–54.

——. *What Do Gay Men Want? An Essay on Sex, Risk, and Subjectivity*. Ann Arbor: University of Michigan Press, 2007.

Hayes, Jarrod. "Proust in the Tearoom." *PMLA* 110.5 (1995): 992–1005.

Heger, Heinz. *The Men with the Pink Triangle: The True Life-and-Death Story of Homosexuals in the Nazi Death Camps*. Translated by David Fernbach. Los Angeles: Alyson Books, 1980. [*Männer mit dem rosa Winkel*. Hamburg: Merlin-Verlag, 1980.]

Higgs, David, ed. *Queer Sites: Gay Urban Histories since 1600*. London: Routledge, 1999.

Hirsch, Marianne. *Family Frames: Photography, Narrative, and Postmemory*. Cambridge: Harvard University Press, 1997.

——. "Projected Memory: Holocaust Photographs in Personal and Public Fantasy." In Bal, Crewe, and Spitzer, ed., *Acts of Memory*, 3–23.

Hocquenghem, Guy. *Homosexual Desire*. Translated by Daniella Dangoor. London: Allison and Busby, 1978. [*Le désir homosexuel*. Paris: Editions universitaires, 1972.]

Hugo, Victor. *La légende des siècles*. Bibilothèque de la Pléiade. Paris: Gallimard, 1950.

——. *Choses vues: Souvenirs, journaux, cahiers*. Paris: Gallimard, 1972.

Hutton, Margaret-Anne. *Testimony from the Nazi Camps: French Women's Voices*. London and New York: Routledge, 2005.

Huyez, Guillaume. "Dix ans de ghetto: Le quartier gay dans les hebdomadaires français." *ProChoix* 22 (2002): 58–81.

Hyman, Paula. *From Dreyfus to Vichy: The Remaking of French Jewry, 1906–1939.* New York: Columbia University Press, 1979.

———. *The Jews of Modern France.* Berkeley: University of California Press, 1998.

It's Always Fair Weather. Dir. Stanley Donen and Gene Kelly. Metro Goldwyn Mayer, 1955.

Jakobson, Roman. *Essais de linguistique générale.* Paris: Minuit, 1963.

Janin, Françoise. "Spoliations d'habitants de 'l'îlot 16.'" In Azéma, ed., *Vivre et survivre dans le Marais,* 409–42.

J'embrasse pas. Dir. André Téchiné. Bac Films, 1991.

Judt, Tony. *Postwar: A History of Europe since 1945.* London: William Heinemann, 2005.

King, J. L., and Karen Hunter. *On the Down Low: A Journey into the Lives of "Straight" Black Men Who Sleep with Men.* New York: Harlem Moon, 2004.

Kriegel, Annie. *Ce que j'ai cru comprendre.* Paris: Laffont, 1991.

Kuperminc, Jean-Claude. "Les mouvements de jeunesse juive en France." In Becker and Wieviorka, ed., *Les juifs de France,* 138–40.

———. "La presse juive en France." In Becker and Wieviorka, ed., *Les juifs de France,* 140–42.

Kureishi, Hanif. *Love in a Blue Time.* New York: Scribner, 1997.

Kurlansky, Mark. *A Chosen Few: The Resurrection of European Jewry.* Reading, Mass.: Addison-Wesley, 1995.

Kushner, Tony. *Angels in America: A Gay Fantasia on National Themes.* New York: Theatre Communications Group, 1993.

La chatte à deux têtes. Dir. Jacques Nolot. Elia Films, 2002.

La grande illusion. Dir. Jean Renoir. Réalisation d'art cinématographique, 1938.

Laloum, Jean. "Entre aryanisation et déportations: Le drame du quartier Saint-Gervais sous l'Occupation." In Azéma, ed., *Vivre et survivre dans le Marais,* 367–90.

Laupts, Dr. [Saint-Paul, Georges]. *L'homosexualité et les types homosexuels.* Paris: Vigot, 1910.

Lebovics, Herman. *Mona Lisa's Escort: André Malraux and the Reinvention of French Culture.* Ithaca: Cornell University Press, 1999.

———. *Bringing the Empire Back Home: France in the Global Age.* Durham, NC: Duke University Press, 2004.

Le Bitoux, Jean. "Marcher dans le gay Marais." *La revue h* 1 (1997): 47–51.

Léry, Jean-Marc. "Evolution du quartier du Marais: Des origines à la fin du XVe siècle." In Babelon, ed., *Le Marais,* 1–61.

Les roseaux sauvages. Dir. André Téchiné. IMA Fils/Les films Alain Sarde, 1994.

Les rosiers du Marais: 15 siècles de présence juive à Paris. Dir. Marc Walter. Novi Productions, 2000.

Lestrade, Didier. *Kinsey 6: Journal des années 80.* Paris: Denoël, 2002.

Levinas, Emmanuel. *Totalité et infini: Essai sur l'extériorité.* The Hague: M. Nijhoff, 1961.

Loret, Eric. "Dustan qui passe." *Libération* (11 Oct. 2005): 3 pp. Online. Internet. 12 Oct. 2005.

Lucey, Michael. *Never Say I: Sexuality and the First Person in Colette, Gide, and Proust.* Durham, NC: Duke University Press, 2006.

Lyotard, Jean-François. *Heidegger and "the Jews."* Translated by Andreas Michel and Mark S. Roberts. Minneapolis: University of Minnesota Press, 1990. [*Heidegger et "les juifs."* Paris: Galilée, 1988.]

Machtan, Lothar. *The Hidden Hitler.* Translated by John Browjohn. New York: Basic Books, 2001. [*Hitlers Geheimnis.* Frankfurt: Taschenbuch, 2001.]

Malino, Frances, and Bernard Wasserstein, eds. *The Jews in Modern France*. Hanover, NH: University Press of New England, 1985.

Marquart, Sharon. "Witnessing Communities and an Ethics of Reading." Ph.D. diss., University of Michigan, 2008.

Martel, Frédéric. *The Pink and the Black: Homosexuals in France since 1968*. Translated by Jane Marie Todd. Stanford: Stanford University Press, 1999. [*Le rose et le noir: Les homosexuels en France depuis 1968*. Paris: Seuil, 1996.]

Maunand, Patrick, ed. *Le Marais des écrivains*. Paris: Pimientos, 2003.

Mendelsohn, Daniel. *The Elusive Embrace: Desire and the Riddle of Identity*. New York: Knopf, 1999.

——. *The Lost: A Search for Six of Six Million*. New York: Harper Collins, 2006.

Mercier, Louis-Sébastien. *Tableau de Paris*. 7 vols. Hamburg: Virchaux & compagnie, 1782.

Miller, D. A. *Place for Us [Essay on the Broadway Musical]*. Cambridge: Harvard University Press, 1998.

Montaigne, Michel de. *Essais*. 3 vols. Paris: Quadrige/Presses Universitaires de France, 1988.

Moreno, Sabine. "Le projet 'Chinois d'Europe et intégration.'" *Hommes et migrations* 1254 (2005): 58–64.

Morrison, Jack G. *Ravensbrück: Everyday Life in a Women's Concentration Camp, 1939–45*. Princeton: Markus Wiener Publishers, 2000.

My Beautiful Laundrette. Dir. Stephen Frears. Channel 4, 1985.

Nancy, Jean-Luc. *The Inoperative Community*. Translated by Peter Conner, Lisa Garbus, Michael Holland, and Simona Sawhney. Minneapolis: University of Minnesota Press, 1991. [*La communauté désoeuvrée*. Paris: Christian Bourgois, 1986.]

——. *Being Singular Plural*. Translated by Robert D. Richardson and Anne E. O'Byrne. Stanford: Stanford University Press, 2000. [*Etre singulier pluriel*. Paris: Galilée, 1996.]

——. "Conloquium." Foreword. *Communitas*. By Roberto Esposito. 3–10.

Nochlin, Linda, and Tamar Garb, eds. *The Jew in the Text: Modernity and the Construction of Identity*. London: Thames and Hudson, 1995.

Nuit et brouillard. Dir. Alain Resnais. Argos Films, 1956.

O'Sullivan, Eileen. Letter. *New York Times*, 17 Aug. 2003, natl. ed., sec. 6:10.

Podselver, Laurence. "De la périphérie au centre: Sarcelles ville juive." In Bordes-Benayoun, ed. *Les juifs et la ville*, 79–90.

Poisson, Véronique. "Les grandes étapes de 100 ans d'histoire migratoire entre la Chine et la France." *Hommes et migrations* 1254 (2005): 6–17.

Powell, Robert Andrew. "Is Key West Going Straight?" *New York Times*, 18 Nov. 2005, natl. ed., D1+.

Priollaud, Nicole, Victor Zigelman, and Laurent Goldberg, eds. *Images de la mémoire juive: Immigration et intégration en France depuis 1880*. Paris: Liana Levi, 1994.

Probetich, Justine. "La construction identitaire d'un quartier: L'exemple de Sedaine-Popincourt." *Hommes et migrations* 1254 (2005): 82–90.

Probyn, Elspeth. *Blush: Faces of Shame*. Minneapolis: University of Minnesota Press, 2005.

Proust, Marcel. *In Search of Lost Time*. Translated by C. K. Scott Moncrieff and Terence Kilmartin. 6 vols. New York: Random House, 1992–93. [*A la recherche du temps perdu*. 4 vols. Bibliothèque de la Pléiade. Paris: Gallimard, 1987–89.]

Rajsfus, Maurice. *Mon père l'étranger: Un immigré juif polonais à Paris dans les années 1920*. Paris: L'Harmattan, 1989.

———. *10 ans en 1938: Souvenirs d'enfance à l'ombre du donjon de Vincennes*. Paris: Verticales, 1998.

Reid, Roddey. *Families in Jeopardy: Regulating the Social Body in France, 1750–1910*. Stanford: Stanford University Press, 1993.

Rémond, René. *Le "fichier juif."* Paris: Omnibus, 1999.

Renan, Ernest. *Qu'est-ce qu'une nation?* Paris: Mille et une nuits, 1997.

Restif de la Bretonne, Nicolas. *Les nuits de Paris ou le spectateur nocturne*. London: 1788–89.

Roblin, Michel. *Les juifs de Paris: Démographie, économie, culture*. Paris: Picard, 1952.

Ross, Kristin. *Fast Cars, Clean Bodies: Decolonization and the Reordering of French Culture*. Cambridge: The MIT Press, 1995.

Royer, Cyril. "Le Marais: Espace à la croisée de dynamiques urbaines et identitaires." Master's thesis. Université Aix-Marseille 3, 2001.

———. "Rue Sainte-Anne." In Eribon, ed., *Dictionnaire des cultures gays et lesbiennes*, 413.

Saidel, Rochelle G. *The Jewish Women of Ravensbrück Concentration Camp*. Madison: University of Wisconsin Press, 2004.

Sartre, Jean-Paul. *Anti-Semite and Jew*. Translated by George J. Becker. New York: Schocken Books, 1948. [*Réflexions sur la question juive*. Paris: Gallimard, 1954.]

Schnapper, Dominique. "Les juifs et la nation." In Birnbaum, ed., *Histoire politique des juifs de France*, 296–310.

Scott, Joan Wallach. *The Politics of the Veil*. Princeton: Princeton University Press, 2007.

Sedgwick, Eve Kosofsky. "Queer Performativity: Henry James's *The Art of the Novel*." *GLQ* 1.1 (1993): 1–16.

Seel, Pierre. *Liberation Was for Others: Memoirs of a Gay Survivor of the Nazi Holocaust*. Translated by Joachim Neugroschel. New York: Basic Books, 1995. [*Moi, Pierre Seel, déporté homosexuel*. Paris: Calmann Lévy, 1994.]

Semprun, Jorge. *The Long Journey*. Translated by Richard Seaver. New York: Grove Press, 1964. [*Le grand voyage*. Paris: Gallimard, 1963.]

———. *Literature or Life*. Translated by Linda Coverdale. New York: Viking, 1997. [*L'écriture ou la vie*. Paris: Gallimard, 1994.]

Shoah. Dir. Claude Lanzmann. Les Films Aleph and Historia Films, 1985.

Sibalis, Michael D. "Paris." In Higgs, ed., *Queer Sites*, 10–37.

———. " 'La Lesbian and Gay Pride' in Paris: Community, Commerce and Carnival." In Cairns, ed., *Gay and Lesbian Cultures in France*, 51–66.

———. "Homophobia, Vichy France and the 'Crime of Homosexuality': The Origins of the Ordinance of 6 August 1942." *GLQ* 8.3 (2002): 301–18.

———. "Urban Space and Homosexuality: The Example of the Marais, Paris's 'Gay Ghetto.' " *Urban Studies* 41 (2004): 1739–58.

———. "Ghetto." In Tin, ed., *Dictionnaire de l'homophobie*, 194–96.

Sidéris, Georges. "Saint-Germain-des-prés." In Eribon, ed., *Dictionnaire des cultures gays et lesbiennes*, 413–14.

Sloterdijk, Peter. *Weltfremdheit*. Frankfirtam Main: Suhrkamp, 1993.

Sodom and Gomorrha. Dir Robert Aldrich and Sergio Leone. Pathé Cinéma, 1963.

Spacks, Patricia Meyer. *Gossip*. New York: Knopf, 1985.

Spector, Scott. *Prague Territories: National Conflict and Cultural Invasion in Franz Kafka's Fin de Siècle*. Berkeley: University of California Press, 2000.

Stendhal. *The Charterhouse of Parma*. Translated by John Sturrock. London: Penguin, 2006. [*La chartreuse de Parme*. Paris: Gallimard, 2006.]

Sternhell, Zeev. *Maurice Barrès et le nationalisme français*. Paris: Colin, 1972.

Suleiman, Susan R. "The Jew in Sartre's *Réflexions sur la question juive*: An Exercise in Historical Reading." In Nochlin and Garb, ed., *The Jew in the Text*, 201–18.

Tagliabue, John. "A French Lesson: Taunts about Race Can Boomerang." *New York Times,* 21 Sept. 2005, natl. ed., A4.

Taguieff, Pierre-André. *La nouvelle judéophobie*. Paris: Fayard, 2002.

Tamagne, Florence. *Histoire de l'homosexualité en Europe: Berlin, Londres, Paris, 1919–1939*. Paris: Seuil, 2000.

———. "Montmartre." In Eribon, ed., *Dictionnaire des cultures gays et lesbiennes*, 328–30.

Tapia, Claude. *Les juifs sépharades en France (1965–1985)*. Paris: L'harmattan, 1986.

Tillion, Germaine. *Ravensbrück*. Paris: Seuil, 1973.

Tin, Louis-Georges, ed. *Dictionnaire de l'homophobie*. Paris: Presses Universitaires de France, 2003.

Tresize, Thomas. "The Question of Community in Charlotte Delbo's *Auschwitz and After*." *MLN* 117 (2002): 858–86.

Turner, Mark W. *Backward Glances: Cruising the Queer Streets of New York and London*. London: Reaktion, 2003.

Vasseur, Nadine. *Il était une fois le Sentier*. Paris: Liana Levi, 2000.

Verlaine, Paul. *Sagesse; Amour; Bonheur*. Paris: Gallimard, 1975.

Villate, Laurent. "La place des gays." In Azéma, ed., *Vivre et survivre dans le Marais*, 501–18.

de Vleeschouwer, Olivier. *La vie des morts est épuisante*. Paris: Anne Carrière, 1997.

Warner, Michael. *The Trouble with Normal: Sex, Politics, and the Ethics of Queer Life*. New York: Free Press, 1999.

Watney, Simon. *Practices of Freedom: Selected Writings on HIV/AIDS*. London: Rivers Oram Press, 1994.

Wheeler, Breana. Letter. *New York Times,* 17 Aug. 2003, natl. ed., sec 6:10.

Wiesel, Elie. *Night*. Translated by Stella Rodway. New York: Bantam Books, 1982. [*La nuit*. Paris: Minuit, 1958.]

Yerushalmi, Yosef Hayim. *Zakhor: Jewish History and Jewish Memory*. Seattle: University of Washington Press, 1982.

Yuen, Tai Hong. "L'immigration chinoise en France: Histoire et caractéristiques." *Migrations sociétés* 9.54 (1997): 33–42.

Yun, Gao. "Nouvelles formes d'esclavage parmi les Chinois récemment arrivés en France." *Hommes et migrations* 1254 (2005): 29–44.

Index